Contents

A Note FROM THE AUTHORS

This book is dedicated to you, the trailblazers in the information revolution. As strange as may seem to be called a pioneer at this point in time, there is little doubt that we have only just begun. Some 30 years ago we had the pleasure of meeting a true pioneer in the information revolution, the late Commodore Grace Hopper, whose work on behalf of the U.S. Navy is still the foundation upon which much business computing is based today. She told our group of know-it-all graduate students that we had not yet reached the Model-T Ford stage in computing. Those of us who were present heard her words and thought that her age was beginning to influence her thinking, because we believed that we were doing some incredible work. As the years have passed her foresight becomes more incredible with each technological breakthrough. Every time we reach and exceed limits that were once expected to be the pinnacle of technological development, the more convinced we are that the only limits are those of the creativity of you, the newest users and developers. It is your authors' hope that this text is but your first step in a long, productive, and enjoyable adventure. This is only the beginning of your Model-T ride. We encourage you to hang on tightly because we have so much more to accomplish and it's going to be quite a trip.

We would like to thank a number of persons without whom this effort would not have been possible. Sonja Brown, Michael Sander, and George Provol of EMC/Paradigm and all of the reviewers—Patty A. Anderson, Lake City Community College, Lake City, FL; Michael Feiler, Merritt College, Oakland, CA; Nancy Graviett, St. Charles County Community College, St. Peters, MO; David A. Laxton, Southern Ohio College, Cincinnati, OH; Bernard L. Levite, Jefferson Community College, Steubenville, OH; and James A. Webb, Austin Community College, Austin, TX—have been most supportive in so many editorial and professional ways throughout the development process. For this we extend our deepest appreciation. We are particularly grateful for the contributions of Mary R. Reichardt, Ph.D., University of St. Thomas, St. Paul, MN. We also wish to thank Jacqueline Belcher, Ronald Sheehy, Debra McCurdy, Dennis Harkins, Marcia Mittelstadt, Virginia Carson, Connie Washburn, and Frankie McIntosh of Georgia Perimeter College for the kind of professional home that encourages the search for the limits of technological accomplishment. Finally, we want to express our undying gratitude to our family, whose love and support is what makes life worthwhile, and especially to our daughter Carole. It is, after all, all about you.

Norman and Mary Carole Hollingsworth

Reality INTERFACE

Airline E-Tickets

In the late 1970s, U.S. government officials and economists began to recognize the necessity of deregulating markets to allow the forces of supply and demand to set prices. During this period of deregulation, the U.S. airline industry was completely restructured. An era of price competition began as no-frills airlines began to compete with mainstream carriers by offering discounted prices. These no-frills airlines reduced customer services, downgraded or eliminated meals, and executed a number of other cost containment measures. For their part, consumers demonstrated a willingness to accept tighter seating and fewer services in order to save money on flights. During the ensuing period of intense competition, the industry experienced bankruptcies, reorganizations, mergers, and failures. Only the most creative competitors could—and did—survive in this cutthroat market.

In searching for creative cost-saving measures, some airlines discovered an opportunity to cut a major expense: eliminate the tickets! The printing and handling of airline tickets is a significant airline carrier cost. Moreover, today's computer databases make such paperwork redundant anyway. Airlines began to experiment with ticketless reservation systems, issuing each passenger a confirmation number instead. Some even began offering better prices on seats booked and paid for over the Internet. After booking a flight on a Web site, a customer receives confirmation of an e-ticket by e-mail. When arriving at the gate, the passenger shows identification and the confirmation number to the airline agent and is given a reusable boarding pass to hold onto until flight time. Through the use of e-tickets, airlines found that they could save millions of dollars annually. In addition, the reduced consumption of paper and energy is good for the environment. While eliminating tickets was not an issue in deregulation, this simple step has had a huge impact, and it was all made possible through the use of computers that can store, maintain, and report information more efficiently than any paper trail can. The e-ticket revolution in the airline industry is just one of numerous situations in our world today where computers have changed our lives in profound ways.

COMPUTER TECHNOLOGY

Changes, Challenges, and Choices

C. Norman Hollingsworth
Georgia Perimeter College, Dunwoody Campus

Mary Carole Hollingsworth
Georgia Perimeter College, Clarkston Campus

Senior Editor	Sonja M. Brown
Developmental Editor	Michael Sander
Editorial Consultant	Mary R. Reichardt, Ph. D.
Special Projects Coordinator	Joan D'Onofrio
Senior Designer	Jennifer Wreisner
Cover Designer	Design Center
Illustrator	Colin Hayes
Photo Researcher	Desiree Faulkner
Copy Editor	Sharon O'Donnell
Proofreader	Joy McComb
Indexer	Nancy Fulton

Publishing Team: George Provol, Publisher; Janice Johnson, Director of Product Development; Lori Landwer, Marketing Manager; Shelley Clubb, Electronic Design and Production Manager.

Library of Congress Cataloging-in-Publication Data
Hollingsworth, C. Norman.
Computer Technology: Changes, Challenges, and Choices / C. Norman Holliongsworth, Mary Carole Hollingsworth
p.   cm.
Includes index.
ISBN 0-7638-1075-4

© 2002 by Paradigm Publishing Inc.
Published by **EMC**Paradigm
875 Montreal Way
St. Paul, MN 55102

(800) 535-6865
E-mail: educate@emcp.com
Web Site: www.emcp.com

Printed in the United States of America
10 9 8 7 6 5 4 3 2 1

1 Computers: Here, THERE, and EVERYWHERE

OBJECTIVES

After reading this chapter, you will be able to. . .

➤ Characterize the information age and discuss its influence on our culture and economy

➤ Identify common uses of computers in everyday life

➤ Define the different categories of computers and give examples of how they are used

➤ Describe the use of computers in finance, human resources, research and development, manufacturing, marketing and sales, and management

➤ Explain the effects of the Internet on our personal and work lives

KEY Terms

information age Our current time period, when work is dominated by manipulation, analysis, and dissemination of information via computers.

knowledge worker One whose work consists of manipulation, analysis, and dissemination of information.

Internet Network of linked computers that has created a worldwide electronic community for communications, research, commerce, and entertainment.

Welcome to the Information Age!

Every so often, civilization reaches major crossroads in technology that completely alter its direction in the future. The harnessing of electricity, the invention of steam and petroleum power systems, and the development of the automobile are but a few inventions that mark such important turning points. In each of these cases, many decades passed between the technology's invention and its wide-scale acceptance in society. Today, however, technological advancement is occurring at such a rapid pace that the time period between invention and proliferation is much shorter.

To classify the course of Western human development, historians and social scientists tend to label eras. The agrarian age, for instance, represents a period of many hundreds of years when agriculture dominated the economy. The industrial or machine age began in 1785 when James Watt's steam engine was first applied to the production of cotton. Today, our era is referred to as the **information age,** a time period in which the manipulation, analysis, and dissemination of information via computers is at the core of our economy and our cul-

ture. During this period, the **knowledge worker,** a term coined by social analyst Peter F. Drucker, has become the dominant member of the workforce. And, say some historians, never before has our civilization been completely changed in so short a period by technological advancements. Consider, for example, that the first operation of computers took place little more than fifty years ago, yet today our personal and work lives are dependent on them. Recent research conducted by Rutgers University and the University of Connecticut, for example, suggests that time spent on a computer accounts for 35% of U.S. employees' workday. In addition, 70% of respondents use office computers at least one hour a day, and 36% use the computer for at least half of the workday. Employees spend 23% of working hours on the **Internet**, the network of linked computers that has created a worldwide electronic community. Another study, conducted by Stanford University's Institute for the Quantitative Study of Society, reports that 55% of Americans have access to the Internet at work or at home.

The linked computers in our **networked economy** have redefined the world of business, education, and entertainment, and contributed to our growing sense of being part of a global society. Since computer use will continue to increase in importance, every person today needs to have an understanding of computer technology. In our information society, each person needs to be **computer literate,** or able to understand fundamental computer concepts, operate a computer, and navigate the Internet. Moreover, every person must be committed to ongoing education as the pace of technological change accelerates. This textbook will provide you with knowledge of how computers operate so that you have a strong basis on which to build your computer skills and adapt to change in the future.

How Wired Are You?

To be **wired,** or **plugged in,** means to be a computer user. So, how wired are you? The complete answer may come as a surprise, for you may use computers at work and at school, but you probably also interact with these machines at least 10 to 12 times every day in ways you never considered. To illustrate this fact, consider a typical day in the life of Elena Carter, a 27-year-old divorced mother from San Antonio, Texas.

Elena's day begins at 6:30 a.m., when an alarm activated by a computer chip inside her clock awakens her. In the kitchen, a cup of coffee awaits, brewed automatically according to instructions programmed the night before into the tiny computer inside her coffee machine. An hour later, Elena is in her car, taking her three year old, Jason, to preschool. As she drives, computers under her car's hood monitor and control coolant flow, fuel injection, and other functions. All day at work, in her job as a dispatcher, Elena uses local, national, and international computer networks that automatically switch and route telephone calls. When she calls Directory Assistance, a computer-generated voice greets her and asks, "What city?" and "What listing?" In between calls, Elena reads her e-mail messages on her computer monitor and sends responses as necessary. At lunchtime, Elena stops at an ATM to get some cash; a computer records her transaction and debits her account. She buys a birthday card at a shop. A computer reads the bar code on the card, identifies the item and its price, and calculates the change she should receive. A computer at the post office will use **optical character recognition (OCR)** to decipher Elena's handwriting and route her envelope with other mail going to the same ZIP code destination.

That evening, Elena leaves her son with her sister and goes to her night class at a local community college. There she takes a test that her teacher has written on a personal computer. Her grade, like her registration information, transcript, and other school records, will be stored on the college's computer system.

Back at her sister's apartment, Elena learns that her son is running a slight fever (as determined by the small digital computer in the thermometer that

KEY Terms

networked economy
Linked computers that have redefined the world of business, education, and entertainment.

optical character recognition (OCR) The capacity for a computer to recognize as system input letter and number characters that have been written by humans.

her sister used). She gives her son a children's medication produced by a pharmaceutical company that used computers to develop, test, and market the product. At home again, she glances at some computer-generated bills that have come in the mail. Then she reads a story to Jason from a children's book containing a computer chip that produces sound effects when the pictures are pressed. The book was typeset, and its illustrations were produced, using computers.

At the end of the day, Elena relaxes by watching a television program. The computers inside her television and cable converter box pick up signals relayed from across the country by a complex computer-operated telecommunications network. Finally, she programs the computers in her coffeepot and alarm clock and goes to sleep. If you asked Elena, "Do you use computers?" she would probably reply, "Only for e-mail and communications at work."

The Computer and Internet Revolution

In numerous ways, computers and the Internet have reshaped the world of work. As they penetrate nearly all occupations, computers have not only increased productivity but also changed marketing and sales techniques. In addition, they have redefined our work lives and work responsibilities. Because of their influence, one can truly speak of a computer/Internet "revolution" in the business world and in society as a whole.

Computers, Productivity, and Future Employment

The most efficient way to determine what an economy will produce, how products are made, who acquires goods or services, and what prices are levied is the free market system. If a business produces goods that consumers do not want, those goods will remain unsold and the firm will fail. Businesses that produce goods inefficiently will incur higher costs and lose their competitive edge to more savvy competitors. In an economy, **productivity** is the measure of output per unit of input. Today, business owners understand that computers and networks, including the Internet, have increased productivity so much over the past two decades that they must keep pace with technological developments or fail to survive in the marketplace.

In attempting to become more efficient producers in today's market, many large firms such as AT&T, Microsoft, Disney, Time-Warner, Viacom, and major television companies have recently formed alliances or mergers with each other. Today's trend toward the merger of the data, entertainment, and communications industries is often referred to as **convergence.** Eventually, the very large firms that result from such mergers will offer consumers an array of telephone, television, Internet, and other communications and entertainment services. Those firms with the best alliances or subsidiaries will offer more options and therefore have the competitive advantage.

In the search for greater efficiency in producing goods, organizations throughout the world are investing heavily in computing hardware and software and in skilled computer workers. Indeed, the phenomenal growth in market productivity in recent years could not have been realized without the computer. Such productivity gains mean more dollars of

KEY Terms

convergence Recent trend toward merging of data, entertainment, and communications industries.

revenue, which, in turn, makes possible a higher wage rate for the technology worker. A strong link thus exists between higher productivity and higher wages. As a result, the income gap between technologically skilled and unskilled workers today is increasing. Moreover, the use of computer technology creates higher paying job opportunities in capital-intensive industries and, in many cases, reduces the number of jobs in labor-intensive industries. Consequently, industries have tended to move labor-intensive jobs to lower cost countries around the world. In countries such as Mexico and China, for example, both wages and operating expenses are lower, allowing firms to produce goods more cheaply than in the United States. Therefore, the United States is now importing labor-intensive products such as clothing and electronics and exporting such technology as robotics hardware and software. This rapid change in the U.S. labor market means that higher paying positions for technologically competent workers are opening at a dramatic rate. Such workers have a strong future promise of high earnings and advancement opportunities. On the other hand, workers who are not computer literate will find themselves in the unskilled labor pool competing for fewer—and lower paying—jobs.

Since computers and the Internet play such a vital role in the enhancement of productivity and since productivity advances the United States in the world economy, it is no surprise that educational leaders and policy makers have moved aggressively in recent years to promote computer literacy and Internet access for all. As a result, today's high school graduates are increasingly computer literate and often at levels of skill far above their parents' generation. The question now becomes one of how to update the computer skills of those adults who have completed school. Although many workplaces offer continuing education in computer technology, individuals must take responsibility for their own skill development throughout their careers. Both basic computer training and advanced skills can be obtained through self-study, hands-on experience, community or technical college classes, or employer-sponsored training courses.

Computers Remake the Workplace

Besides enhancing productivity and reshaping the workforce into one of technically trained knowledge workers, computers have significantly altered the ways in which we perform our jobs. Nearly every occupation—from business management, to government, to education, to travel, to medicine—has been changed by the use of

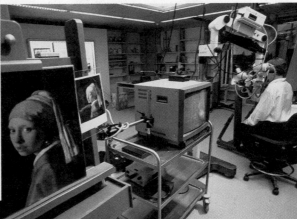

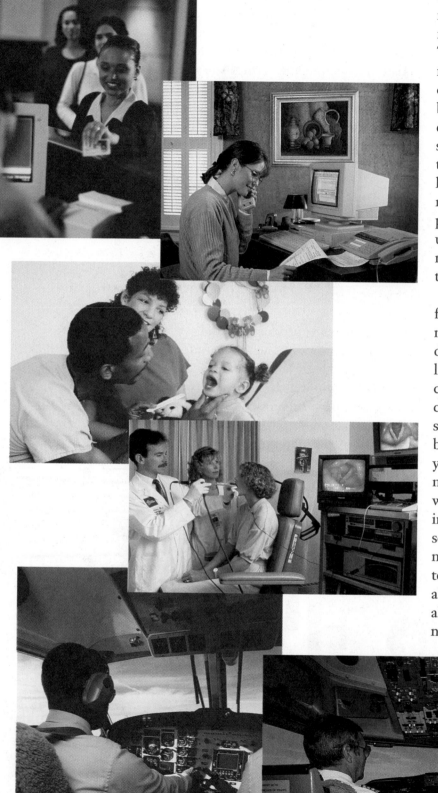

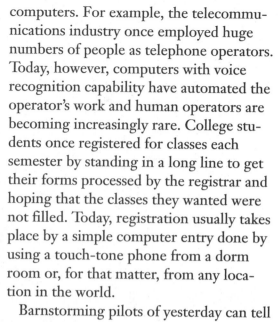

computers. For example, the telecommunications industry once employed huge numbers of people as telephone operators. Today, however, computers with voice recognition capability have automated the operator's work and human operators are becoming increasingly rare. College students once registered for classes each semester by standing in a long line to get their forms processed by the registrar and hoping that the classes they wanted were not filled. Today, registration usually takes place by a simple computer entry done by using a touch-tone phone from a dorm room or, for that matter, from any location in the world.

Barnstorming pilots of yesterday can tell fascinating tales about their skilled flying maneuvers, but they would be seriously disoriented in the cockpit of a modern jetliner. Newer jumbo jets have systems so complicated that they rely entirely on computers. Imagine, for instance, a barnstormer's dismay in finding a **joystick** beside the captain's seat and no steering yoke! And who among us would like our medical care to be delivered by a system without the latest advances in magnetic imaging, arthroscopic surgery, or endoscopic examinations? In medicine, as in many other professions, computer-based technological advances have not only altered the way work is performed, but also opened exciting career paths that did not even exist a few years ago.

EXPANSION CARD

(Bold indicates computer history significance)

The History of Computers

1938	Photo copier demonstrated
1939	World War II begins
	DuPont introduces Nylon
	First jet airplane produced in Germany
	Konrad Zuse completes first programmable digital z computer in Germany
	John Atanasoff creates first electronic digital computer, the ABC
1940	Color television demonstrated
1942	First controlled nuclear reaction
1943	Penicillin developed by Alexander Fleming
	Alan Turing and Thomas Flowers complete the Colossus computer in Britain
1944	**Howard Aiken completes the Mark I**
1945	First atomic bomb and end of World War II
1946	Mass production of television
	Formation of Tokyo Telecommunications (later to become Sony)
	ENIAC completed by John W. Mauchly and J. Presper Eckert
1947	**Transistor invented by William Shockley and others at Bell Labs**
1948	Xerox formed—xerography perfected
	First long-playing record album
1951	First color TV broadcasts
	Univac I developed by John W. Mauchly and J. Presper Eckert
1952	First Holiday Inn (Memphis, Tennessee)
	Salk polio vaccine human trials begin
1954	**IBM mass produces first computer, the 701**
1955	First Kentucky Fried Chicken
1956	Organization of European Common Market
	Transatlantic Cable Telephone Service established
	Bell Labs builds first transistor-based computer
1957	Russia launches *Sputnik I*
	First nuclear power plant
	Boeing 707 produced—the first successful passenger jet airplane
1958	**Integrated circuit patented by Jack Kilby and Robert Noyce**
1960	First weather satellite
	Ray Kroc begins McDonald's Hamburgers national expansion
	Laser invented
1962	First American in orbit, John Glenn
	First communications satellite, *Telestar*
	DEC creates first minicomputer
	First time-sharing computer
	RAND Corporation begins research that leads to the Internet
1963	**Mouse pointing device created by Doug Englebart**
1964	Beatles' first visit to the USA
	First computer crime is prosecuted
1965	First home videocassette recorder
1966	First human heart transplant, Dr. Michael De Bakey
1968	**Organization of INTEL by Robert Noyce and Gordon Moore**
1969	First man on the moon, Neil Armstrong
	Organization of the ARPANET
1970	**ROM developed**
	Xerox establishes Palo Alto Research Center (PARC)
	First basic patent on microprocessor by Gilbert Hyatt

1971	Origin of Federal Express by Fred Smith
	Shipment of INTEL's first microprocessor, the 4004
	First e-mail message by Ray Tomlinson
1974	First computer-controlled industrial robot
1975	USA and USSR link in space
	Formation of Microsoft Corporation by Bill Gates and Paul Allen
	Cray-I supercomputer introduced
	Ed Roberts sells first personal computer, the Altair 8800
1976	**Apple Corporation formed**
1977	Freddie Laker forms Laker Airways—the first discount-priced airline
	Apple II introduced
	Founding of Oracle Corporation
	Xerox introduces the Graphical User Interface (GUI)
1978	Airline industry deregulated
1979	**First spreadsheet program, VisiCalc, introduced by Dan Bricklin and Bob Frankston**
1980	Walkman introduced
	Japan surpasses USA in auto production
	Smallpox virus eradicated worldwide
1981	First space shuttle
	Organization of Compaq
	IBM PC available to public
	Development of the Internet
1982	**Term "Internet" first applied to ARPANET**
1983	CD player debuts
1984	**Apple introduces Macintosh**
1988	Organization of Time-Warner
	Internet Worm virus, the Internet's first virus, corrupts 6,000 systems for two days
1989	Berlin Wall falls
	Tim Berners-Lee proposes the establishment of the World Wide Web
1990	**Pocket computers introduced**
	Windows 3.0 introduced by Microsoft
1991	USSR breaks up
	Failure of Pan American Airlines
	Microcomputer multimedia era begins
1993	**Corporate convergence merger era begins**
	NCSA Mosaic—first graphical web browser
1994	**Apple and IBM introduce PowerMac and PowerPC**
1995	**Netscape stock goes public—$28 to $71 price increase in the first day**
	Merger of Walt Disney and Capital Cities—major move toward convergence
1996	Dolly the sheep is first mammal to be cloned
	Personal computers outsell televisions in USA for the first time
1997	**WorldCom buys MCI—another telecommunications combination**
	Advent of Network PC computer stations
	U.S. Supreme Court supports free speech rights for the Internet
1998	**Justice Department and 20 states sue Microsoft for antitrust violations**
1999	HDTV broadcasts in USA
2000	**Microsoft ordered to break into two companies for monopolistic practices—appeal process begins**

Types of Computers

So, what kinds of computers are used in homes, schools, and in the workplace—whether it's the business office, research lab, hospital, or government center? Computers come in many different forms, with varying levels of capability. The following list describes the types of computers most widely used today.

A **mainframe** is a very large computer used, typically, in a large organization to handle high-volume processing (see Figure 1-1). A typical use of a mainframe computer would be to process the financial transactions and maintain the accounts of a large bank.

Figure 1-1: Mainframe Computer

A **dumb terminal** is a keyboard or a keyboard and a display connected to a mainframe or other computer and used, generally, to input raw information, or **data** (see Figure 1-2). Bank tellers often make use of dumb terminals, which take their name from the fact that they have no processors of their own (a **processor** is the brain of the computer, the part that actually carries out the instructions fed into the machine). In the early days of computers, the mainframe/dumb terminal configuration was the only one available for computing.

Figure 1-2: Dumb Terminal

A **supercomputer** is a mainframe capable of very high volume and very fast processing. Supercomputers are typically used in research and defense applications (see Figure 1-3).

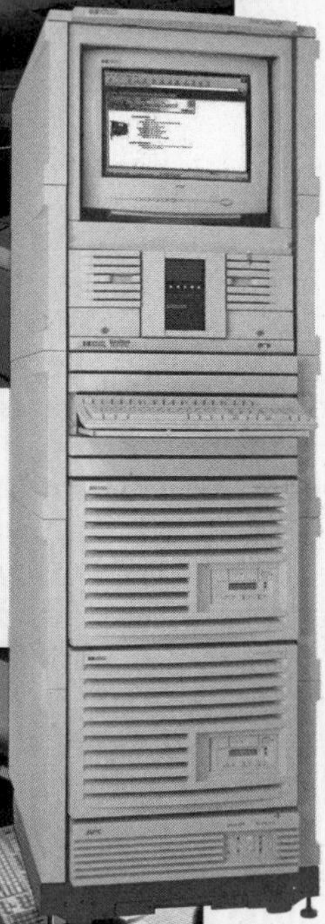

Figure 1-3: Supercomputer

A **minicomputer,** or **mini,** is a midsized computer widely used in universities, research labs, and smaller corporations (see Figure 1-4). For example, a college might use a minicomputer to process financial aid applications, course registrations, and the reporting of grades.

Figure 1-5: Workstation

Figure 1-4: Minicomputer

A **workstation** is a desktop computer powerful enough to rival the performance of a minicomputer or, in some cases, of a small mainframe. Workstations are widely used for scientific, engineering, and research applications (see Figure 1-5).

A **network** is a means by which computers are connected with one another so that they can share data and programs (see Figure 1-6).

A **personal computer,** or **PC,** is a desktop computer (see Figure 1-7) that is less powerful than a workstation. In practice, as personal computers have become more powerful, the distinction between them and workstations has blurred. During the 1980s and early 1990s, networked personal computers took over many of the functions previously performed by larger machines, the mainframes and minis. (Note: The abbreviation *PC* is sometimes used more narrowly to refer to IBM PCs and compatibles.)

Figure 1-6: Networked Computers

A **network computer,** or **NC,** accesses programs and data over a network and has little or no disk storage built in, making it a less expensive alternative to the PC (see Figure 1-8). Despite price advantages, the network computer is not widely used.

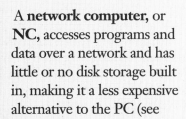

Figure 1-7: Personal Computer

A **laptop,** or **notebook, computer** is small enough to be placed in a lap or carried by its user from place to place (see Figure 1-9).

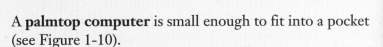

Figure 1-8: Network computer

Figure 1-9: Laptop Computer

A **palmtop computer** is small enough to fit into a pocket (see Figure 1-10).

A **personal digital assistant,** or **PDA,** is a palmtop specialized to store telephone numbers, calendars, schedules, and other personal information. Some PDAs can recognize handwriting and have fax, modem, e-mail, and Internet capabilities.

Figure 1-10: Palmtop Computer

KEY Terms

supercomputer Mainframe computer capable of very high volume and very fast processing; typically used in research and defense applications.

personal digital assistant (PDA) Palm-sized computer specialized to store telephone numbers, calendars, schedules, and other personal information; some offer fax, e-mail, and Internet capabilities.

Computers in Business

The workplace is the arena that has experienced the initial and perhaps most dramatic wave of technological change. At the turn of the twentieth century, most Americans worked in agriculture. The early to mid-century period saw a shift from agriculture to manufacturing. Then, in the last third of the century, another shift occurred away from manufacturing and toward service and information sector jobs. Today, most Americans work in service- or information-oriented businesses that employ computers. Industry analysts estimate that beginning with the year 2001, nearly 90% of all jobs will require some degree of computer use. The Gartner Group, a research firm, predicts that by 2005, 75% of global enterprises will require a major restructuring of their workforce policies and planning due to knowledge becoming the center of wealth production.

COMPUTERS IN
SCIENCE/MEDICINE

From DNA to Outer Space

Some common uses of computers in science are to store and analyze data collected from field work or from experiments, to represent data graphically, to create models and simulations, to control scientific equipment, and to do numerical calculations that would be difficult or impossible to do otherwise.

- The California Institute of Technology (CalTec), the United States Geological Survey (USGS), and the California State Department of Conservation have created a system, called TriNet, to predict earthquakes in southern California. The system consists of over six hundred seismometers that send information about seismic activity to central computers at CalTec and the USGS. A similar system, created by the USGS and the University of California at Berkeley, operates in northern California.

- The Department of Defense uses supercomputers, very powerful computers that make billions or even trillions of calculations per second, to model the movements of individual particles during simulated nuclear blasts. This enables scientists to conduct nuclear tests without physical explosions in the atmosphere or underground.

- Biochemists use computers to create models of complex molecules and to make predictions, based on the shapes of these molecules, about how they will behave. For example, computers are being used to design compounds for the treatment of AIDS and other diseases.

- Scientists at the National Aeronautics and Space Administration (NASA) use computers to calculate trajectories of spacecraft, to control instruments in space, and to collect and analyze data from satellite dishes, cameras, telescopes, and other instruments.

- Until recently, most psychologists in the United States and Great Britain were behaviorists, scientists who believed that the proper province of psychology was the study of observable behaviors. They dismissed discussion of the mind as unscientific. Beginning in the 1960s, however, analogies between the operation of the brain and the computer helped psychologists begin to view the brain as a mechanism (so-called "wetware") for the processing and storage of information. Thus was born an entirely new field of scientific inquiry, called cognitive science, that combines studies in computer science, biochemistry, neurology, and psychology. One field of study within cognitive science is **artificial intelligence**, which involves using computers to simulate human thinking.

- All of the information required to create a human being is contained in a single molecule, called DNA, found in cell nuclei. In the summer of 2000, researchers completed a draft map of the DNA molecule as part of the Human Genome Project, the largest single scientific undertaking in history. The purpose of the project was to create a computer database showing the structure of the human DNA molecule and the locations, on that molecule, of the estimated 100,000 human genes. This project, overseen by the National Institutes of Health and the Department of Energy and completed significantly ahead of schedule because of advancements in computer processing capability, will provide information useful in the treatment of over 4,000 genetic diseases, from cystic fibrosis to certain forms of breast cancer. Scientists in laboratories around the world divided up the task of analyzing (sequencing) human DNA, and the results of their work are posted on the Internet for other scientists to use.

- Health care providers use computers to maintain databases of health records; to monitor patients' vital signs automatically; to control devices, such as pacemakers, implanted in the human body; to extend the capabilities of persons with disabilities; and to peer inside the body by means of computerized axial tomography (CAT) scans, positron emission tomography (PET) scans, and magnetic resonance imaging (MRI).

KEY Terms

artificial intelligence Field of study within cognitive science that involves modeling intelligent or learning behaviors on computers.

Types of Business Applications

Computer systems consist of **hardware,** or machinery, and **software,** or instructions that run on the machines and process information. A piece of software that performs on a particular kind of function is called an **application.** Business applications can be roughly categorized into three types: vertical applications, individual applications, and workgroup applications.

A **vertical application** is integrated software created for a narrowly defined market, such as banking, insurance, or retail merchandising. Usually, the one software product performs all of the functions of the business. For example, a bank might have a mainframe computer at its corporate headquarters connected to ATM machines and to conventional terminals used by managers, tellers, loan officers, and other employees in branch offices. All transactions are fed to and processed by the central computer, which then generates managers' reports, account statements, and other essential documents. A retail pharmacy chain might have a large central computer, linked to terminals in all of its stores, running a single, custom-built application that keeps track of prescriptions, customers' medical histories, cash and charge sales, purchases, inventory, and many other kinds of information.

Most businesses use **application software,** which are programs that perform specific tasks and are used by each worker individually, generally on a workstation, PC, laptop, palmtop, or PDA. Types of application software used in business include:

- **spreadsheets** (software for doing accounting and other types of calculations)
- **word processors** and **desktop publishing programs** (software for writing and doing page layouts)
- **databases** (software for storing and manipulating large amounts of information)
- **graphics programs** (software for producing drawings and other types of illustrations)
- **electronic mail,** or **e-mail** (software for sending messages by computer)
- **personal productivity programs** (software for scheduling and project-planning tasks)
- **software suites** (collections of commonly used programs)

Large corporations often adopt a standard set of application software such as Microsoft Office for their employees. Sometimes, businesses also have cus-

tomized applications written to perform highly specific tasks. For example, an environmental engineering firm might have a program written specifically to help the company's hydrologist analyze the potential for groundwater contamination at construction or manufacturing sites.

In recent years, one of the more promising developments in business computing has been the emergence of **groupware,** which are applications that enable people at separate personal computers or workstations to work together on a single document. Using modems and a groupware application, a designer in Rio de Janeiro can work with a copywriter in Rome to create an ad layout for a marketing manager who watches the work in progress and adds comments or new lines of text to the document from an office in Tokyo.

Computers in the Functional Areas of a Business

Traditionally, business functions have been divided into the following areas:
Finance
Human Resources
Research and Development
Manufacturing
Marketing and Sales
Management

In the area of **finance,** employees use computers to maintain a company's accounting records and to generate its financial statements and reports. Workers use computers to access information about the company's assets, liabilities, costs and expenses, and profits and losses. Computers are also used to prepare payroll checks, to maintain payroll and tax

KEY Terms

computer-aided design (CAD)
Sophisticated computer systems used to design and test products before manufacturing.

computer-aided manufacturing (CAM) Computer systems that enable manufacturing companies to control and change production processes to meet design specifications.

virtual reality Software and hardware used to create simulated environments and a method to view versions of finished products prior to manufacture.

just-in-time inventory Efficient inventory method that automates purchase and delivery of raw materials, ensuring their delivery to assembly lines exactly when needed.

Figure 1-11: Engineers and architects cut drafting time dramatically by using CAD systems in their design work

records, and to produce budgets and financial projections. Today, all financial accounting functions in most midsized and large businesses are fully computerized.

In the area of **human resources,** employees use computers to identify job candidates, to develop wage scales and benefit plans, to keep employee records, to create training materials, and to monitor hiring and promotion data for compliance with fair employment laws.

In the area of **research and development,** businesses use computers to design new products and services. In fact, some of the most sophisticated computer systems today design and test products ranging from airplanes and automobiles to running shoes, pharmaceuticals, and mutual funds. **Computer-aided design** and **computer-aided manufacturing** systems, known as **CAD/CAM** applications, enable manufacturing companies to design and change products without having to waste time and money redoing drawings or old models (see Figure 1-11). Some large companies have gone beyond CAD/CAM systems and are using **virtual reality** software and hardware to create simulated versions of finished products such as buildings, automobiles, and artificial hearts. The advantage of a virtual reality system is that it allows the designer to interact with the simulation in a "walk-through" that efficiently pinpoints

potential problems. Currently, virtual reality is being used to design cars, planes, medical equipment, and many other items. When a design is complete, many CAD/CAM systems can furnish a complete list of necessary materials, along with estimates of manufacturing costs.

In **manufacturing,** computerized **control systems** regulate assembly lines and often, via **robotics,** do the actual assembly and testing. Computerized **just-in-time inventory** systems save manufacturing companies millions of dollars annually by automating purchase and delivery of raw materials, ensuring that these materials will be purchased and delivered to assembly lines exactly when needed.

Marketing and sales departments use databases to gather and store the names, addresses, telephone numbers, tastes, and buying habits of potential customers. Marketing personnel use computers to plan and analyze the results of market surveys, to design promotional materials, to devise pricing strategies for their products, to create and post direct-mail solicitations, to make telephone calls to potential customers, to check customers' credit histories, to bill customers, to check customer orders against inventory, and for many other purposes (see Figure 1-12).

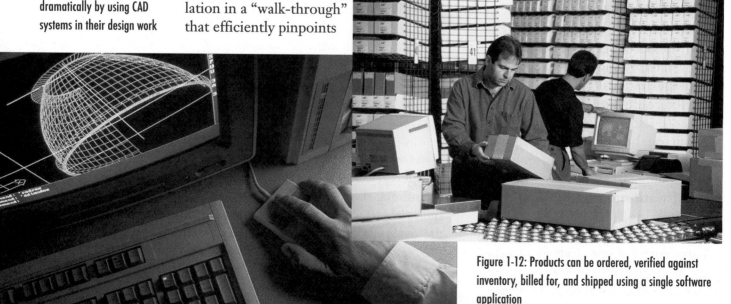

Figure 1-12: Products can be ordered, verified against inventory, billed for, and shipped using a single software application

Management can be defined as the gathering, allocation, and direction of resources—human, financial, and material—to achieve an organization's objectives, one of the most important of which, in a business, is to make a profit. To meet this fundamental objective, managers must gather information, make decisions, and communicate these decisions to employees. Computers have proved indispensable tools in each of these areas. Computer-generated reports of all kinds provide managers with the information that they need. Managers use specialized applications software to generate budgets and schedules, to plan projects in great detail, and to create and deliver training materials. They also use decision support software to project various scenarios and to make decisions based on these projections. Increasingly, communication in the workplace is computerized; memoranda, schedules, reports, agendas, bulletins, and newsletters are composed and printed by computer or transferred directly from computer to computer via electronic mail, or e-mail.

E-Commerce: One Economy, One Market

Business conducted on the Internet, or **e-commerce**, is growing at an extremely fast rate, and the future looks particularly bright for those firms that have made quality Internet investments. To sell their products to a worldwide market, organizations need to have well-designed and carefully monitored **Web sites** (see Figure 1-13). They need to have updated hardware and software equipment, and be committed to ongoing change and employee education. Those firms, on the other hand, that have chosen to ignore the trend in e-commerce may not survive. In fact, the information age has the potential to reward well those who participate in e-commerce and greatly disadvantage those without Internet connections or up-to-date computer hardware and software. For this reason, some people today believe that governments should regulate Internet use or provide Internet ser-

vice on a universal basis to empower economically disadvantaged individuals. Otherwise, they argue, our society will merely help encourage an information-deficient underclass. But calls for more government regulation in these areas have been opposed by those who insist such measures would curtail freedoms of enterprise and of speech. We can expect that such battles will be fought increasingly in the near future.

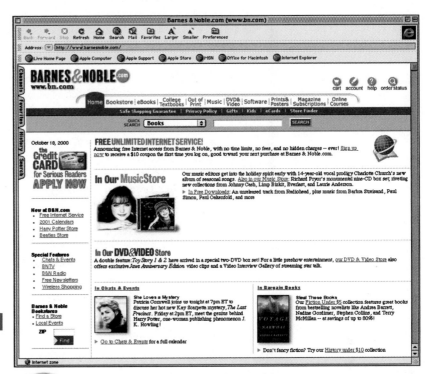

Figure 1-13: E-Commerce Web Site

Redefining Workday Responsibilities

Computers and the Internet have helped redefine work responsibilities for today's knowledge workers. Many jobs no longer fit into the traditional eight-hour-day block. Fewer and fewer people work from nine to five, with the weekend off. Today's knowledge workers, in fact, find that their duties are a twenty-four-hour-a-day affair. Our networked economy engages in commerce around the clock, and successful businesses need to keep pace to compete in the fast-paced, "information-everywhere" market. Employees can use e-mail, pagers, cell phones, and other

e-commerce Business conducted on the Internet either between firms or directly with customers through Web sites.

COMPUTERS IN
GOVERNMENT

One of the first electronic computers, the Colossus, was developed by the Allied forces during World War II to decipher codes created by the German Enigma machines. The first all-purpose, all-electronic computer, the ENIAC, completed in 1946 by J. Presper Eckert and John W. Mauchly, was used to calculate trajectories of projectiles. One of the greatest of the first-generation computers, the UNIVAC I, was built in 1951 by Eckert and Mauchly for use by the U.S. Bureau of the Census. From their beginning, electronic computers have served the needs of government and defense.

All modern government bureaucracies use computers as their primary means for storage, manipulation, and dissemination of information. Government bureaucracies use computers, for example, to store demographic statistics; to process enormous payrolls; to calculate payments to entitlement recipients; to store, analyze, and cross-check records; to track regulatory compliance; to produce budgets; and to generate such documents as the Congressional Record.

In this age of technological warfare, computers have become a key component of defense systems. Computers are used, for example, by the U.S. Department of Defense to simulate potential military scenarios and determine defensive strategies; to guide equipment, from satellites to nuclear submarines; to analyze satellite photos for locations of missile sites, weapons factories, and troop movements; and to keep records for the largest payroll and benefits system on earth.

In the 1970s, many people feared that increased use of computers would lead to increasingly centralized control by government. A popular movie of the period, *Colossus: The Forbin Project,* described two enormous supercomputers, built to control the U.S. and Soviet defense systems, that began to communicate with one another and, as a combined entity, started dictating terms to both countries. The fear of centralized, computer-based control expressed in such science fiction works has proved to be unfounded. Indeed, computers have been as great a force for individual freedom and democratization as they have for tightening of centralized authority. Today, for example, a citizen of the United States can use the Internet to call up a bill under consideration by the Senate and can then send his or her senators an opinion about it via e-mail. This is not to say, however, that governments have not abused the fact-gathering power that computers offer. It remains for citizens to be vigilant about the information governments (and private corporations) collect about them via computers.

Key Terms

embedded computer
Computer that performs its work behind the scenes to automate tasks without special human training or intervention.

telecommute Act of performing a job that involves information management or is creative in nature and does not require the worker to be in a particular location.

devices with **embedded computers** to perform their work at any time. Moreover, twenty-four-hour responsibilities provide today's employees with opportunities to establish a variety of **flexible work schedules**. Rotating shifts, staggered schedules, job sharing, and the increased use of part-time workers can fully meet the needs of a particular organization if well coordinated.

Employees in some jobs do not need to be physically present at the business's central office at all. Using computers, they can **telecommute** from their homes or from any remote location around the world (see Figure 1-14). Many newspaper reporters and other writers or editors, for instance, do much of their work outside of the office. So do certain sales representatives and con-

sultants in various business areas. As the information age moves forward, increasing numbers of jobs that involve information management or are creative in nature will not require the worker to be in a particular location. Another factor driving the increased use of telecommuting is the high cost of lease rates in modern urban office buildings. According to a September 18, 2000, *Business Week* article, some 18 million

Figure 1-14: Telecommuter

U.S. employees worked from home at least one day a week in the year 2000, and that number will only grow as mobile computing becomes a way of life.

Many firms are now experimenting with telecommuting options. When Atlanta played host to the Centennial Olympic Games in 1996, the city that is famous for its extraordinarily congested rush-hour traffic suddenly found its freeway system to be virtually empty. The reason was that significant numbers of employers, fearing that their employees would get hung up in traffic, encouraged them to stay home and telecommute. To everyone's surprise, Atlanta's workers were able to perform the same tasks that they would have done in the office by using computers and other telecommunications devices in their homes. For example, one Atlanta hotel chain routed incoming reservation calls to their employees' homes, and customers' needs were handled as efficiently as ever. Another firm used mini-video cameras to facilitate interaction among employees at different office locations.

Telecommuting also expands employment opportunities for the physically impaired or for those unable to travel to work for any reason. Hearing-impaired persons have used TTY Teletype units for communications for the last few decades, but these have now been supplanted by the use of e-mail. Persons with physical injuries, those in wheelchairs, and those caring for elderly relatives or for small children can now hold full-time jobs by telecommuting from their homes.

Computers in Everyday Life

Just as computers and the Internet have remade the workplace, so too have they dramatically changed the ways in which we communicate, shop, learn, and play. Fewer and fewer people handwrite letters anymore as family members use home Internet access to communicate by e-mail. More and more people shop **online**, where today everything from pet food to houses can be purchased (see Figure 1-15). Online banking and investment services fill many personal finance needs and help streamline record keeping. All aspects of travel planning, including booking airline tickets and making hotel reservations, can be transacted instantly online from anywhere in the world. Home Internet connectivity also provides around-the-clock and around-the-world access to a vast array of all types of information, research materials, and discussion groups. Almost anything a person wishes to know can be found on a Web site posting or in someone's conversation posted in a discussion group. Some people read the daily news on the Web. Others use computers for entertainment. Interactive games, some of which use Internet connections with others around the world, can be especially exciting to play. Other Web-linked applications turn computer games into learning experiences to teach math, reading, and spelling skills painlessly. The Web is also increasingly used for multimedia applications, including downloading and playing music, watching videos, and virtual reality experiences. It is expected that all of these leisure and educational activities will increasingly rely on computers and the Internet in the future.

KEY Terms

online Performing tasks of work, communications, commerce, or entertainment while connected to a network.

Figure 1-15: Groceries purchased online can be delivered directly to the purchaser's home.

EMBEDDED TECHNOLOGY

Computers are embedded in even the most commonplace items today—watches, calculators, remote controls, telephones, and numerous household appliances. Embedded computers are also increasingly found in our cars. Since 1975, pollution control systems, for example, are run by computers. At a rate of thousands of times per second, these intricate systems monitor emission output and regulate variables in the fuel-air mix and ignition timing. Other embedded computers in cars regulate temperature, radio tuning, and seat position. Researchers are developing single, centralized computers to handle all of these needs. In addition, a new breed of computing use has recently entered automobile technology. Microsoft's Windows CE operating system is being adapted for automobile use in order to support more new car features. One of these latest features is the availability of navigation instructions that are linked with Global Positioning Satellites (GPS) and that can provide a driver with directions to an intended location. General Motors has launched its OnStar service (see Figure 1-16), a feature linked to a center where staff members can offer drivers various types of assistance. The OnStar system will also automatically call for help in the event of any deployment of airbags. In addition, some 2001 car models will introduce Internet e-mail service that will use spoken input and audible output. In fact, manufacturers are currently developing versions of such in-car computer systems for consumers to purchase for any car. Clarion, for example, has already introduced the "AutoPC" on the retail market. In our automobiles, embedded computers are providing a greater level of convenience and a wider choice of purchasing options.

Figure 1-16: General Motors' OnStar links drivers to a central office for emergency assistance

A Worldwide Wired Society

Computers and the Internet have altered the way we work, live our daily lives, and enjoy ourselves. But they have done much more than this. They have accomplished another major revolution, that of helping forge a worldwide connected society. Today, metal and fiber optic cables, microwave towers, and satellites with earth stations work together around the globe to create vast telecommunications systems that connect people to each other through the Internet. Previously inaccessible people, countries, ideas, and cultures are now available at our fingertips as we sit in our homes using the Internet. Our world is indeed growing smaller all of the time as people and nations are coming closer through this extraordinary medium.

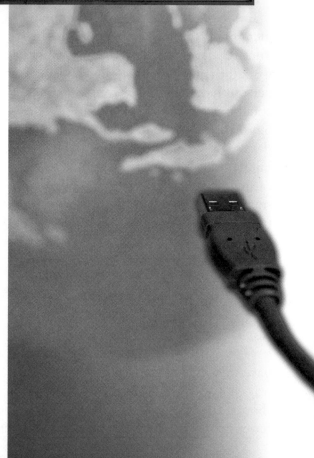

Computers of Tomorrow

In less than one generation, computers have revolutionized our business and personal lives, and the rate of technological change is expected to increase even more dramatically in the future. Future computers will, of course, be smaller and faster with greatly enhanced processing power. But we can hardly imagine today what extremes may be achieved. As an example, researchers are working on computers the size of dust particles that have data collection and reporting capabilities. Still other scientists and technicians are developing miniature robots that can assemble, dismantle, and reassemble themselves to form different structures to meet each task at hand. These robots would be useful, for example, in searching for survivors in a collapsed building following a disaster. Once a survivor has been located, the robots could form themselves into a jack or support device to stabilize the victim as well as a phone to call for help. In a similar manner, researchers suggest the possibility of micro-robots that could be injected into a heart patient. Once inside the patient, the robots could re-form themselves into devices that would perform internal medical procedures, eliminating the trauma of surgery and the loss of blood.

But while such inventions are exciting and have the potential to increase our quality of life, the rapid rate of technological change is also creating serious challenges for society. Research is under way to ensure that computers do not have a negative ecological impact on the environment. Energy consumption and the disposal of outdated computers and other hardware devices are issues of concern. As with any new era, the information age has brought both opportunities and challenges to human society, and we go forward to meet these challenges.

KEY Terms

microtechnology Research into the tiniest designs of computers and robotic machines, with sizes approaching a millionth of a meter.

INNOVATIONS
Computers Smaller than a Human Cell

Perhaps computers should be called incredible shrinking machines! Ever increasing computer-processing power has been accompanied by constantly decreasing physical size. For example, just compare the massive room-sized computers of the 1960s with today's Palm Pilot! Private, university, and government researchers are working on the tiniest designs imaginable. The area known as **microtechnology** is developing machines with sizes approaching a millionth of a meter. These robotic devices have sensing and processing power, and they can report data such as temperature, pressure, humidity, and other physical variables. Such a device could be dropped from an airplane, for instance, so that it could ride the winds of dangerous weather patterns to capture data. This technology has never been possible before.

One major scientific endeavor along these lines is called the Smart Dust project, directed by Kristofer S. J. Pister at Berkeley. Pister envisions systems being taken up into tornadoes much like the devices that were depicted in the movie *Twister*. Pister's view, however, is that the sensors portrayed in the movie were much too large. By contrast, his design is only one millimeter cubed. These same tiny computers could be used for thousands of other applications as well. For example, they could perform espionage functions behind enemy lines in a military conflict. They could also be employed by medical science to circulate through a human body and trace changes in biological systems. Molecular biologists are currently researching even smaller units that are being constructed atom-upon-atom for use in other types of physical research. In fact, the ability to construct tiny computers has opened up marvelous opportunities to explore biological frontiers, such as human genetics, which may someday halt diseases that have plagued the human species for centuries.

Chapter SUMMARY

Computers have truly pervaded our world today. In both visible and embedded forms, they work to enhance our lives and create new opportunities for work and play. Over the last few decades, the advent of computers and the Internet in business has reshaped the world of work in numerous ways. Computers and the Internet have helped increase productivity, a phenomenon that in turn has created a higher paid, professional labor force. It is predicted that income disparities will continue to grow between those who have technological competence and those who do not. Today's knowledge workers in our information society, therefore, need to not only understand basic computer operation, but also be committed to a program of ongoing education as technology changes. In addition, computers and the Internet have fundamentally redefined the nature of work itself. More and more people today are working around-the-clock, on a flexible work schedule, or at home or on the road via telecommuting. The traditional nine-to-five office worker is almost a thing of the past.

Computers have also reshaped our daily lives. Among other activities, we can shop, bank, play games, find information, do research, and send letters on the Internet. Today as well, multiple convergences of telecommunications, data, and entertainment media are taking place. This combined media, the next stage in Internet development, will use high-speed links to open up a new era of integrated computing, communication, and entertainment. At the same time, computers are becoming much, much smaller and faster. Already, embedded computers work behind the scenes to automate many appliances, our automobiles, and other items we use every day. In the future, embedded computers, including tiny robots, will continue to pervade our daily lives, helping us live and work better. Exciting times in the world of computer technology lie ahead! We have designed this textbook to help you gain the computer literacy skills that will allow you to thrive in the changing times to come.

Key terms are presented here in the order in which they are cited in the text. A complete list of key terms in the text, in alphabetical order with definitions, can be found in the Glossary at the end of the book.

information age (p. 4)
knowledge worker (p. 4)
Internet (p. 4)
networked economy (p. 4)
computer literate (p. 4)
wired (p. 5)
plugged in (p. 5)
optical character recognition (OCR) (p. 5)
productivity (p. 6)
convergence (p. 6)
joystick (p. 8)
mainframe (p. 10)
dumb terminal (p. 10)
data (p. 10)
processor (p. 10)
supercomputer (p. 10)
minicomputer (mini) (p. 10)
workstation (p. 10)
network (p. 11)
personal computer (PC) (p. 11)
network computer (NC) (p. 11)
laptop or notebook computer (p. 11)
palmtop computer (p. 11)
personal digital assistant (PDA) (p. 11)
artificial intelligence (p. 12)
hardware (p. 12)
software (p. 12)
application (p. 12)
vertical application (p. 12)
spreadsheets (p. 13)
word processors (p. 13)
desktop publishing programs (p. 13)
databases (p. 13)
graphics programs (p. 13)
electronic mail (e-mail) (p. 13)
personal productivity programs (p. 13)
software suites (p. 13)
groupware (p. 13)
finance (p. 13)

human resources (p. 14)
research and development (p. 14)
computer-aided design (CAD) (p. 14)
computer-aided manufacturing (CAM) (p. 14)
CAD/CAM applications (p. 14)
virtual reality (p. 14)
manufacturing (p. 14)
control systems (p. 14)
robotics (p. 14)
just-in-time inventory (p. 14)
marketing and sales (p. 14)
management (p. 15)
e-commerce (p. 15)
Web site (p. 15)
embedded computer (p. 16)
flexible work schedule (p. 16)
telecommute (p. 16)
online (p. 17)
microtechnology (p. 19)

Changes, Challenges, and CHOICES

CONFIGURING KNOWLEDGE

Multiple Choice Questions

Choose the best answer from those provided.

1. Today's economy is known as a(n) _____ economy due to the widespread use of linked computers in the business world.
   a. computer
   b. agrarian
   c. mechanical
   d. automated
   e. networked

2. Computer technology has increased _____, a concept that means that workers create more output per unit of input.
   a. slack
   b. time
   c. costs
   d. productivity
   e. communications

3. Today's merging of the computing, entertainment, and communications industries is commonly referred to as _____.
   a. WEBtv
   b. convergence
   c. merger
   d. antitrust
   e. networking

4. One effect of the information age is the increased use of _____ to produce labor-intensive goods such as textiles and small appliances.
   a. illegal aliens
   b. workers in foreign countries
   c. high-tech workers
   d. skilled laborers
   e. none of the above

5. The income disparities between workers with and without computer competence is expected to _____ in the coming years.
   a. increase
   b. decrease
   c. remain unchanged
   d. increase and then decrease
   e. decrease and then increase

6. Persons who have specific training or experience in an area that can be applied to the evaluation of information are called _____.
   a. technicians
   b. information specialists
   c. learned workers
   d. knowledge workers
   e. none of the above

7. When workers can perform their tasks from a distant location using network connectivity, they are said to be _____.
   a. remotely performing
   b. distance learning
   c. teleworking
   d. infocommuting
   e. telecommuting

8. The information age network feature that has virtually replaced TTY communications for the deaf is called _____.
   a. Braille-mail
   b. e-mail
   c. info-mail
   d. TTY-mail
   e. none of the above

9. When a computer is integrated into the design of a product to perform tasks in an unseen manner, it is called a(n) _____.
   a. integrated computer
   b. stand-alone computer
   c. hidden computer
   d. embedded computer
   e. holistic computer

10. _____ refers to business activities conducted through the use of the Internet and other network linkages.
   a. i-commerce
   b. Internet commerce
   c. e-commerce
   d. linked commerce
   e. none of the above

True or False?
Rewrite each false item to make it a true statement.

1. The correct chronological order of the following historical time groupings is the agrarian age, the information age, and the industrial age.
2. The networked economy provides a foundation that results in the increased productivity that characterizes the information age.
3. Technology changes are bringing about a convergence of the telecommunications, entertainment, and computing industries.
4. Computer literacy means possessing an advanced level of computer skills.
5. Few workers in the future will job share or have flexible work schedules due to the increased pressure to always be on the job.
6. The Internet opens up new work possibilities for physically impaired persons.
7. Computers are often embedded in household appliances as control systems without the user even knowing they are there.
8. A vertical application is a program written for generic business use that is usually run on a personal computer.
9. CAD/CAM applications enable manufacturing companies to design and change products without having to revise drawings and models.
10. Very powerful computers that perform billions or trillions of calculations per second are called networked computers.

TECHNOLOGY IN CONTEXT

Prepare to discuss each of the following questions, drawing upon the material presented in this chapter as well as additional information you may have researched on your own.

1. Describe how embedded computers can carry out their actions without the user being aware of their existence. Identify three examples of embedded computers that you use daily, and describe both how they function and how they enhance your lifestyle.

2. Explain how computers and the Internet have reshaped the world of work. How is a worker's life different today than a worker in a) your parents' generation; b) your grandparents' generation? What do you think a worker's life will be like in the year 2025?

3. Explain what kind of employees are valued in the information age and what kind of skills and education are particularly sought after. Identify some examples of interesting new career paths that use computer technology. Discuss how computer technology is changing your current career or the career you wish to pursue in the future.

4. Explain why today's worker can expect job responsibilities to be a twenty-four-hour-a-day task. How have computer and Internet technologies both created this environment and provided solutions to it?

5. Explain why computer literacy is a vital survival skill for today and the future. Identify the challenges that are likely to be faced by individuals who fail to take the responsibility to become computer literate.

6. Seek out Internet or written materials that describe the problems associated with a society split into computer literate and illiterate members. In what ways should society members who are computer competent help those who are not? Should individuals who dislike or distrust technology be forced to learn it—for example, should schools have mandatory computer classes? Should the government interfere in computer development and use? Explain from the perspective of a free society.

DEVELOPING MINDSHARE

1. Locate a firm or organization that has made a significant change in the way work is performed due to computer and Internet technology. Interview an employee affected by this change, or form an evaluation on your own of how successful the change has been. Identify any difficulties that might have impeded a smooth transition to the new methods. What improvements would you suggest to make the change easier or more effective?

2. Visit a car dealership in your area to view the new line of cars that employ so-called "smart car" technology. Discuss with a salesperson what such technology entails, who is interested in purchasing such a car, and what the future of computer technology in automobiles may be.

3. Use the Internet or library sources to identify computer and telecommunications equipment that is available to enable physically challenged users to enhance their lifestyles. Identify jobs that have opened to these individuals because of computer and Internet technology. Describe tasks where telecommuting might be the most efficient way to perform a job for those unable to travel to work.

4. Research the Internet and find out what libraries and resources are on the Net to help you in college. Answer these questions: What is a full-text library? Can you check out books online? Is your college library online? How do the online services compare to the "real thing"? What site offers the best place to find dictionaries, language translators, and reference tools?

5. Research distance learning at your school. Are any distance learning courses offered? How do they function compared to traditional classes? Think about learning style. What do you like or dislike about distance learning classes?

THINK TANK

Review the Reality Interface at the beginning of this chapter and consider other major changes to workplace environments brought about by computer technology. The changes in the airline industry that are replacing tickets and saving millions of dollars are also impacting other workers and society as a whole. The employees who create, print, handle, and dispose of tickets are now without jobs. In addition, less printing will occur, less paper will be required, fewer trees will be harvested, and so on down the economic supply chain. Some of the displaced jobs are skilled workers, but many are not. If lesser skilled workers ultimately lose their jobs, there will be an increased demand for public assistance and social services. In the face of foreign competition for labor-intensive manufacturing, a significant problem seems to be arising for unskilled workers in America that has implications for all of society.

Team Challenge: Write a report describing another industry that has made changes to its operations to reap savings through the use of computers and technology. Identify the kinds of jobs that will ultimately be omitted within the firm. Which other firms that supply goods or services to the initial firm will also be affected by the decreased demand for their output? Describe the compound effects of the cuts, and suggest possible areas of saving in resources other than labor. Conclude by weighing the positive versus the negative effects of the changes. Is the overall change good or bad for the firm, individuals, or the economy as a whole? What role, if any, should the federal government play in mediating the effects of this change? Should the government intervene? Should companies be offered incentives to help employees displaced by technological improvements? Defend your position.

Answers to Configuring Knowledge Questions

Multiple Choice: 1 – e; 2 – d; 3 – b; 4 – b; 5 – a; 6 – d; 7 – e; 8 – b; 9 – d; 10 – c
True-False: 1 – F; 2 – T; 3 – T; 4 – F; 5 – F; 6 – T; 7 – T; 8 – F; 9 – T; 10 – F

Reality INTERFACE

Using Computers to Prevent Medical Errors

Did you know that the eighth leading cause of death in America is medical error? According to the Institute of Medicine, nearly 98,000 patients die each year because of medical mistakes. That's more than die of breast cancer, diabetes, or in traffic accidents. In today's managed care environment, many different professionals collaborate in the care of a single patient. Each time a patient is seen by yet another medical professional or a treatment change is made, a potentially dangerous situation for the patient arises. Combining certain drugs, for example, can pose deadly risks. So can patients who are allergic to certain medications. Sadly, one of the most common causes of medical error is poor handwriting on medical charts, prescriptions, and treatment instructions.

One of the greatest benefits of today's computer technology is its ability to significantly reduce human error. In the medical field, computer monitoring systems can be used to identify potential conflicts between prescribed medicines and to warn of possible health risks. A Boston hospital, Brigham and Women's Hospital, recently installed just such a computerized prescription system. Its interactive warning system alerts healthcare providers to any existing patient allergies to drugs, harmful dosing levels, or other problems associated with prescribing and administering medication. As a result, medication errors in this hospital have decreased by an astonishing 81%. Yet, despite its remarkable success rate, only 5% of the nation's hospitals currently use this kind of computer monitoring system.

Today, computer technology that can send prescriptions directly from the computer to a selected pharmacy is available in many doctors' offices. Moreover, the online pharmacy Rx.com offers a linked PocketScript wireless pad that physicians can carry on their rounds: a doctor creates an electronic prescription for her patient that is transmitted directly to the pharmacy. No more struggling to read handwritten prescriptions! As in so many fields, computer technology is revolutionizing the healthcare industry by reducing human error. In the future, we can expect insurance firms to put more pressure on medical professionals to use these safety measures routinely.

2 Understanding COMPUTER HARDWARE

OBJECTIVES

After reading this chapter, you will be able to. . .

➤ Explain the concept of information systems

➤ Describe how computers process data

➤ Identify the main components in a personal computer system

➤ Explain the parts and function of a microprocessor

➤ Distinguish among various types of memory, such as ROM, RAM, cache memory, and virtual memory

➤ Explain the major factors affecting a computer's speed

➤ Describe the differences between magnetic, optical, and magneto-optical storage devices and give examples of each

➤ Identify the most common input and output devices and describe their uses

KEY Terms

information systems (IS) Process through which data is collected, processed, delivered, or stored.

central processing unit (CPU) Part of computer that transforms data–the microprocessor or "brain" of the system.

memory Chip storage area used by CPU as workspace while it transforms data.

storage Permanent location of programs and data, primarily hard and floppy magnetic disks and optical media.

How Computers Work: An Overview

In today's world, businesses and individuals use computers to manage huge amounts of **information,** or data, to create a wide variety of communications. **Information Systems (IS)** refers to the four-part process centered around data:
1. Collecting or **inputting** data.
2. Transforming or **processing** data.
3. Delivering or **outputting** data.
4. Storing data.

Information systems theory doesn't just apply to computers; biological ecosystems, cameras, and music reproduction equipment are just a few examples of other areas that use systems theory. Study Figure 2-1 to learn how the information systems concept applies to computers and other seemingly unrelated areas.

To operate effectively as an interconnected system, a computer requires certain devices for inputting, processing, outputting, and storing. Users typically enter data into the computer by typing (keying) on a **keyboard.** That data is transformed by the **central processing unit (CPU),** the microprocessor "brain" of the system with its chip memory. Output of data occurs through peripheral devices such as a printer, and data is stored typically on magnetic disks either on a hard drive within the system unit or in an external floppy disk drive. System output can also be recycled as **feedback.** Feedback allows users to compare the results received with the results expected. If the output differs from expectations, users can modify the input and reprocess the data. It is the processing of data that changes it into usable information—thus the origin of the term **data processing.**

Electricity: The Lifeblood of the Computer

But where does the system of interrelated components that comprise a computer obtain its "heartbeat" or "lifeblood" to operate? It does so through electricity. Computers use electrical switches to process and store data. In order for the processing chips in the CPU to hold and work with their data, a constant stream of electric power is required. If the power is turned off, the data being processed (in memory) is lost. However, data can be stored permanently through the use of magnetic and optical media (which will be discussed below).

It is not uncommon to confuse **memory** and **storage,** but they are very different functions. Internal memory is made up of chips that the CPU uses as workspace while it transforms data. Storage, on the other hand, holds data permanently. In fact, storage is sometimes called "external storage," because its function is performed essentially *outside* the CPU. The term "external" may also be confusing since the most common form of storage is the hard disk that is typically located *inside* the computer's hardshell case. But both hard and floppy disks, and all other storage media, are still technically external, relative to the CPU, even though they are housed inside the case. Figure 2-2 shows the CPU, the hard disk, and other elements on the interior of a computer system unit.

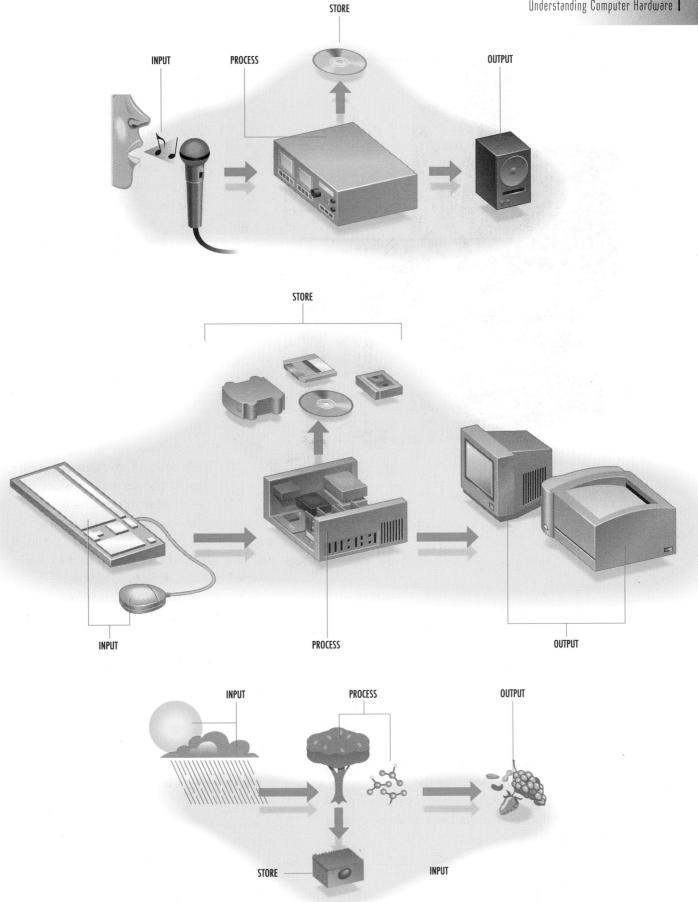

Figure 2-1: Systems Theory
A system is comprised of inputs that undergo a transformation. The result of the transformation is called output. In a system, all components are necessarily interrelated. Any change in one part of the system could alter another part. Systems theory is the study of how components in a system interact.

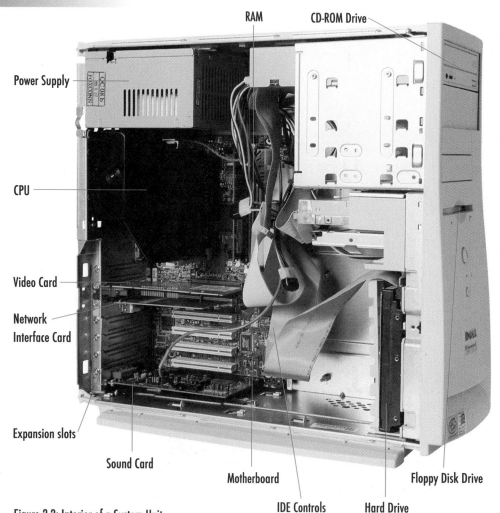

Figure 2-2: Interior of a System Unit

RAM   CD-ROM Drive

Power Supply

CPU

Video Card

Network
Interface Card

Expansion slots

Sound Card

Motherboard

IDE Controls   Hard Drive

Floppy Disk Drive

imal number system in which numbers are indicated by the symbols 0 through 9. Soon, however, engineers hit upon a much simpler system that used **binary numbers,** which are constructed solely of the symbols 0 and 1. All computer storage uses this **binary code.** Engineers settled on a **base-2** system because, as we have seen, the electrical storage chips can only store data in one of two states: off (0) or on (1). Therefore, the base-2 system was a perfect match for the electrical circuitry of the CPU.

Base-10 Decimal System

By contrast, the familiar **base-10** decimal system uses ten elements, 0 through 9. When using the decimal number system, a person counts from zero up to nine and then, to represent the number ten, carries a 1 to the tens place and writes a 0 in the ones place: 0, 1, 2, 3, 4, 5, 6, 7, 8, 9, 10

When using the **binary number system**, a person counts from zero to one and then, to represent the number two, carries a 1 to the twos place and writes a 0 in the ones place: 0, 1, 10, 11 (0, 1, 2, 3 in decimal). Table 2-1 compares counting from one to nine in binary and in decimal.

How Computers Process Data

After you've input data, what goes on inside the computer to transform that data into output? That depends in part on your computer's operating system program and the particular software application package you are using. But with all computers, data must move through electronic pathways to different storage locations and accessories, all of which are under the control of the CPU. To understand the variables that affect the processing of data, you need to know how the data is represented inside the system.

How Computers Encode Information

All computers perform the data-to-information transformation by using a simple number system to represent data. The first large computers made use of the dec-

binary code System of numbers comprised solely of the symbols 0 and 1.

Table 2-1: Counting in Binary and in Decimal

Binary	Decimal
0	0
1	1
10	2
11	3
100	4
101	5
110	6
111	7
1000	8
1001	9

Binary numbers are a powerful tool for computing because they can easily be represented by simple electrical switches. An open switch (in an electromechanical relay, a vacuum tube, or a transistor) can represent a 0, and a closed switch can represent a 1. By this means, the switches in a computer can be made to represent numbers (and anything else that can be encoded as numbers). Figure 2-3 illustrates how an on/off electrical switches system equates to decimal and binary numbers.

10011010 is a byte. Several systems have been developed for using binary numbers to encode symbols and characters. The most commonly used today is the **American Standard Code for Information Interchange,** or **ASCII.** ASCII code uses 8 storage bits and can represent 256 items. See Table 2-2 for the ASCII codes of the alphabet letters and numbers 0 through 9.

Figure 2-3: Binary and Digital Numbers in On/Off Code

Decimal Number	Binary Equivalent				
0	OFF	OFF	OFF	OFF	0
1	OFF	OFF	OFF	**ON**	1
2	OFF	OFF	**ON**	OFF	10
3	OFF	OFF	**ON**	**ON**	11
4	OFF	**ON**	OFF	OFF	100
5	OFF	**ON**	OFF	**ON**	101
6	OFF	**ON**	**ON**	OFF	110
7	OFF	**ON**	**ON**	**ON**	111
8	**ON**	OFF	OFF	OFF	1000
9	**ON**	OFF	OFF	**ON**	1001
10	**ON**	OFF	**ON**	OFF	1010
11	**ON**	OFF	**ON**	**ON**	1011
12	**ON**	**ON**	OFF	OFF	1100
13	**ON**	**ON**	OFF	**ON**	1101
14	**ON**	**ON**	**ON**	OFF	1110
15	**ON**	**ON**	**ON**	**ON**	1111

For example:
0   0

=1

=0

Light switches in on and off positions

Using Binary to Encode Text and Other Items

In computer jargon, a single piece of data, which can be either a 1 or a 0, is referred to as a *binary digit,* or **bit.** To represent other items, such as alphabetic letters, punctuation marks, special symbols, and codes for directions such as backspace, one can assign each item an arbitrary binary number that becomes its code. An eight-digit binary number, referred to as a **byte,** can be used to represent one of 2^8, or 256, separate symbols and characters. For example, the eight-digit sequence

Table 2-2: Alphabet Letters and Numbers in ASCII Code

Character	ASCII Binary Code							
A	0	1	0	0	0	0	0	1
B	0	1	0	0	0	0	1	0
C	0	1	0	0	0	0	1	1
D	0	1	0	0	0	1	0	0
E	0	1	0	0	0	1	0	1
F	0	1	0	0	0	1	1	0
G	0	1	0	0	0	1	1	1
H	0	1	0	0	1	0	0	0
I	0	1	0	0	1	0	0	1
J	0	1	0	0	1	0	1	0
K	0	1	0	0	1	0	1	1
L	0	1	0	0	1	1	0	0

(continued)

KEY Terms

byte Eight-digit binary number that can be used to represent any one of 256 separate symbols or characters.

American Standard Code for Information Interchange (ASCII) Standard code used internally to represent entire standard keyboard's characters with a binary equivalence.

M	0	1	0	0	1	1	0	1
N	0	1	0	0	1	1	1	0
O	0	1	0	0	1	1	1	1
P	0	1	0	1	0	0	0	0
Q	0	1	0	1	0	0	0	1
R	0	1	0	1	0	0	1	0
S	0	1	0	1	0	0	1	1
T	0	1	0	1	0	1	0	0
U	0	1	0	1	0	1	0	1
V	0	1	0	1	0	1	1	0
W	0	1	0	1	0	1	1	1
X	0	1	0	1	1	0	0	0
Y	0	1	0	1	1	0	0	1
Z	0	1	0	1	1	0	1	0
Numbers								
0	0	0	1	1	0	0	0	0
1	0	0	1	1	0	0	0	1
2	0	0	1	1	0	0	1	0
3	0	0	1	1	0	0	1	1
4	0	0	1	1	0	1	0	0
5	0	0	1	1	0	1	0	1
6	0	0	1	1	0	1	1	0
7	0	0	1	1	0	1	1	1
8	0	0	1	1	1	0	0	0
9	0	0	1	1	1	0	0	1

All data is stored and processed using these codes. The data storage and processing capabilities of a computer are sometimes expressed in bytes, although today the number of bytes is typically so large that other terms such as **megabyte** (about 1 million bytes) or **gigabyte** (about 1 billion bytes) are used. See Table 2-3 for more of these terms.

Table 2-3: Measures of Data Storage

Abbreviation	Unit of Storage	Equivalent Amount
Bit	Binary Storage	Takes value of 0 or 1
Byte	8 Bits	1 byte usually represents one keystroke
K	Kilobyte	1,024 bytes or 2^{10}
MB	Megabyte	1,024,000 bytes or about one million bytes
GB	Gigabyte	1,024,000,000 bytes or about 1,000MB
TB	Terabyte	1,024,000,000,000 bytes or about one million MB

Although the ASCII code is adequate to support most common communications, worldwide computing tasks that use many languages require far more characters. Therefore, a new and much larger coding system called **Unicode** has been developed. Unicode uses 2 bytes, or 16 binary digits, and can represent more than 65,000 separate characters. As such, it can meet the needs not only of the English language, but also of most written languages throughout the world.

Hardware Basics

Computers use a variety of hardware devices for processing data. The following section takes a look at the devices designed for each stage of information processing: input, processing, output, and storage.

Input Devices: Entering Data into the Computer

No computer can transform data into information unless data is first entered for processing. Several different types of data entry devices exist, including tactile, audio (voice) and sensory, and optical hardware. What works best in one situation may not be appropriate for another. For example, the situation of a physician transmitting a prescription directly to a pharmacy might best be handled by a voice-activated device. Optical devices, on the other hand, might be the appropriate input device for pictures or graphics. In all cases, it is important to select the input device that will collect the data accurately and efficiently to produce the desired output.

Tactile Entry

Many input devices require a human user and "hands-on" operation to enter data into a computer. One of the most common types of these devices, the keyboard, has actually been around a long time. The **QWERTY** typewriter keyboard (named for the first six keys at the left of the first row of letters) took on its current configuration more than a century ago when time and motion study engineers arranged the typewriter keyboard in a layout they thought would prevent keys from jamming and thus speed up the typing process. Unfortunately, this meant that the weakest small fingers were assigned to press the most frequently used letters of the alphabet. Since then, new designs have been introduced, including the DVORAK keyboard, which places the most commonly used keys close to the user's fingertips. However, most people have rejected learning a new key layout, and the QWERTY keyboard remains the most common keyboard design.

Besides the alphabetic and numeric/symbol keys, today's computer keyboards include specialized keys, such as modifier keys, cursor keys, and function keys. **Modifier keys** enable the user to change the symbol or character that is entered when a given key is pressed. The Shift key, for example, makes a letter uppercase. **Cursor keys** allow the user to change the location of the **cursor,** a symbol that appears on the monitor to show where in a document the next change will appear. The cursor keys are the up, down, left, and right arrows on a standard keyboard. **Function keys** are labeled F1, F2, F3, and so on. These keys allow the user to issue commands by pressing a single key. (See Figure 2-4.)

Point-and-Click Devices

Engineers continue to propose keyboard design and screen changes to enhance computer users' ease and comfort. "Point-and-click" devices for a **graphical user interface (GUI)** such as Windows 98 or Windows 2000 are available in a wide variety of styles, as shown in Figure 2-5. A GUI is easier to use than a command-line interface because the user can interact with onscreen **icons,** or thumbnail pictures, representing familiar objects such as a trash can, a file folder, or a printer. With a GUI, the screen itself becomes a virtual **desktop,** a place where the user can click on icons or buttons to execute a command, drag items in the screen to other locations, and pull down menus of options. A user points and clicks with a **mouse,** which next to the keyboard is the second most common input device. A mouse moves the cursor in the computer screen to correspond to directional movements made with the mouse. It can be designed generically or custom fitted for right- or left-handed users. A **trackball** is much like a mouse turned on its back with the roller sensor facing up. Unlike a mouse, which is moved over a pad, a trackball remains stationary, and the user moves the ball with his fingers or palm. Popularized by video games, this

graphical user interface (GUI) Technique through which the user can click icons or buttons to execute a command, drag items on the screen to other locations, and pull down menus of options.

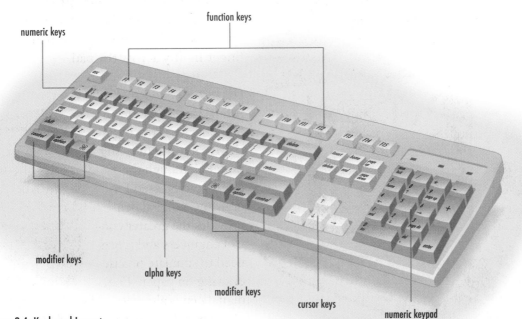

Figure 2-4: Keyboard Layout

EXPANSION CARD

What Happens to Discarded Computers?

Technology is advancing so rapidly that today's computer systems need to be replaced at least every three years to maintain maximum efficiency. However, the disposal of outdated computers poses a significant problem for our society. An individual's computer can easily be given to a person with less advanced computing skills. But large numbers of discarded systems in a business or organization are a much different matter. Although many such systems are donated to institutions or charities, statistics show that 62% of these donated machines are abandoned within the first six weeks.

Typically, discarded machines are utterly obsolete, not worth repairing and incompatible with newer systems. Since only about 20% of electronic equipment can be reused for parts, 80% must be disposed of. Most U.S. companies still take their unwanted computers to a dumpsite. It is estimated that by 2005, 150 million used computers will be dumped into landfills at a disposal cost of more than 1 billion dollars. A single monitor may take several thousand years to decompose biologically. But attempting to recycle computers also creates hazards: incineration generates toxic smoke and only recovers small amounts of precious metals. Such high recovery costs and small payoffs have driven much of this recycling work to less developed nations where stringent pollution controls don't exist. While nations and firms worldwide continue to seek solutions, the problem of disposing of outdated computers remains one of society's great challenges in the future.

Figure 2-5: Common Point-and-Click Devices

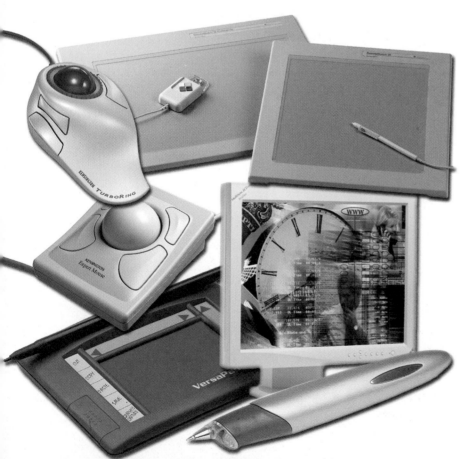

type of pointing device performs particularly well in work environments where mouse movement space is limited. Other pointing devices for special circumstances also exist. Information kiosks in many hotels and airports, and ATM cash machines use a **touchscreen** for input. It works just as the name implies: a user chooses options by touching appropriate parts of a screen. To save space, laptop computers often use a **touchpad** rather than a mouse or trackball. The touchpad operates by the user simply moving her finger lightly across the pad.

Digitized Pens and Tablets

A final type of tactile input device is the **digitizing pen** and **drawing tablet**. Although the mouse can be used for drawing, a digital pen provides the greater control engineers and artists need to simulate precise drawing on paper. The digital pen is also part of the popular personal

Figure 2-6: Handspring Visor Deluxe Personal Digital Assistant

digital assistant, such as the Newton Message Pad, the Handspring Visor, or the Palm Pilot. Users choose menu options and write information on the screen with the special pen (see Figure 2-6).

Audio and Sensory Entry

Most likely, keyboards and other tactile input devices will be around for some time. However, today's computer designers are increasingly committed to voice input and embedded computer designs that require little or no human interface with the computer.

But how is sound represented in the computer? To explore that question, you need to know that all sounds in nature are made up of vibrations that are **continuous,** called **analog waves.** Analog waves oscillate at different rates for high or low pitches. Such sounds can be input digitally by converting them into binary numbers and then storing them. These numbers are processed through equipment that can then synthesize a very close approximation of the original sound. But the key word for such sounds is *continuous.* This means that any numerical representation of sound data must contain an infinite number of decimal places. However, computer memory and storage deal with finite, or fixed, amounts. So, the solution to this problem is to take a sample of what the desired sound is like in an instant and record the binary number that it represents. Since this sound has a start and an end, it is finite and can be represented in a computer. By taking many thousands of such samples of the sound

per second and then replaying them in the same time sequence, the fragments are "squeezed" together so that the multiple starts and ends are fused, creating the effect of continuous sound. Figure 2-7 illustrates the process of converting analog sounds to digital data.

This **sampling** technique converts analog sounds into **digital storage.** In essence, this is how a music CD stores a musician's performance digitally. That performance can be replayed without mechanical distortion since the numbers don't change in storage. In fact, a process similar to this sampling technique can convert any analog state of nature, such as temperature or pressures, into a digital equivalent for storage. For example, an infinite number of sample temperatures between 71.0 and 72.0 degrees exists. The fact that we could add an enormous number of decimal places representing many billions of samples is not really necessary since few of us can feel the difference between 71 and 72 degrees. So, an appropriate digital representation might be at a single decimal place and then rounded up at .5 degree. These variations help us use the power of digital technology by providing a digital equivalent that is "close enough" to reality.

Voice recognition software uses this same technology to create human oral interaction with computers. You can dial some handheld or automobile cellular telephones, for example, by using voice-activated controls. To do so, you speak into a microphone that converts the sounds through voice recognition software into the binary equivalent. Such

Figure 2-7: How Analog Sounds Are Converted to Digital Data

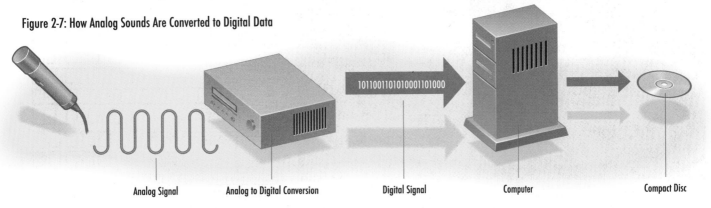

Analog Signal Analog to Digital Conversion Digital Signal Computer Compact Disc

KEY Terms

Universal Product Code (UPC)
Barcode made up of lines and spaces that appears on virtually every product sold in the United States, which the computer translates into a useful product number.

point of sale terminal (POS)
Computer terminal that serves as a cash register as well as a data collection device.

magnetic ink character reader (MICR) Device that can read and process at high speed somewhat strangely shaped numbers printed with magnetic ink, as on the bottom of a cancelled check.

Figure 2-8: Universal Product Code (Barcode)

technology is especially useful for hands-free data entry and for the physically challenged. The computer industry is committed to wide-scale development and marketing of computer voice interfaces, and we can expect to see much more of this technology in the near future.

Optical Entry

No doubt you've already encountered optical digital recognition in grade school when you took standardized tests. Marking answers in the spaces with a #2 pencil and being admonished not to make stray marks on the paper have introduced a generation of students into the world of **optical mark recognition (OMR).** Scanning devices called readers use light reflectivity to sense the presence or absence of a mark—a binary condition that can be digitally stored. A similar technique is used by retail stores with **barcode readers** and the **Universal Product Codes (UPCs)** that now appear on virtually every product sold in the United States (see Figure 2-8). The lines and spaces in the barcode contain symbols that the computer translates into a number. The computer then uses this number to find information about the product, such as its price, purchase date, or quantity ordered, in a computerized record, or database. Moreover, a version of readers called **wand readers,** which look like pens, can interpret alpha and numeric data preprinted onto sales tags, charge slips, or inventory records. These devices usually accompany computer terminals that serve as cash registers and are typically called **point of sale (POS) terminals** (see Figure 2-9).

Another widely used version of optical input is optical character recognition (OCR), technology that can read numbers and letters that are handwritten. For OCR to read printing, the letters and numbers must be formed in a standard manner and placed inside defined boxes. This input device, for example, is used for the United States Federal Tax Form 1040-EZ so that any taxpayer can directly enter data into the government's computers (see Figure 2-10). Yet another high-speed reader, the **magnetic ink character reader (MICR),** is used in banking for rapid account settlement and

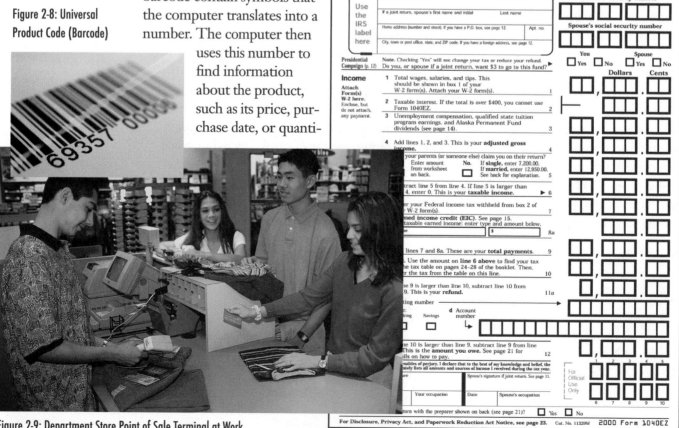

Figure 2-9: Department Store Point of Sale Terminal at Work

Figure 2-10: Federal Tax Form 1040-EZ

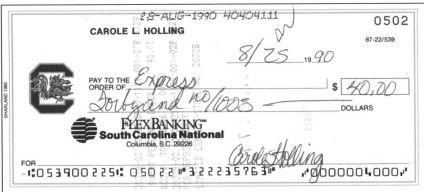

Figure 2-11: Cancelled Check with Account Numbers in Magnetic Ink

routing of checks. You may have seen the strangely shaped numbers, printed with magnetic ink, on the bottom of a cancelled check, as shown in Figure 2-11.

Scientists are currently developing other optical input methods that can store facsimiles of actual data in almost photographic quality. High-speed digital cameras with extremely high resolution, for instance, can convert any visible object into binary equivalent code (see Figure 2-12). Any picture, drawing, or diagram can thus be stored in database files. The consequences of this developing technology are exciting and wide ranging. A company's database of employee profiles, for instance, can now include a digital photo of the employee and her fingerprint alongside text data. An arborist firm's database can include digital photos or diagrams of the trees or shrubs marked for pruning beside textual information such as the homeowner's address and phone number. It is no exaggeration to say that this remarkable type of data-object storage is currently revolutionizing the way databases are created and maintained throughout the world.

Scanning

The use of **scanners** has grown significantly over the last few years as prices have fallen. These optical input devices use a form of a video camera to sense a sample of a spot on a page that is then represented by a number that registers its color, brightness, and

density. Most computer pictures are stored as a combination of the primary colors red, green, and blue **(RGB).** One byte is typically used for each color, which means that one 24-bit number represents each spot on the image. Scanners are used for a variety of purposes. Text can be scanned and then analyzed by OCR software to provide a document that can be modified in an appropriate editor such as a word processor. Drawings and pictures can also be scanned for storage

Figure 2-12: How a Digital Camera Works

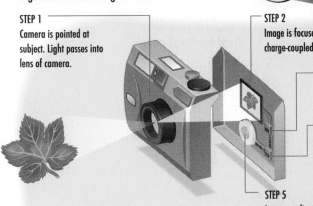

STEP 1
Camera is pointed at subject. Light passes into lens of camera.

STEP 2
Image is focused on a chip called a charge-coupled device (CCD).

STEP 3
The CCD generates an analog signal that represents the image.

STEP 4
The analog signal is converted to a digital signal by an analog-to-digital converter (ADC).

STEP 5
Image quality is adjusted by a digital signal processor (DSP) and the image is stored on a PC Card, disk or other media in the camera.

STEP 6
Images are transferred by a cable going from the camera to the computer, or a PC Card or disk inserted into the computer. Images can be copied to the computer's hard disk.

STEP 7
Images can be viewed on screen using software supplied with the camera.

and modification by graphics software packages. Video and **animation** files are simply a succession of still images that are then shown rapidly to simulate action. In fact, with today's technology, all graphic images can be converted into digital format for storage, although some large files, such as video and still image files, usually require a form of **data compression,** or data shrinkage, for long-term storage or transfer. See Figure 2-13 for an illustration of how a scanner works.

data compression Process for shrinking size of binary data files for long-term storage or transfer.

bus One of a number of electronic pathways through which signals travel inside a computer, allowing communication among the various components of a system.

Processing Devices: Transforming Data into Information

Once data is entered into the computer, it needs to be converted into useful information. As we have seen, all pro-

Figure 2-13: Scanner Technology

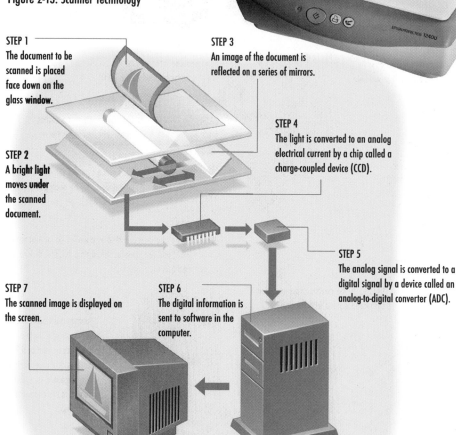

STEP 1
The document to be scanned is placed face down on the glass window.

STEP 2
A bright light moves under the scanned document.

STEP 3
An image of the document is reflected on a series of mirrors.

STEP 4
The light is converted to an analog electrical current by a chip called a charge-coupled device (CCD).

STEP 5
The analog signal is converted to a digital signal by a device called an analog-to-digital converter (ADC).

STEP 6
The digital information is sent to software in the computer.

STEP 7
The scanned image is displayed on the screen.

cessing action is performed by the central processing unit or CPU. But other internal hardware devices also enable the data transfers that will make these processing actions possible.

The Internal Hardware

The components in your computer are manufactured in many places throughout the world by a wide variety of companies. Those components are then assembled into complete computer systems by other firms. Computer components include the system board, or motherboard, with its CPU and memory, and additional peripheral devices for input, output, and storage. Differences in each of these components affect the system's performance. It is, therefore, important for all parts to be **compatible** with each other in order for the system to perform efficiently. This section introduces each of these components and describes some of the configurations that can result from their combination.

System Board, or Motherboard

The central processing unit transforms the data that is entered into the system into useful information. The CPU chip itself is connected to its memory and other components of the system by being plugged into the **system board,** or as it is commonly called, the **motherboard,** as shown in Figure 2-14. The motherboard is the main circuit board in the computer and consists of a collection of electrical pathways. Each motherboard contains a number of major electronic pathways called **buses.**

Signals travel inside a computer by these buses, and they allow communication between the various components in the system (see Figure 2-15). Think of them as kinds of vehicles for carrying data and instructions. The primary bus is the main connecting link for the system, and special buses are used for other applications such as for data. Early computers used an eight-bit bus; as of mid-2000, the common widths are 32 bits and, in limited applications, 64 bits. It is through these different buses that the binary code representations of the data input into the computer flow through the stages of processing.

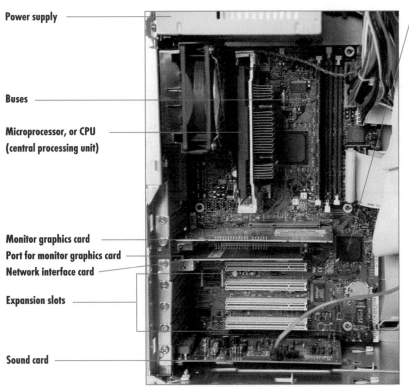

Figure 2-14: System Board with Buses

The Central Processing Unit (CPU) Chip

The CPU is comprised of a number of major components that perform individual tasks but work together as a single unit. The **control unit** operates likes a traffic officer, directing the traffic or instructions on the computer's electrical highways, or buses. It organizes work and directs all data movement and processing. The **arithmetic logic unit (ALU)** is where all mathematical and logical operations are performed. A third major component of the CPU is primary memory or storage. Primary storage is usually provided in chips that are external to the

arithmetic logic unit (ALU)
Component of the CPU where all mathematical and logical operations are performed.

Figure 2-15: How Electrical Signals Travel on Buses

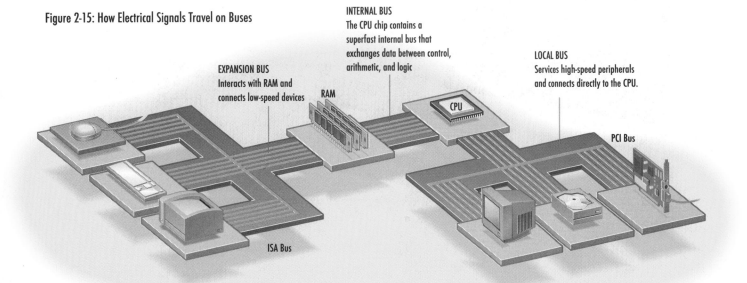

CPU, but are connected by a bus that provides instantaneous access to them. See Figure 2-16 for an example of a CPU.

Processing Speed

For the circuits within a computer to operate properly, the electrical signals that reach them must arrive at the same time. For this reason, every personal computer has an internal clock that synchronizes events within the computer, in effect turning the processor on and off very rapidly. This internal clock determines its speed by the number of electric pulses it creates, and the speed is reported in units of millions of cycles per second, called **megahertz (MHz).** With the development of ever more powerful CPUs, processing speed keeps climbing. But speed alone is not an adequate measure for comparison. The number of bits simultaneously processed has also increased. A CPU that processes 16 bits of data at 200MHz performs less work than one that can process 32 bits concurrently. Most modern systems are 32- or 64-bit processors, and speeds have already exceeded 1,500MHz, although most personal computers in use today have speeds of around 400MHz.

To better understand how the variables of speed and bits processed impact computer performance, imagine that the 8-bit bus is an 8-lane highway. Your data is a car traveling at 65 miles per hour. If more traffic flow is needed on the highway, engineers can simply increase the number of lanes or raise the speed limit. As personal computers have developed, bus width has increased first to 16 bits, then to 32 bits, and now to 64 bits to correlate with the increasing speed and capabilities of the CPUs. The bus speed has also increased from 100MHz, then to 133MHz, and now to 400MHz. Our "highway" now has up to 64 lanes of traffic moving at around 400 miles per hour without wrecks! This impressive performance growth is expected to continue into the near future. In fact, to gain even more speed, some manufacturers have simplified the programming code that enables a CPU to gain in performance. These simplified instructions are called **reduced instruction source code (RISC)** as opposed to **complex instruction source code (CISC).** In the future, the RISC programming approach may dominate the industry because of its speed advantage.

CPU Memory

The primary memory of a computer typically consists of chips that can be accessed directly at any time and reused at a

Figure 2-16: Central Processing Unit (CPU)

intel® pentium®4
1.5GHZ/256/400/1.7V
SL4SH COSTA RICA
3038A629-0144
i®©'00
9048A666

RAM

PCI Bus

Local Bus

BUS INTERFACE

ALU

REGISTERS

Control Unit

CPU

INNOVATIONS

Mass Data Processing for Tomorrow

The large-scale integrated circuits and microprocessors that power today's computers use a process called photolithography to etch the circuitry onto silicon wafers (see Figure 2-17). But there are technological limits to the smallness of the etched circuitry. Even with newer methods being discovered, a limit to the use of silicon will be reached eventually. Researchers are currently working on alternative methods of data storage and manipulation. For instance, scientists are now performing interesting research on data manipulation at the molecular level using protein as the medium instead of a silicon chip. They are programming it at the level of the atom using quantum physics to reflect different values (see Figure 2-18). Not only is extreme speed attained by this method, but the speed also occurs in a smaller amount of space. Another alternative currently under study is a completely new way to handle information using holographs.

Binary data can be stored in a holographic pattern that can be read in parallel meaning so that the data in the image is all read or written in one single operation. Researchers expect to develop storage media no larger than a deck of playing cards that will hold 1TB (one trillion bytes) of data and can be accessed at 1GB (one billion bytes) per second. Mass data processing and storage of this magnitude is absolutely astonishing and something incredible to anticipate in the not-too-distant future.

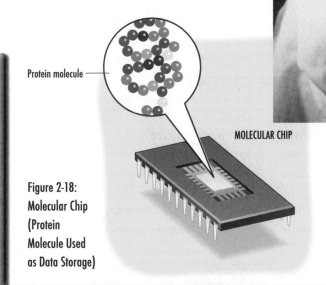

Protein molecule

MOLECULAR CHIP

Figure 2-18: Molecular Chip (Protein Molecule Used as Data Storage)

Figure 2-17: Silicon Wafer with Etched Circuitry

computer user's control. These chips are called **random access memory (RAM)** because any bit of data in this memory can be reached by its specific **storage address** when called for by the control unit. When a user works on a personal computer, the data that she enters, along with large portions of the computer's operating system and of the application programs that are running, are written to RAM and read from it as needed. However, RAM chips lose their data if the flow of electricity is interrupted, and so they are also referred to as **volatile memory.** RAM chips are usually mounted in single or double rows onto small boards that snap into place on

the motherboard (see Figure 2-19). These are called either **single in-line memory modules (SIMMs)** or **double in-line memory modules (DIMMs).** When a consumer decides to purchase a computer, he must consider carefully how much RAM his computing needs and his wallet allow. Today, most personal computers range from 64MB to 128MB of internal memory.

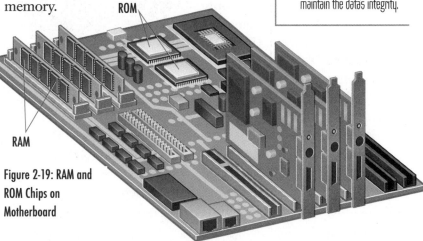

ROM

RAM

Figure 2-19: RAM and ROM Chips on Motherboard

EXPANSION CARD

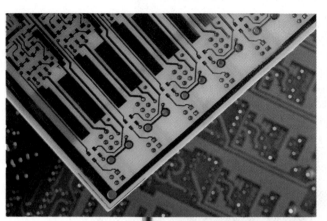

When people buy computers, they often inquire about different "brands" of systems. But the "brand name" of a computer is usually only the trade name of the firm that assembled the parts. Those parts were probably manufactured elsewhere. In fact, generic parts can be purchased by any assembler anywhere in the world, installed into a $25 metal and plastic case, and labeled with the assembling firm's "brand" name. This practice means that used, recycled, or refurbished components can easily be labeled and sold as a "new" system without the consumer's knowledge. Most computer "manufacturers" engage in this practice. Though many firms jealously work to protect their reputations by honoring warranty claims, their recycled goods are merely turned into other computers often because the cost of discarding repaired parts is too great.

Yet another purchasing dilemma for the consumer occurs when large national computer companies create a proprietary method for installing components into their configuration for their own assembly-line convenience or so that generic parts cannot be used as replacements. This often means that parts with a much higher replacement cost must be purchased from the original assembler when the warranty period is over. For the average consumer, therefore, standardized or generic industry designs offer an advantage if the computer has a defective part or needs an upgrade. Since no single firm can possibly be the world's best at producing every computer part, a generic design makes possible the configuration of a system that matches the consumer's needs by providing the ability to select each component independently. When consumers opt for packaged computer deals, *caveat emptor*–let the buyer beware!

KEY Terms

Read only memory (ROM) Type of computer memory that is permanent, programmed into the chip by the manufacturer, and cannot be changed or erased by the user.

flash memory Chips whose memory content can be changed by the user but continue to hold their data even without the use of electricity.

cache Chip memory holding area in which data and instructions most recently called from RAM by the processor are temporarily stored for possible repeated use.

Read only memory (ROM) is another type of memory that is used in most computers for start-up instructions or data that is too important to lose. Unlike RAM, the data in a ROM chip is permanent, or nonvolatile. It must be programmed into the chip by the manufacturer, and it cannot be written over or erased by the user. It remains even when the computer is shut off. Finally, other types of specialized memory chips exist such as **erasable programmable read only memory (EPROM),** ROM chips that are re-programmable, and **flash memory,** chips that hold data without the use of electricity. These special chips essentially belong to the ROM or RAM families of chips, and ROM and RAM designs will likely remain the mainstays for computer memory in the immediate future.

Figure 2-20: Cache Memory in a CPU

Cache Memory

CPU performance is also enhanced by the use of an internal unit of memory that anticipates the need for data in order to avoid a slowdown in processing. This internal memory device is called a **cache** (see Figure 2-20). Cache memory is essentially a holding area in which the data and instructions most recently called from RAM by the processor are temporarily stored. When a processor needs an instruction from RAM, it first looks for that instruction in cache memory and, because some instructions are called frequently, finds it there often enough to speed up processing. Most currently manufactured CPUs use this caching technique.

Ports and Expansion Slots

A computer that is not connected to input, output, or storage devices is like a brain with no connections to arms and legs. Generally, one connects an external device to a computer by plugging it into a port that is built into the computer or provided by an expansion card.

A **port** is a connector, generally found on the back of a personal computer, that allows a user to connect devices to the computer. A **serial port,** also referred to as a **communications (COM) port,** transmits one bit of data at a time and is used on IBM PCs and compatibles to connect devices such as keyboards, modems, and mice. A **parallel port,** which transmits eight bits of data at a time, is used on PCs to connect devices such as printers and scanners. A **video port** is used to connect a monitor. See Figure 2-21 for examples of ports.

The primary bus on the motherboard is connected to a number of empty locations where expansion may take place. **Expansion cards** inserted into one of the **expansion slots** add various capabilities to the computer. Originally, expansion cards were needed for monitor output, telephone or network connections, and similar peripheral devices. But newer computers actually build these features into the motherboard as a cost-saving measure. Expansion cards can also be purchased for special functions such as networking, video, sound, and increased speed. The number and types of expansion slots that are available in a computer depends on the design of the mother-

board. A computer with more expansion slots usually costs more than one that has fewer, and consumers should remember that there is no reason to purchase extra expansion capacity if it will not be used. Figure 2-22 shows expansion cards inserted into expansion slots.

A type of expansion card called a **PCMCIA card,** or **PC card** for short, is used in portable computers. PC cards are credit card-sized adapters that can connect a portable system to networks, telephone connectors, auxiliary storage, or other peripheral devices. Although some PC card connections are used in desktop computers as a convenience for those who also use the connection in a laptop, further growth in the PC card industry for desktop use is not expected. Desktop computer components that perform these same functions are sold in much larger volumes and thus at lower cost than the price of separate PC card connections.

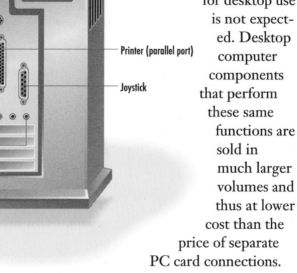

Figure 2-21: Serial, Parallel, and Video Ports

Labels: Mouse, USB ports, Keyboard, Serial port, Monitor, Speaker, Phone/modem, Microphone, Power, Printer (parallel port), Joystick

Output Devices: Receiving Information after It Has Been Processed

Once data is introduced into a computer and processed, the information created from the raw data is produced as output. Output can be sent to another control unit, for example, as on a cold winter evening when the temperature sensor in your living room thermostat instructs a control unit to turn on your furnace. Output can also be sent to a human user in the form of a display on the computer

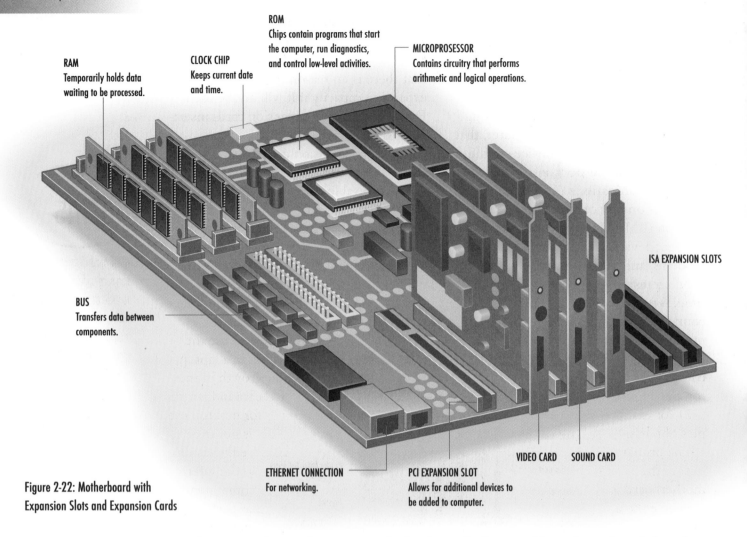

RAM
Temporarily holds data waiting to be processed.

CLOCK CHIP
Keeps current date and time.

ROM
Chips contain programs that start the computer, run diagnostics, and control low-level activities.

MICROPROSESSOR
Contains circuitry that performs arithmetic and logical operations.

ISA EXPANSION SLOTS

BUS
Transfers data between components.

VIDEO CARD   **SOUND CARD**

ETHERNET CONNECTION
For networking.

PCI EXPANSION SLOT
Allows for additional devices to be added to computer.

Figure 2-22: Motherboard with Expansion Slots and Expansion Cards

monitor or a printout from an attached printer. In fact, a wide variety of **peripheral output devices** can be customized to meet nearly any output need.

Monitors

Perhaps the simplest way of receiving output is by viewing a computer **monitor** or **video display terminal (VDT),** an example of which is shown in Figure 2-23. This type of output is sometimes called **soft copy** as opposed to the **hard copy** of a permanent printed version of the information. Monitors have the advantage of immediate feedback: they show the data as it is entered along with the results of the processing, if any, as it is performed.

The display you see on your monitor's screen consists of tiny dots called **pixels,** which stands for "picture elements." An expansion board on the motherboard called a **video adapter** creates the display from the flow of data from the CPU. To create the pixels, the computer requires a form of memory called **video RAM (VRAM).** Most computers today use from 2MB to 16MB of VRAM, although some of the newer models have 32MB. The larger the VRAM memory, the greater the picture details and quicker the display of the picture.

Figure 2-23: Standard Monitor

Typically, a monitor creates images by arranging approximately 72 pixels on each side per square inch. These pixels are displayed through a matrix grid, as shown in Figure 2-24. A space called a **dot pitch** exists between the pixels of this grid. A smaller dot pitch results in a higher **resolution,** or image quality, and high-resolution monitors produce less eyestrain. Most monitors today have a 15- to 17-inch screen and a .28mm dot pitch. The higher the number of pixels, the sharper and clearer the image displayed on the monitor will be. Monitors today are often described by the number of rows and columns of pixels that can be displayed. For example, an **S-VGA** monitor can display 1,024 columns and 768 rows of pixels, thus it is said to have a 1,024 x 768 image.

Monitors are categorized by certain characteristics. They can be either monochromatic or color. They may also use either a glass **cathode ray tube (CRT),** which is what a television uses, or a **liquid crystal display (LCD),** which is the type of display in digital watches, calculators, and laptop computers. Each type of monitor requires a particular video adapter to define the screen image. Monochrome monitors, for instance, contain a predominantly black and white background, although sometimes amber and green colors are also used. Since each pixel can take on only two colors, just one memory bit is needed to define a monochrome monitor's screen image value—either darker or lighter. Color monitors, on the other hand, must reproduce a much greater spectrum of value. Each individual pixel, when assigned a single byte of memory, can take on 256 different values. This means that numbers representing various combinations of the primary red, green, and blue colors can create a palette of 256 different hues. Such a video display is called 8-bit color. By adding two additional memory bytes, the resulting 24-bit display creates a

palette in excess of 16 million shades, and is thus referred to as **true color.** Since more than enough hues in a true color palette can represent the color spectrum needed for all photo and video applications, this technology is rapidly becoming the industry standard. Figure 2-25 illustrates how CRT color monitors display color.

Figure 2-24: Monitor with Section of Type Enlarged to Show Pixels

YOUR WORLD-WIDE SOURCE

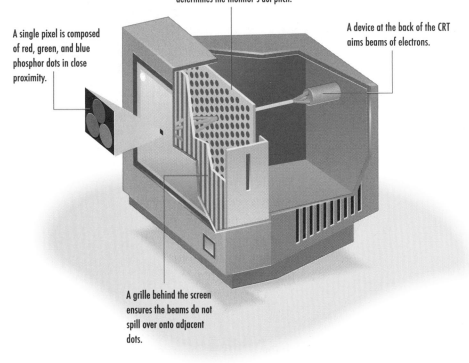

Figure 2-25: CRT Color Monitor

A single pixel is composed of red, green, and blue phosphor dots in close proximity.

The beams pass through a phosphor coated grid containing holes. The number of holes determines the monitor's dot pitch.

A device at the back of the CRT aims beams of electrons.

A grille behind the screen ensures the beams do not spill over onto adjacent dots.

LCD displays are generally standard for portable computers because, unlike CRTs, they are thin, lightweight, and consume very little power. They are sometimes hard to read, however, because of inadequate contrast. Although they produce images that are inferior to those produced by CRTs, LCDs have improved in recent years and are now making their way onto desktops. In locations where space is a factor, **flat panel LCD** displays are ideal, but their cost so far has been prohibitive for the average consumer. LCD technology is also used for output projection devices that project images for group settings. As is generally true of all such technology, computer hardware prices have decreased as production methods have improved. Flat panel and projection displays will probably become much more affordable in the near future. Figure 2-26 shows a standard monitor next to a flat panel LCD.

Figure 2-26: Standard Monitor and Flat Panel LCD

Printers

Printers provide hard copy, a permanent written record of a computer's output. Three general categories of printers currently exist. The first general type, **impact printers,** make contact with the paper through a carbon source, somewhat like a typewriter. Smaller capacity personal printers of this type create by impact a series of dots that are arranged in the shape of the letter or number. This **dot matrix** technique is similar to the

arrangement of light bulbs that show numbers on a scoreboard at an athletic event. As with screen resolution, the greater the number of dots per inch, the better the quality.

Another kind of impact printer, a **line printer,** can print entire lines of text at very fast speeds in mainframe large-volume settings. Both dot matrix and line printers get readable text onto a page successfully, but their print quality is generally not very professional looking and graphics, if even accommodated, are poor.

A second category of printers, **ink-jet printers,** create hard copy without impacting the page. Rather, these printers spray ink in dot form to create text and graphics equally well. Ink jet printers create up to 2,400 dots per inch (DPI) and blend primary colors to simulate a palette quite close to the one used by the monitor. A third type of printer, **laser printers,** use technology similar to a photocopier to create output. A laser beam creates points of electrical charge on a cylindrical drum. Toner, composed of particles of ink with an opposite electrical charge, sticks to the charged points on the drum. As the page moves past the drum, heat and pressure fuse the toner to the page. Some other types of laser printers use alternative sources of color such as wax sticks or color transfer sheets to perform essentially the same task. With all laser printers, the quality of the text and graphics is usually superb. Figure 2-27 shows examples of the three types of printers.

Besides printers, another type of hard copy output device is widely used in the engineering and design fields. **Plotters** use ink to draw designs, diagrams, maps, and blueprints and print them onto large format paper, as shown in Figure 2-28. A plotter has several pens with different color cartridges. A computer sends binary data to the plotter, which translates the signals into coordinates and places pen marks on each specified location. Some plotters move the paper vertically under

Figure 2-27: Dot-Matrix, Ink-Jet, and Laser Printers

static pens, while others use a flatbed design that moves the pens over static paper. In years gone by, engineers had to draw blueprints and diagrams by hand, and then go through a lengthy process to create copies. Additionally, any changes to the diagrams had to be laboriously entered by hand. Today's technology makes the entire process, including corrections, immensely more efficient. Engineers who use plotters proficiently are able to do much faster work, reducing the need for drafters. Output devices such as plotters have truly revolutionized the ways in which engineers draft and produce documents.

Figure 2-28: Plotter Printing in Large Format

Other Output Devices

Other kinds of specialized output devices have been developed to meet a wide variety of needs. Output can be both enlarged by projection onto screens for group presentations and reduced to tiny sizes for filing in archives. You are probably familiar with output that has been photographed onto **microform** media, either roll film or small sheets (see Figure 2-29). **Multimedia** applications can mix sound and motion video to produce stimulating presentations. Or, a computer expansion board can convert a computer's sampled sounds into output that can be played through traditional stereo speakers. Yet another expansion board can be used for motion video input and output that permits both editing and the mixing or blending of media. Such multimedia computer applications are currently an exciting and creative area of growth.

Storage Devices: Keeping Data Secure

Collected data and the output generated are typically saved into a nonvolatile form of storage. As computer output has grown more complex, particularly in multimedia applications and video, the demand for larger storage devices has increased. There are two main types of storage devices: magnetic and optical.

Magnetic Storage

The most common storage devices are magnetic. A **magnetic storage device** is the dominant form of data storage today. Hard disk drives come in a wide variety of capacities, up to 73GB and soon even higher. Most home computer systems, however, have capacities of less than 30GB. See Figure 2-30 for examples of magnetic storage devices.

Figure 2-30: Floppy Diskette, Hard Disk, Tape Reel, and Tape Cartridge (clockwise from upper left)

Optical Storage

Optical storage devices are read by means of lasers, much the way music CDs are read by CD players. This medium operates by directing the laser light onto the surface of the disk and then back to an opto-electronic device that detects changes in light. The areas holding data reflect light differently than the rest of the aluminum layer, and it is these

Figure 2-29: Student Using Microfiche Reader

magnetic tape Inexpensive data storage that uses continuous tape to store content, but is slow because tape needs to unwind to find storage location.

works by applying electrical charges to iron filings on a revolving media, orienting each filing in one direction or another to represent a 0 or a 1. One of the earliest storage formats was **magnetic tape.** While this type of storage was inexpensive, the data stored on tape was slow to recover. To locate particular data, a user first had to unwind the tape to find the storage location. This access is referred to as **sequential access.** By contrast, **magnetic disks,** from **floppy diskettes** (1.44MB) to large-scale **hard disk drive** packs, are accessible to the CPU almost immediately. This **direct access** method

INNOVATIONS
Tomorrow's Computers, Today's Daydreams

What will tomorrow's computers look like? Predictions are as varied as their predictors. Only one thing is certain: they will not look at all like they do now. Today, we think of a personal computer as a monitor, keyboard, mouse, and CPU box. But the computer systems of tomorrow will probably be more like a network that controls virtually every function in the home. Video panels will be available in each room to provide computing, telephone, and entertainment functions by voice control or by graphic touch panels. The home's temperature, security system, and even its cooking apparatus will be controlled by this central system. Homeowners will be able to program the system from anywhere in the world.

In tomorrow's computers, system security will recognize users by biological methods such as eye, fingerprint, or photo rather than by ID numbers or passwords. Computer processors will be dramatically faster than we experience today, and storage capacity will increase to accommodate greater demands. Computer displays will increasingly employ flat panel technology, and portable output will be flexible enough to fold for storage. In the world of the future, in fact, computers will be seen as an integrated and necessary everyday working partner, as opposed to a separate piece of machinery. While the rapid proliferation of new technology ensures that no one can really know the future, such integrated home computer systems are currently being developed and tested.

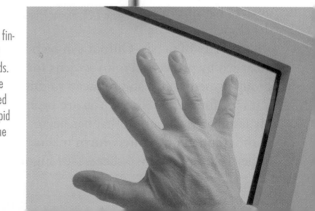

changes in reflectivity that are interpreted as bits and bytes. Four widely used types of **optical storage media** include:

- Compact disk with read only memory (CD-ROM).
- Write once, read many compact disk (CD-WORM).
- Rewriteable compact disk (CD-RW).
- Digital video disk with read only memory (DVD-ROM)

The earliest optical storage form developed for a computer was the compact disk with read only memory, or **CD-ROM** (see Figure 2-31). These round disks on which data, sounds, or images can be stored are still widely used. One CD-ROM has the capacity to hold almost 600 floppy disks, and any one floppy disk can hold all of the text in this book two times over! Table 2-4 compares the storage capabilities of various storage media, including optical storage disks.

Another optical storage device is the family of drives called write once, read many, or WORM. A **CD-WORM** drive allows the user to write data to the disk once, but data thus written is permanent and cannot be erased. By contrast, a version called compact disk rewriteable, or **CD-RW** drive, allows the user to erase and rewrite data on the disk many times. A final type of optical storage device is the **DVD-ROM.** The introduction of high-definition television around the world is creating a demand for higher

capacity digital recording and playback devices for home use. **DVD (digital video disk),** a high-capacity format that saves digital data onto a CD-sized disk, has been adopted as the new industry standard and will most likely soon replace the VCR. DVDs can hold binary data for a computer with a capacity up to 17 gigabytes, an amount of storage that would fill from 2,600 to almost 12,000 floppy disks depending upon the format chosen. The DVD-ROM drive used in computers can also play standard CD and CD-ROM disks. Moreover, if the DVD replaces the VCR, it will also need to have the recording capability of home video. In future computer applications, we may even see **DVD-RAM** become the storage device of choice.

Figure 2-31: CD-ROM and CD-RW Drive

Table 2-4: Secondary Storage Capacities

Type	Medium	Capacity
High-Density Floppy Diskette	3.5-inch Magnetic Disk	1.44MB
Zip Drive - 100	3.5-inch Magnetic Disk Cartridge	100MB
Zip Drive - 250	3.5-inch Magnetic Disk Cartridge	250MB
Laser Servo - Superdisk	3.5-inch Magnetic & Optical Cartridge*	120MB
Sony HiFD Drive	3.5-inch HiFD Technology Cartridge*	200MB
CD-ROM	Optical Disk	to 700MB
WORM CD-R	Magneto Optical Disk	to 700MB
CD-RW	Magneto Optical or Phase Change	to 700MB
DVD, DVD-R, DVD-RAM	Optical Laser	4.7 to 17GB

* Also reads and writes standard 3.5-inch floppy diskettes.

EXPANSION CARD

Managing Your Hard Drive

The primary storage medium used with most personal computers today is the hard drive. Typically, the hard drive stores the computer's operating system, application programs, fonts, and data files created with the application programs. However large or small the hard drive, at least 10 to 15% of its total capacity should be left free. If the hard drive becomes too full, the user is likely to experience various difficulties, such as printing problems caused by an inability to write temporarily to the drive the files that are to be printed.

Both internal and external hard drives generally come preformatted. When setting up a hard drive for the first time, the user should follow the manufacturer's guidelines for installing the drive and for formatting it, if necessary. When the user installs programs and files onto the hard drive, the operating system should be loaded first, followed by fonts, application programs, and data files, in that order.

As the operator uses a hard drive—writing files to it, erasing files, and writing more files—the files may become fragmented, or written to different sectors of the hard drive, causing the drive eventually to operate more slowly. To correct such fragmentation, users can run a disk defragmenter, shipped with many hard drives or available as a separate application, to rewrite files so that all sections of each file are written to contiguous sectors of the drive. Utility programs can also be used to check a hard drive for unreliable portions, or sectors, and to block data from being written to those sectors.

When a hard drive fails for any reason, it is said to have crashed. Hard drives these days are generally quite reliable, but hard drive failure is always a possibility, so it is essential to have back-up copies of all important programs and files. Some people back up such data onto floppy disks or some large-capacity removable medium such as a Zip disk, a CD-RW, or a DVD-ROM.

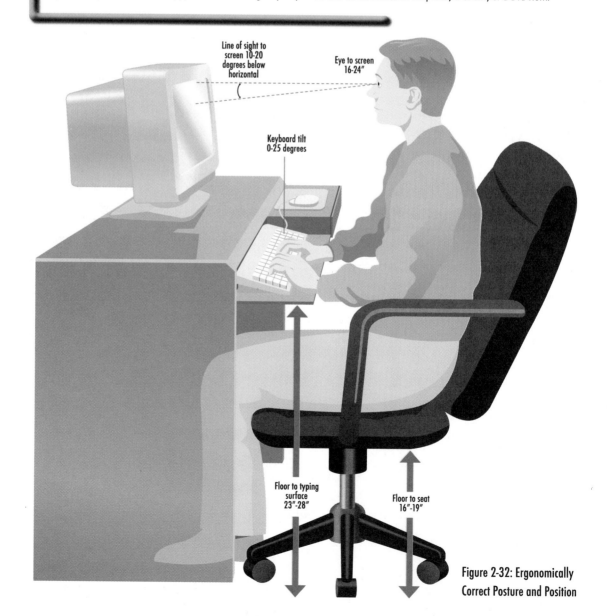

Line of sight to screen 10-20 degrees below horizontal

Eye to screen 16-24"

Keyboard tilt 0-25 degrees

Floor to typing surface 23"-28"

Floor to seat 16"-19"

Figure 2-32: Ergonomically Correct Posture and Position

Ergonomic Design—Health and Safety Issues

Any discussion of computer hardware needs to include information on the effect computer use has on one's health. **Ergonomics** is the science of examining the design of a work environment to improve workers' safety and health—and thus their productivity. While ergonomics involves much more than the design of a computer workstation, many of the problems associated with continual work on a computer are common to jobs that require repetitive movements. Any activity that involves repeated motion or places a strain on parts of the body can lead to repetitive-stress injuries. One such injury, **carpal-tunnel syndrome,** is a medical con-

dition that causes pain and numbness in the hands and lower arms. Frequent computer users also face the problem of poor sitting posture. Maintaining poor posture over an extended period of time can lead to cardio-vascular, neuromuscular, and orthopedic complications (see Figure 2-32 for an illustration of *correct* posture at a computer). In addition, radiation from long periods of viewing a VDT monitor can result in eye-strain. Such problems associated with computer use and the larger issue of **ergomatics** have recently been studied by the United States Department of Labor. If implemented, the guidelines they recommend may mean significant cost increases for an organization that chooses to ignore problems in this area.

Key Terms

ergomatics Broad study of the issues of physical harm that can come to users from extended computer use, such as radiation and repetitive stress injury.

EXPANSION CARD
OSHA and the Costs of Computer-Based Injuries

The U.S. Department of Labor estimates that 1.8 million workers annually experience musculoskeletal injuries related to ergonomic factors. The Occupational Safety and Health Administration, or OSHA for short, has calculated that up to 600,000 employees miss some work time annually due to such injuries. These injuries have been called the most prevalent, expensive, and preventable workplace injuries in the country. Assembly-line workers, jobs where heavy lifting is required, and computer use are the worst offenders. Recently, the Department of Labor has proposed new work regulations that, if approved, will take effect in early 2001. The proposed regulations state that an employee who is diagnosed by a physician with a work-related injury can expect to have his work environment corrected to relieve the cause. His income will also be protected should he require medical care. OSHA estimates that the cost of implementing these regulations will total $4.2 billion a year. Estimates of costs due to ergonomic injuries currently are $15 billion to $20 billion for workers' compensation, and $30 billion to $40 billion for related expenses such as medical care. However, the U.S. Chamber of Commerce and other business groups have argued that these costs are grossly understated. Rather, the National Association of Manufacturers estimates the cost to be 2.5 to 15 times greater than the OSHA figures. As is obvious from these numbers, the problem is an enormous one. Clearly, responsible employers want to protect the health of their workers and avoid such exorbitant expenses.

If the Department of Labor's proposed regulations take effect, changes will no doubt occur in the way computer work is performed. While various different keyboard, mouse, and chair designs are currently on the market (see Figure 2-33), soon consumers may see "OSHA Approved" labels on such products. A National Academy of Sciences long-term study of workplace injury should be completed in 2001 and will no doubt provide additional insight and guidance into the manufacture of such ergonomically correct products.

Figure 2-33: Wrist Pad for Keyboard

Chapter
SUMMARY

A computer's hardware performs the input, processing, output, and storage functions required to implement the information systems concept. The central processing unit, or CPU, is essentially the "brain" of the computer where all of the work is done. The CPU is comprised of a control unit, arithmetic logic unit (ALU), and internal memory. Internal memory chips are either read only (ROM) or randomly accessible (RAM). ROM memory holds its content without the need for electrical current, while RAM chips are volatile and lose unsaved data when the power fails. When entered into the computer, data must be processed and stored using a binary number code because electrical currents exist in only two states—on or off.

The CPU and memory chips plug directly into a main system board, or motherboard, that has openings where expansion boards can be attached. These expansion slots enable the connection of types of input, communication, and output devices to the system. In the computer, data travels along an electronic pathway called a bus to perform the activities directed by the CPU. Bus capacity plus speed are important measures of a computer's performance. Input hardware for a computer include keyboards, pointing devices, and scanning devices that convert real-world analog data into digital form. Output can be displayed in a soft-copy form such as on a monitor, or printed in hard-copy form on a variety of printing or plotting devices. Processed data is stored in either magnetic or optical forms. While magnetic disk format is currently the most common form of storage, optical storage devices show promise for the future. Ergonomic design is important for the health and safety of frequent computer users in the workplace. Designs to reduce the chance of user injury are being developed and governmental regulations on the industry may be on the immediate horizon.

Key Terms

Key terms are presented here in the order in which they are cited in the text. A complete list of key terms in the text, in alphabetical order with definitions, can be found in the Glossary at the end of the book.

information (p. 28)
information systems (IS) (p. 28)
inputting (p. 28)
processing (p. 28)
outputting (p. 28)
information systems theory (p. 28)
keyboard (p. 28)
central processing unit (CPU) (p. 28)
feedback (p. 28)
data processing (p. 28)
memory (p. 28)
storage (p. 28)
binary numbers (p. 30)
binary code (p. 30)
base-2 (p. 30)
base-10 (p. 30)
binary number system (p. 30)
binary digit (p. 31)
bit (p. 31)
byte (p. 31)
American Standard Code for Information
   Interchange (ASCII) (p. 31)
megabyte (p. 32)
gigabyte (p. 32)
Unicode (p. 32)
QWERTY (p. 32)
modifier keys (p. 33)
cursor keys (p. 33)
cursor (p. 33)
function keys (p. 33)
graphical user interface (GUI) (p. 33)
icons (p. 33)
desktop (p. 33)
mouse (p. 33)
trackball (p. 33)
touchscreen (p. 34)
touchpad (p. 34)
digitizing pen (p. 34)
drawing tablet (p. 34)
continuous waves (p. 35)
analog waves (p. 35)
sampling (p. 35)
digital storage (p. 35)

voice recognition software (p. 35)
optical mark recognition (OMR) (p. 36)
barcode readers (p. 36)
Universal Product Code (UPC) (p. 36)
wand reader (p. 36)
point of sale terminal (POS) (p. 36)
magnetic ink character reader (MICR) (p. 36)
scanner (p. 37)
RGB (p. 37)
animation (p. 38)
data compression (p. 38)
compatible (p. 38)
system board (p. 38)
motherboard (p. 38)
bus (p. 38)
control unit (p. 39)
arithmetic logic unit (ALU) (p. 39)
megahertz (MHz) (p. 40)
reduced instruction source code
   (RISC) (p. 40)
complex instruction source code
   (CISC) (p. 40)
random access memory (RAM) (p. 41)
storage address (p. 41)
volatile memory (p. 41)
single in-line memory module
   (SIMM) (p. 41)
double in-line memory module
   (DIMM) (p. 41)
read only memory (ROM) (p. 42)
erasable programmable read only memory
   (EPROM) (p. 42)
flash memory (p. 42)
cache (p. 42)
port (p. 43)
serial port (p. 43)
communications (COM) port (p. 43)
parallel port (p. 43)
video port (p. 43)
expansion card (p. 43)
expansion slot (p. 43)
PCMCIA card (p. 43)
PC card (p. 43)

peripheral output devices (p. 44)
monitor (p. 44)
video display terminal (VDT) (p. 44)
soft copy (p. 44)
hard copy (p. 44)
pixel (p. 44)
video adapter (p. 44)
video RAM (VRAM) (p. 44)
dot pitch (p. 45)
resolution (p. 45)
S-VGA (p. 45)
cathode ray tube (CRT) (p. 45)
liquid crystal display (LCD) (p. 45)
true color (p. 45)
flat panel LCD (p. 46)
printers (p. 46)
impact printer (p. 46)
dot matrix (p. 46)
line printer (p. 46)
ink-jet printer (p. 46)
laser printer (p. 46)
plotter (p. 46)
microform (p. 47)
multimedia (p. 47)
magnetic storage device (p. 47)
magnetic tape (p. 48)
sequential access (p. 48)
magnetic disk (p. 48)
floppy diskette (p. 48)
hard disk drive (p. 48)
direct access (p. 48)
optical storage device (p. 48)
optical storage media (p. 49)
CD-ROM (p. 49)
CD-WORM (p. 49)
CD-RW (p. 49)
DVD-ROM (p. 49)
digital video disk (DVD) (p. 49)
DVD-RAM (p. 49)
ergonomics (p. 51)
carpal-tunnel syndrome (p. 51)
ergomatics (p. 51)

Changes, Challenges, and CHOICES

CONFIGURING KNOWLEDGE

Multiple Choice Questions

Choose the best answer from those provided.

1. Computers use a two-digit system of numbers called a _____ to represent all of the characters in our language.
   a. schematic diagram
   b. hexadecimal
   c. compucode
   d. binary code
   e. decacode

2. The hard drive inside the computer is classified as a form of _____ because it is outside the CPU.
   a. external storage
   b. external memory
   c. secondary memory
   d. primary memory
   e. primary storage

3. The base-2 set of code that is used to represent data in most microcomputers today is called _____.
   a. ANSI number system
   b. ASCII binary code
   c. Unicode
   d. binary conversion
   e. byte conversion

4. A collection of binary bits that is adequate to represent any key on the keyboard is called a _____.
   a. databit
   b. keystroke
   c. colbit
   d. field
   e. byte

5. The primary system board that holds the CPU is often called a(n) _____.
   a. primary board
   b. CPU board
   c. motherboard
   d. memory board
   e. expansion board

6. The electrical pathways through which data flows in a computer are called _____.
   a. current paths
   b. buses
   c. powerways
   d. data paths
   e. circuits

7. A connection for an S-VGA monitor will typically require the use of a _____ .
   a. serial port
   b. motherboard
   c. line printer
   d. video port
   e. parallel port

8. All mathematical and logical work is performed by the _____ component of the computer.
   a. control unit
   b. primary memory
   c. MPU
   d. ALU
   e. secondary memory

9. The programming that runs a CPU will run faster if _____ techniques are used.
   a. RISC
   b. RAD
   c. CISC
   d. excel
   e. CAD

10. A CPU is able to perform more quickly by using a memory space called a(n) _____ to hold the next commands that may be needed.
    a. chip
    b. SIMMs
    c. DIMMs
    d. address
    e. cache

11. The primary memory used by the CPU to perform all of its work uses a kind of chip that is called _____.
    a. PROM
    b. RAM
    c. ERAM
    d. EPROM
    e. ROM

12. Music and other analog data can be converted to digital form by using a technique called _____.
    a. fractioning
    b. MP3
    c. digitizing
    d. posting
    e. sampling

13. Point of sale terminals are able to read price and inventory information from a system of manufacturer-imprinted _____.
    a. MSRP units
    b. MICR symbols
    c. UPC codes
    d. POS codes
    e. Unicodes

14. Each tiny picture element on a monitor is called a _____ and is represented by a number to express its color.
    a. color dot
    b. pixel
    c. VGA
    d. pica
    e. dot pitch

True or False?

Rewrite each false item to make it a true statement.

1. The term *memory* refers to data stored in a computer's chips or internal disk drives.
2. A base-2 number system is used to create the ASCII code that runs almost all personal computers today.
3. The smallest unit of binary data storage is called the bit.
4. The international multi-language-coding scheme for internal data representation is called Unicode.
5. The use of a motherboard in a computer eliminates the need for secondary storage.
6. The bus in a computer moves data under the control of the CPU.
7. A PCMCIA card extends the power of a CPU in a desktop to a laptop computer.
8. Any true/false or other logical comparisons made by a computer must take place in the ALU.
9. A computer CPU will perform tasks much more quickly if the design does not use a cache.
10. RAM chips are a type of memory chip that can hold their data values in the event of a power failure.
11. The technique of repeatedly sampling fractional music sounds allows analog data to be saved in a digital format.
12. UPC codes appear on virtually all commercial products for data collection reasons.
13. The smaller the number of pixels a monitor uses, the clearer will be its output.
14. Generally speaking, additional VRAM memory on a video adapter will make a monitor perform more quickly.

TECHNOLOGY IN CONTEXT

Prepare to discuss each of the following questions, drawing upon the material presented in this chapter as well as your own experience and additional information you may have researched on your own.

1. Define and compare internal computer memory and data storage. Give examples of each type of hardware. Cite the advantages and/or disadvantages of each.
2. What are the component parts of the central processing unit (CPU)? Define each and explain the role it plays in the overall performance of the computer.
3. Explain the electronic data bus on the computer's motherboard. How does changing the characteristics of the bus impact the performance of the computer?
4. Explain how the number of pixels in a monitor or LCD panel can have an impact upon image quality in a computer system. Describe the way a binary number is used to represent the color of each pixel in the display. How much memory would it take to represent the *true color* of nature? Explain.
5. Compare impact versus nonimpact printer types for image quality. What printing feature requirement has driven the growth of ink jet and laser printers? Explain.

DEVELOPING MINDSHARE

1. Locate a number of computer advertisements and compare features and prices. Search for a variety of CPU speeds, bus speeds, memory installed, and cache size. Explain the relationships you find between capabilities and prices.
2. Use literature or the Internet to search for the growth in CPU processing power that has evolved since the advent of the personal computer. How does this

increase in clock-speed compare with any personal computers that you have used? Can you tell a difference when using a fast or slow CPU? Explain. *(Hint: Check processor manufacturer Web sites such as Intel, AMD, and so on.)*

3. Find a number of examples of peripheral devices that facilitate a conversion of real-world analog data into digital form for processing. Locate as many different types as possible—temperature, pressures, sounds, weight, and so forth. Describe the insignificance of decimal places being dropped in the process of conversion.

4. Locate copies of computer printouts from a dot matrix impact printer, an ink jet, and a laser printer to compare for quality. Identify the features that lead you to prefer one as opposed to the others. Locate several examples of color printer output. Compare each for quality. Describe the advantages or disadvantages that may be found.

5. Find examples of ergonomically redesigned computer components in advertising or on Internet sites. Explain the advantages you see in the redesigns of the mouse, keyboard, chairs, and monitors (eyestrain—radiation). Do the improvements appear to be effective and/or worth their prices?

THINK TANK

In the Reality Interface at the beginning of the chapter, you learned about a growing use for computers in the medical field—monitoring drug prescriptions to prevent medication errors. A new initiative launched by Microsoft in 2000, called "the .Net," is designed to include the software and services that automatically link various Web sites and thus automate processes, such as the delivery of healthcare, which could reduce the potential for human error. Picture this scenario, for example. You break an arm and seek treatment at your local clinic. The identification card you present upon checking in contains a chip that checks your insurance and displays your medical record on the Internet. The software also pages your doctor and checks to ensure that the doctor is authorized to view your medical information. During the exam, the doctor dictates her notes into her handheld computer, which then sends the notes to your online file and links to the x-rays just taken. Completing the diagnosis, your doctor enters into her computer a prescription for a painkiller. Another program checks to ensure you are not allergic to the drug and are not taking any other medications that would cause interaction problems. The prescription is sent online to your neighborhood pharmacy, where it is filled and then delivered to your home.

Team Challenge: Think about the possibilities of Microsoft's ".Net" system. As a group, brainstorm the ways in which this new product could help prevent errors in the healthcare industry. Or, do you think it opens up *more* possibilities for mistakes? Explain your thinking and propose solutions to any problems you identify. Then try to identify other ways in which computer technology could be used to improve accuracy in patient care. What is the ideal system, from the patient's point of view? Provide your ideas in an oral presentation to the class. Make sure that each member of the team has contributed to the project, either with written research summaries, visual displays, or as part of the oral presentation.

Answers to Configuring Knowledge Questions

Multiple Choice: 1 – d; 2 – a; 3 – b; 4 – e; 5 – c; 6 – b; 7 – e; 8 – d; 9 – a; 10 – e; 11 – b; 12 – e; 13 – c; 14 – b **True-False:** 1 – F; 2 – T; 3 – T; 4 – T; 5 – F; 6 – F; 7 – T; 8 – F; 9 – F; 10 – F; 11 – F; 12 – F; 13 – F; 14 – T

Reality INTERFACE

My Portable Telephone Has a Windows Operating System!

From pagers to digital telephones, all portable communication devices contain embedded computers that perform their operations. To grab a part of this growing market, hardware and software companies have forged some intriguing business alliances. Adding to the frenzy of activity is the trend toward the convergence of computing, communications, and entertainment industries. The alliance of communication device manufacturers Ericsson (a Swedish company), Nokia (Finnish), and Motorola already has a significant stranglehold on telecommunications hardware standards. Meanwhile, Sun Microsystems and other software companies have been developing operating system technology for the portable communicator industry, leaving Microsoft Windows potentially vulnerable.

Enter the Microsoft Windows CE operating system, which suits the invisible dedicated applications perfectly. Microsoft has aggressively marketed and made agreements with manufacturers and service providers all over the world. The firm developed a new component called MS Mobile Explorer—a Windows CE-driven Internet browser that can be installed in personal communication devices. This capability lets users see full-screen Web pages on their phone as well as have full access to e-mail functions. Ericsson and Microsoft announced that they would use this new operating system and browser in their next generation of personal communicators. This move gives Ericsson an alternative operating system and opens the door for Microsoft to enter into the Ericsson-Nokia-Motorola alliance. Essentially any computing function that is available to Windows 2000 applications can be programmed into the digital communicator. So, the next time your portable phone rings, it may be calling invisibly through the Microsoft CE operating system.

3 SOFTWARE:
UNDERSTANDING
Computer Operating Systems

OBJECTIVES

After reading this chapter, you will be able to. . .

➤ Describe the major functions of operating systems and how operating system software interacts with system and application software

➤ Track the evolution and major milestones of operating systems

➤ Distinguish between command-line interfaces and graphical user interfaces

➤ Explain the significance and impact of the Windows operating system from the perspective of users and programmers

➤ Identify how new-generation operating systems will impact computing trends in the future

What Is an Operating System?

A computer system without software is like an array of chemical compounds without the formula to combine them, a car without an engine, or an airplane without a pilot: that is, useless. Computer hardware is, after all, merely machinery that contains no innate intelligence or ability. In order to come to life, computers need to employ mathematical algorithms, the step-by-step instructions that explain the basic actions necessary for carrying out a task. In a modern computer, this system software is called the **operating system (OS).** A computer's operating system is its most important piece of software. It gives a particular personality or "feel" to the computer. In fact, it is common to refer to a certain computer type, or **platform,** by the operating system it uses. A computer running Microsoft's Windows 2000 operating system, for instance, is called a **Windows platform.**

The operating system's work takes place behind the scenes. When a user starts a computer, instructions built into the machine's ROM look for an OS, first on any disk inserted into a floppy drive at start-up, and then on the system's primary hard drive. When found, the OS is loaded, in part, into the computer's RAM memory from its permanent hard-drive storage. This process is called **booting,** and the operating system remains in RAM until the computer is turned off. Once loaded, the OS takes over, creating a display on the monitor and assisting in every operation the user performs.

KEY Terms

operating system (OS)
Software that includes step-by-step instructions for controlling all of the functions necessary for a computer to carry out its tasks.

user interface Environment displayed on computer screen with which the user interacts to cause actions to occur.

The Operating System's Tasks

The operating system manages all of the operations of the CPU, enabling it to coordinate and use accurately and efficiently all of the hardware and software that is installed in the system (see Figure 3-1). This "brainwork" includes the following tasks:

- Loads during start-up; recognizes the CPU and the devices connected to it such as the keyboard, monitor, hard drive, and CD drive.
- Creates a **user interface,** an environment displayed on the computer screen with which the user interacts when working on the computer.
- Manages files by organizing the data, system, and software files stored in memory so users can locate needed material. The OS creates and maintains a file system, or **directory,** for each storage device attached to the computer. This directory shows the location of each file on each storage device, and thus allows the user to access programs and documents quickly. Within a directory, users can create a personalized file system of **folders** and **subfolders,** similar to the filing system for paper documents in a filing cabinet.
- Supports operations performed within other software programs, such as opening and closing programs, calling resources such as fonts and sounds, and saving and printing documents.
- Controls all of the system's peripheral devices by carrying out the complex chores associated with running the screens, disk drives, printers, scanners, and other hardware attached to the computer.
- Manages the communications links to outside resources such as networks and to the Internet. (Networks are discussed in more detail in Chapter 5, and the Internet is discussed in Chapter 6).

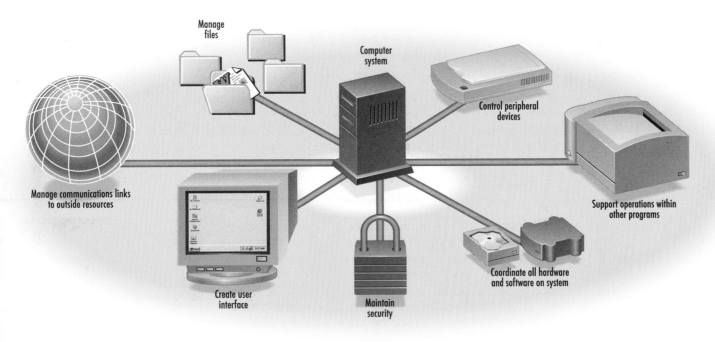

Manage files

Computer system

Control peripheral devices

Manage communications links to outside resources

Support operations within other programs

Create user interface

Maintain security

Coordinate all hardware and software on system

Figure 3-1: Operating System Functions

The newest operating systems also enable a user to have multiple software programs running concurrently, a capability called **multitasking.** A user working with a multitasking OS can, for example, simultaneously run a page layout program and an image-editing program, making it easier to create a graphic and then fit it into a page layout. Or, the user can have spreadsheet and word processing applications running at the same time and can be reading or transferring data between them. The operating system manages this timesharing role of multitasking to ensure that resources are properly timed and directed. No encroachment must be made into the memory space allocation of one program by another. If a shortage of memory available for processing occurs, the operating system uses a portion of the hard drive as an extension of chip memory. This virtual extension of memory keeps the processing under way, although the work is slower than that performed by chips.

The operating system also contains a security function that operates as a gatekeeping device to regulate access to the system. Authorized users are required to enter a private password to log onto the system as verification of their identity. Other necessary security and housekeeping functions are performed by utility programs built into the operating system. For example, changing file format for different storage devices or repairing damaged data files are accomplished by utility programs. Some of these programs run automatically, and some the user must launch. Certain **utility programs** to enhance the operating system, such as antivirus software, may be purchased and added to the system.

Evolution of Operating Systems

In the early days of the computer industry, using a computer required that programmers create both its operating instructions and its **programs,** or instructions for manipulating data. By developing operating systems, technicians made computers much simpler to use because an operating system automatically takes care of routine, often-repeated tasks. One of the first operating systems for personal computers was Gary Kildall's CP/M, or

EXPANSION CARD

In a capitalist economy, the production and price of goods are largely determined by the market. Products that do not satisfy consumers or whose costs are too high soon disappear from the market. In a similar manner, a number of operating systems over the years have been proposed, produced, and then rejected by consumers. Certainly the most significant event in Microsoft's history was when IBM invited that company to create the original version of DOS for their first personal computer. Although it is said that IBM may have preferred other firms besides the fledgling company, Microsoft managed to close the deal—and the rest is history. As Microsoft continued to improve its operating system and other computer manufacturers adopted it, Microsoft became a powerhouse. Since a capitalist system rewards successful entrepreneurs with profits for their risks and efforts, many Microsoft employees have become millionaires and Microsoft's CEO, Bill Gates, is one of the richest persons in the world.

To help regulate the market, the United States also has laws that protect citizens from the unscrupulous pricing associated with monopoly profiteering. In May 1998, the United States Department of Justice filed an antitrust lawsuit against Microsoft, alleging that the company harmed consumers by using its market muscle to block competition. Some of Microsoft's competitors have supported these allegations. For its part, Microsoft has vigorously defended its pricing policies and has fought, additionally, for the right to integrate its Internet Express browser program into its operating system.

Microsoft faced perhaps its darkest day on November 5, 1999, when Justice Thomas Penfield Jackson of the United States District Court in Washington, D.C., issued a finding that the firm was indeed abusing its power. As a solution, the government insists that Microsoft should be broken into two separate businesses, but Microsoft has maintained its right to improve and add features to its operating system. Both sides seem to be bound by conflicting objectives as they move toward resolution through the appeals process.

As with most successful market ventures, Microsoft has achieved its status through a combination of product excellence, savvy marketing, and a bit of luck. Certainly, Microsoft would not be a household word today if its products did not satisfy the public. But anything can happen in a capitalistic society. The recent growth in popularity of the Linux operating system, for example, shows that even small firms with an excellent product can successfully develop a following even if the market is dominated by a giant.

Gary Kildall

Control Program for Microcomputers, written in 1974. CP/M made it possible for personal computers created by different manufacturers to run the same software and so helped to jump-start the personal computer software industry.

Later in the decade, Tim Patterson of Seattle Computer Products created an operating system for personal computers using the Intel 8086 microprocessor. Patterson called it OS 86-QDOS, or 8086 Quick and Dirty Operating System. In

Bill Gates

1980, IBM approached Bill Gates, cofounder of the then small software company named Microsoft, looking for an operating system for its new IBM PC. Gates licensed QDOS from Patterson's company, renamed it **MS-DOS,** or Microsoft Disk Operating System, and negotiated a deal whereby IBM would distribute the OS with its computers under the name **PC-DOS,** or Personal Computer Disk Operating System. This deal made computing history; IBM PCs and compatibles, running PC-DOS or MS-DOS, captured the lion's share of the personal computer market, and Gates's tiny company grew into a multibillion-dollar giant. For many years, DOS was the most widely used OS in the world.

MS-DOS and Other Command-line Interfaces

Any instruction or command given to a computer's OS requires an interaction between the computer and a human person. The format or structure of this interaction is the **interface.** Over the years, the way that the computer-human interface occurs has changed. The earliest personal computer operating systems, like CP/M and DOS, used what is known as a **command-line interface.** In other words, they presented the computer user with a prompt such as C:\, to which the user would respond by typing in a **command,** a string of abbreviated codes telling the computer what to do. After the introduction of the IBM PC in 1981, millions of users became familiar with the DOS command-line interface. After booting up the computer that runs DOS, the user saw a prompt naming the drive on which the computer had found the OS. Usually that drive was the internal hard drive, most commonly designated as the C:\ drive. At the C:\ prompt, the user typed a command. For example, the user might have typed a command telling the computer to format a floppy disk, erase a file, launch a particular application program, or create a directory. The following command would copy a document called MKTRPT to a directory on the hard drive called QTR1: C:\COPY MKTRPT.DOC C:\QTR1. To open a particular document, the user keyed the **pathname,** a command that specified the document's location on a storage medium. For example, this pathname shows the location on the C:\ drive of a document called "EXAM1": C\MY DOCUMENTS\ EXAMS\EXAM1. The document is located in a **subdirectory** called "EXAMS," which is inside a subdirectory called "MY DOCUMENTS." Figure 3-2 shows the path the computer would follow to find the file "EXAM1."

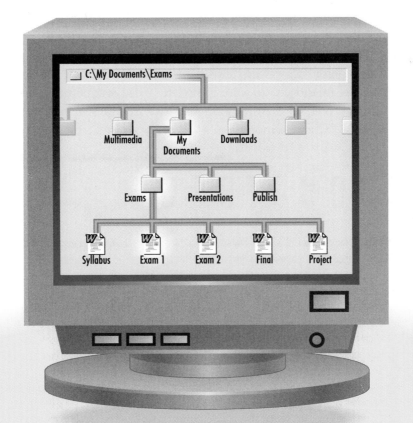

Figure 3-2: Path Computer Follows to Find a File

Limitations of Command-line Interfaces

Command-line interfaces were ideal for early personal computers with their limited graphical display capabilities but, as the above example illustrates, they could also be complicated and difficult to learn. Users had to remember long sequences of cryptic commands and be proficient touch typists. A mistyped command would lead to an error message, forcing the user to type the command again. DOS also restricts file names to eight characters. An additional three characters can be added after a period, called an **extension.** In the first example above, MKTRPT is called the **file name,** and DOC is the extension. This naming limitation caused DOS file names to be quite artificial. In this case, the user has chosen MKTRPT as the file name to represent "First Quarter Marketing Report," because DOS does not allow for the longer name. Another limitation of DOS is that it can address only 1MB of RAM. When DOS was first introduced, much smaller memory sizes were common. The original IBM, for example, only had 64K of RAM. To access more than 1MB of RAM, a computer user running DOS on today's computers must make use of special software, an EMS or XMS driver, that recognizes the additional memory. Yet another problem with DOS is that it was created for computers that used 16-bit data bus architectures and cannot make use of the faster 32-bit architectures of contemporary personal computers. Although widely used in the past, DOS has now been largely replaced by Windows GUIs.

Figure 3-3: An Early Apple Macintosh Computer

Graphical User Interfaces, or GUIs

In 1983, Apple Computer introduced a computer that had an entirely new kind of OS, the graphical user interface (GUI). Because this new type of interface was based on visual graphics rather than command lines, it was much more intuitive and user-friendly. Although the first line of Apple computers with a GUI failed on the market, in 1984 Apple released the Macintosh (see Figure 3-3), which also employed a GUI for its operating system. The Macintosh revolutionized personal computing and ignited a new era of market competition.

INNOVATORS
The Person for the Job

Steve Jobs is the prototype of America's computer industry entrepreneur. A college dropout fascinated with the counterculture and Eastern thought, Jobs transformed himself into a millionaire by the age of 30. Jobs's efforts changed the computer from a huge machine accessible only to big business and government into a small, user-friendly tool for the masses. In doing so, he revolutionized the computer industry.

Jobs started his career as a video game designer at Atari. He and a friend, Steve Wozniak, built their first computer in Jobs's basement. Then they each sold a few prized possessions to raise $1,300 to start their new company. Fondly recalling a summer working at an orchard in Oregon, Jobs named the company Apple Computer. Apple went public in 1980 and was soon worth $1.2 billion.

Apple originally had the personal computer market to itself, but when IBM started elbowing in, the company faltered. Jobs got involved in a power struggle and was eventually forced to resign. Jobs spent ten long years and almost his entire $100 million fortune in an effort to match the success of Apple. When his animation company Pixar went public after the release of the hit movie *Toy Story*, Jobs became a billionaire.

An even bigger coup was his invitation in 1996 to return to the floundering Apple as an informal advisor. Jobs has been the driving force behind the iMac computer and Apple's complete turnaround. In September 1999 at the Macworld convention, he was once again named CEO of Apple Computer. It was a long road back to what he calls "the best job in the world."

As discussed in Chapter 2, a GUI is easier to use than a command-line interface because it enables the user to interact with onscreen simulations of familiar objects (see Figure 3-4). For this reason, GUIs have rapidly evolved into the most popular form of interaction between humans and computers. The screen becomes a virtual desktop, and users "point and click" on icons representing the action they desire, such as moving, printing, or restoring text. The mouse pointer, in fact, was designed to be like an extension of the human hand that can reach to the screen and merely point to the picture or button that controls the desired activity. Programs and files are also represented by icons. A calculating program, for example, can be represented by a tiny calculator on the screen. A note pad program can be represented by a tiny note pad. In addition to icons, GUIs offer such convenient features as **pull-down menus,** which enable the user to carry out such functions as opening a program or formatting a disk; **shortcuts,** icons that act as proxies for files or programs and can be used to open the program or file with a simple double click; and **dialog boxes,** particular types of windows that give users various options in completing the desired task. Because of their intuitive, graphics-based operating systems, Macintosh computers were widely adopted for use in graphics-intensive industries such as publishing and advertising. DOS-based machines, on the other hand, with their command-line operating systems, remained standard in most businesses for many years.

Evolution of the Windows Operating System

In 1985, Microsoft responded to the popularity of the MAC-OS by introducing **Microsoft Windows** software, its own version of a GUI for use on IBM PCs and compatibles. The early Windows operating system provided a **shell** that essentially converted the graphical choices selected by a user into the DOS-equivalent commands. Like the MAC-OS that preceded it, the Windows graphical environment also contained such features as pull-down menus, icons, file folders, and dialog boxes (see Figure 3-5). In fact, Apple sued Microsoft, claiming that the latter company had copied the "look and feel" of the MAC-OS. The failure of Apple's suit, however, left the door open for the development of successive versions of Windows and of other GUIs. The first two releases of Windows were not very

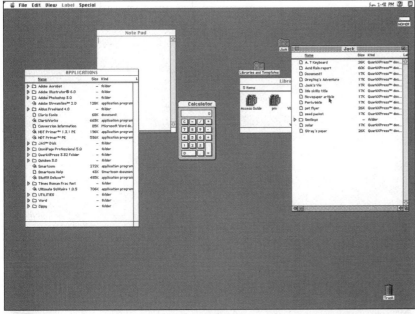

Figure 3-4: A Macintosh Graphical User Interface (GUI) from the Early 1990s

successful, perhaps because of the commitment of PC users to the DOS command-line interface. Windows 3, however, became extremely popular, and today most PC users run some version of Windows.

Windows 95

With the release of **Windows 95** in August 1995, Microsoft adopted a version-naming convention that was tied to the year of release. Windows 95 was a 32-bit operating system that replaced the DOS and shell concept with a completely new integrated approach. It offered improved networking capabilities and memory handling, a superior interface (see Figure 3-6), an intuitive file-management tool called Explorer, and Internet access. Early on, Windows 95 achieved widespread success because it was compatible with a broad range of hardware and software. In addition, it allowed the user to create file names of up to 256 characters long, including spaces. Some of the utilities that came with Windows 95 were a calculator, calendar, note pad, card file, clock, paint program, and clipboard. Minimum system requirements for running Windows 95 included:

- 486/25MHz or higher processor
- 8MB of memory (RAM)
- 40MB of available hard-disk space
- VGA or higher resolution display
- Microsoft mouse or compatible pointing device

Windows NT

Released in 1993 in response to the growing use of networks in business, **Windows NT** was a sophisticated **multiuser OS** that became widely used by network administrators and professionals in MIS (management information services). Offering a graphical user interface (see Figure 3-7) like that of Windows 95, this Windows OS is the only one (prior to Windows 2000) not built on DOS. It included built-in networking, multitasking, Internet access, and a security system to prevent other programs from manipulating the hardware or operating system without authorization. This security feature made Windows NT particularly suitable for file servers and computers that are accessed remotely.

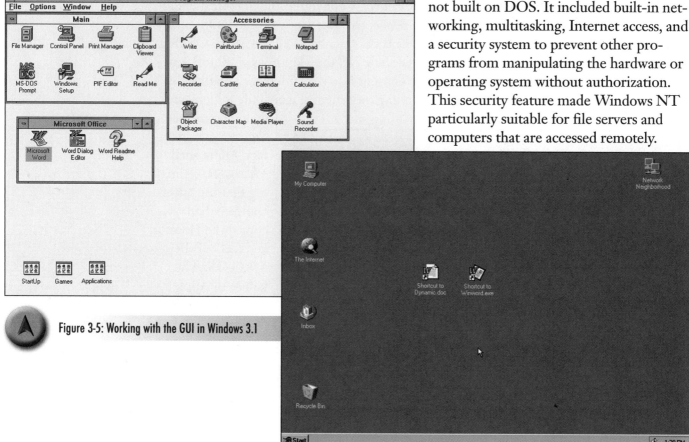

Figure 3-5: Working with the GUI in Windows 3.1

Figure 3-6: Windows 95 Desktop

EXPANSION CARD

Managing a Graphical Desktop: Files, Folders, and Directories

To open a document using a command-line OS, you type a pathname, a command that specifies the document's location on a storage medium. For example, the pathname C:\word\mydocs\letters\memobob shows the location on the C:\ drive of a document called "memobob." The document is located in a subdirectory called "letters," which is inside a subdirectory called "mydocs," which is inside a subdirectory called "word."

In a GUI, the path, or location, of a file remains the same as in a command-line interface, but that path is represented graphically rather than by a command. Instead of finding a file by using a pathname, the user sees on the screen graphic icons that stand for the drive, for folders (directories and subdirectories), and for documents within those folders.

The folders in a GUI can be nested, or placed inside one another, in a way that shows their hierarchical organization. GUIs allow nested folders to be viewed as folder icons or as an indented outline. Using a command-line system, one would have to issue a complicated command containing two pathnames in order to change the location of a file from one subdirectory to another. Using a GUI, the user can simply click on a file and drag it from one folder to another.

Without the ability to create hierarchical levels of organization on a storage device, everything on the device would appear at the same level. This would make finding documents quite time consuming. Nested folders, however, make it easy for a user to organize a hard drive in a manner that simplifies finding files.

There is no one correct way to organize a hard drive, but organizing the drive in some way is essential. As hard drives get larger and larger (drives capable of storing several gigabytes are now common), organization becomes increasingly important. One way to organize a hard drive is to create partitions, or sections, of the drive using a kind of software known as a disk utility. One partition might contain system software and be named "My System," another partition might contain application programs and be named "Apps," and yet another might contain documents and be named "Docs." The advantage of partitioning a drive is that doing so improves hard-drive access time because the drive's read/write heads do not have to search the entire drive to find a particular program or file. Instead, the heads can search only the partition in which the file or program is located.

Users can also create folders that imitate partitions. For example, one might create separate folders for applications and for documents.

Here are some other ways to organize files on a hard drive:
1. Create separate folders for different projects.
2. Create separate folders for personal and business documents.
3. Create separate folders for each application program and store documents created by each program within that program's folder.
4. Create separate folders for applications, work in progress, and archived, no longer current, files.

Minimum system requirements for running NT were as follows:

Intel-based Systems
- 486/25MHz or higher or Pentium-based system
- 12MB of memory (RAM); 16MB recommended
- 110MB of available hard-disk space
- CD-ROM drive or access to a CD-ROM over a computer network
- VGA or higher resolution display adapter

- Microsoft mouse or compatible pointing device

RISC-based Systems
- Workstation with Alpha AXP, MIPSW R4x00, or PowerPC processor
- 16MB of memory (RAM)
- 110MB of available hard-disk space
- VGA or higher resolution display adapter
- Microsoft mouse or compatible pointing device

Optional
- Network adapter card
- Audio board

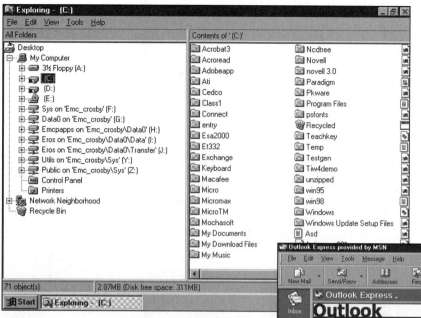

Figure 3-7: Working with the Windows NT Interface

Windows 98

Windows 98 developed some of the capabilities of Windows 95 more fully. Among other changes, Windows 98 increased allowable hard-disk size to two terabytes,

improved hardware support, better integrated Internet access with the operating system, and added enhanced multimedia support. A new Internet connection **wizard,** step-by-step instructions that guided the user through the process, made configuring a system to an **Internet service provider (ISP)** easier. New tools provided for Internet communication included the Personal Web Server and the Web Publishing Wizard, which supported publishing of pages on intranets or the Internet, and Outlook Express, which enabled a user to send and receive e-mail and manage newsgroups (see Figure 3-8).

Windows 98 also added support for software using Intel Pentium MMX technology, which improved the performance of multimedia applications. It provided a new ActiveMovie architecture that supported a wide variety of audio and video and allowed a PC to receive standard television signals. Windows 98 was also more user-friendly than Windows 95. It allowed applications to be started with a single click of the mouse, for example, rather than a double-click. The Start menu was easier to customize, and startup, application launching, and shut-down were faster than in Windows 95 (see

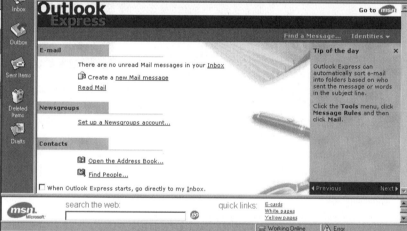

Figure 3-8: Opening Outlook Express in Windows 98

Figure 3-9). Other new features included System File Checker, which automatically scanned the OS, located corrupted or deleted system files, and restored them to proper working order. Minimum system requirements for Windows 98 Second Edition are:

- 486DX/66MHz or higher processor
- 24MB of memory (RAM)
- 205MB of available hard-disk space (more for additional options)
- CD-ROM or DVD-ROM drive
- VGA or higher resolution monitor
- Microsoft mouse or compatible pointing device

The Newest Versions of Windows

As of this writing, a majority of personal computers use either the Windows 95 or Windows 98 operating systems. Microsoft, however, continues to release upgrades and introduce new versions of its Windows technology. **Windows 2000 Millennium Edition** (shortened to **Me**) is the most recent upgrade. Developed primarily for the home computer market, Me features an enhanced capability to work with digital media such as photos, video, and music. New set-up wizards and help utilities make the program easier for users to learn. The Me version also makes the creation of a home network easier for those who have not done it before. Another major upgrade to this software is scheduled to be released in late 2001. Minimum system requirements for Windows Me include:

- Pentium 150MHz or higher processor
- 32MB of memory (RAM)
- 295MB of available hard-disk space
- CD-ROM drive
- 28.8Kbs modem with current Internet connection
- VGA or higher resolution monitor
- Sound card
- Speakers or headphones
- Microsoft mouse or compatible pointing device

Windows NT and Windows 98 have been superseded by three versions: **Windows 2000 Professional, Windows 2000 Server** and **Advanced Server,** and **Datacenter Server.** Each of these offer increasing levels of security, reliability, and features needed in typical business networked environments. Windows 2000 Professional is the mainstream operating system for desktop and notebook computing in all organizations (see Figure 3-10). A direct replacement for Windows 98, it combines ease-of-use features such as plug-and-play and power management techniques from Windows 98 with the networking power of Windows NT.

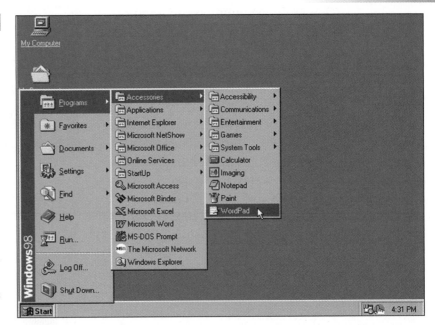

 Figure 3-9: Starting Windows 98 from the Desktop

 Figure 3-10: Windows 2000 Professional Desktop

Replacing Windows NT, Windows 2000 Server has the capability to handle up to 4 processors and up to 4 gigabytes of data. If an even larger environment is needed, the Advanced Server version supports up to 9 processors and up to 8 gigabytes of data. For a truly large network, the Datacenter Server version can handle up to 32 processors and 64 gigabytes of data.

Minimum system requirements for Windows 2000 Professional include:

- 133MHz or higher Pentium-compatible processor
- 64MB of memory (RAM)
- 2GB hard disk with a minimum of 650MB of available space
- CD-ROM drive
- VGA or higher resolution monitor

Windows CE was developed for use in small, dedicated systems such as personal digital assistants (PDAs), what Microsoft refers to as **handheld PCs (HPCs)**. This OS powers such wireless communications devices as pagers, cellular phones, multimedia players, and Internet Web phones, as shown in Figure 3-11. One version of Windows CE is being developed for an aural interface for use in cars. Windows CE is a 32-bit, multitasking OS with special power management capabilities and built-in Internet and e-mail capability. It allows interchange with desktop and networked Windows-based PCs.

Figure 3-11: Windows CE powers wireless communications devices such as handheld computers.

Other Operating Systems

Today, some 90% of personal and business computers throughout the world employ one of the Microsoft family of GUI operating systems. In fact, Microsoft Windows has so dominated the market that the U.S. Justice Department recently argued that the firm has held monopoly power and violated antitrust laws. (See the sidebar called "Microsoft and Antitrust Litigation.")

COMPUTERS IN
GOVERNMENT

Crime Files

Although not exactly a crime capital, Sweden is getting organized about dealing with it. In Stockholm, citizens can now log on to the home page of the police department to report a minor crime such as a stolen car or a purse snatching. Police review the report and then determine if it merits sending out a patrol car.

The law in Sweden requires a report on all lost items such as cell phones or credit cards. Stockholm gets about 50,000 of these reports annually, and would like to see all those minor incidents filed electronically by 2001. The service will eventually expand to other minor crime categories. When crime victims make reports online, the police can concentrate on solving cases instead of filing paperwork.

Macintosh OS 8 and OS X

Despite the dominance of Windows in the personal and business markets, there are other OS choices, as summarized in Table 3-1. Apple Macintosh, reputed to hold a 3.4% share of the computer market worldwide according to the International Data Corporation, is still preferred by some in the graphics or advertising trade. **Macintosh OS 8,** released in 1997, added improved multitasking abilities, enhanced multimedia support, and numerous interface enhancements.

In September 2000, Apple released a beta version of its **Macintosh OS X** operating system software, which has a new interface called Aqua and is based on the UNIX operating system, making it likely to be highly stable. OS X also includes updated, more detailed graphics, preemptive multitasking (increases its work speed and efficiency), and protected memory (prevents the entire system from crashing when an individual program crashes).

UNIX

UNIX has a significant following, particularly among former mainframe users. Developed by AT&T, MIT, and General Electric in the mid-1970s and widely adopted by laboratories and universities, the UNIX OS has a dauntingly complex command-line interface and some extraordinary capabilities. The developers of UNIX sought to create an OS that would provide effective time-sharing, or simultaneous access by many users to a single powerful and expensive minicomputer. Therefore, UNIX, from its inception, has been a multiuser OS. Because of its prevalence in universities and laboratories, UNIX became the first language of the Internet and is used by many Internet service providers to maintain their networks. A **multiplatform** program, it is also the OS of choice for powerful RISC-based desktop workstations like those produced by Hewlett-Packard, IBM, and Sun Microsystems. Many companies, including Apple, IBM, Microport, and Sunsoft, produce versions of this OS. UNIX also provides the backbone for the NeXT Step OS, a graphical user interface

multiplatform Software product able to be used on computers with different operating systems.

Table 3-1: Commonly Used Operating Systems

Name of Operating System	Type of Interface	Platform(s)
PC DOS, MS-DOS	command-line interface	PC
Windows 3.x	graphical user interface	PC
Windows 95	graphical user interface	PC
Windows NT	graphical user interface	PC
Windows 98	graphical user interface	PC
Windows Me	graphical user interface	PC
Windows 2000 Professional	graphical user interface	PC
Windows 2000 Server, Advanced Server	graphical user interface	PC
Datacenter Server	graphical user interface	PC
Windows CE	graphical user interface	PC PDAs or HPCs and other wireless devices
Macintosh OS 8, OS X	graphical user interface	Mac
UNIX	command-line interface	various systems, including Sun, RISC-based, PC
Newton OS	graphical user interface	Newton PDA
NeXT Step	graphical user interface	NeXT
Linux	command-line interface	PC
AU/X	command-line interface	Mac
JavaOS		multiplatform

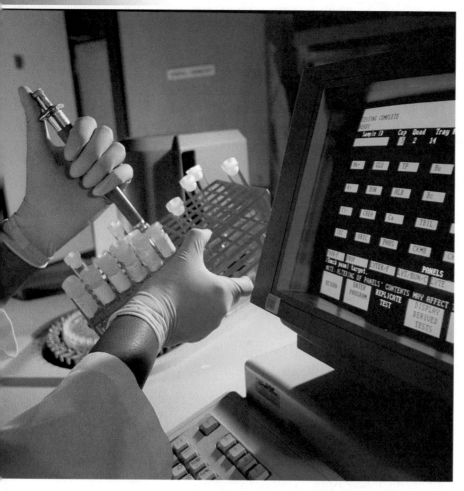

highly reliable OS. It contains features that allow nonprogrammers or inexperienced programmers to create, with ease, their own customized applications. Apple Computer purchased NeXT in 1997 with the intention of incorporating NeXT Step into a future version of the MAC-OS.

Linux

Created as a variant of UNIX in 1991 by Linus Torvalds, a graduate student at the University of Helsinki in Finland, **Linux** is considered an open-source program, in that the internal programming instructions are available freely via the Internet so that anyone can add to, or improve it. In turn, the changes developers make must be shared with the public. Some of Microsoft's competitors, including Sun Microsystems, Oracle, and IBM, have particularly supported the Linux variant of UNIX (see Figure 3-12). However, the considerable difficulty for many users of setting up and operating this OS will likely keep a limit on Linux's growth. In the Microsoft antitrust case, it was determined that Linux was not expected to show enough growth to keep Microsoft from

that combines the power and stability of UNIX with an attractive user interface.

NeXT Step

NeXT Step is the OS created by NeXT for use on the company's RISC-based computers. Based on UNIX, NeXT Step provides a superb graphical user interface that uses a programming language called Display PostScript to create screen images that show a great deal of detail. NeXT Step has proved to be a

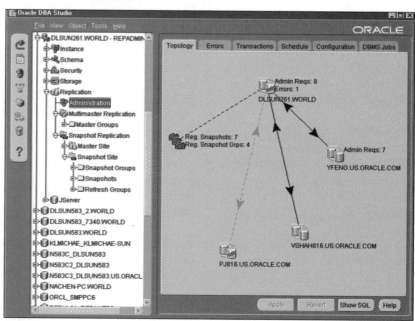

Figure 3-12: Oracle Application Running on Linux Platform

being declared a monopolist in the operating system software market.

JavaOS

A multiplatform operating system growing in popularity among technically competent users is the **JavaOS.** Sun Microsystems originally developed Java as a program in which small applications called **applets** could be run on any computer platform (see Figure 3-13). The major use for these applications has been the creation of Internet-ready files that can be downloaded and run on any computer that can support them. The earliest applications tended to be simple actions such as creating banner headlines that scrolled across the screen, but over time applets have grown increasingly sophisticated. Today the Java™ language has evolved into JavaOS, an independent operating system in its own right.

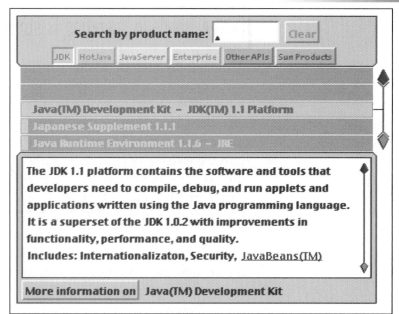

Figure 3-13: Java applets can be run on any computer platform.

EXPANSION CARD

Teaching Computers to Loosen Up

Early in the history of programming, some programmers realized that for many purposes, computers are simply too logical. Computers, being logic machines, tend to be excessively literal. They are superb at brute number crunching and at solving problems that have precise, discoverable, optimal solutions. They are miserable, however, in circumstances that are imprecise or fuzzy, circumstances, for example, in which all of the variable necessary to solving a problem are not known. Of course, most problems in the real world tend to be like that. Therefore, programmers realized very quickly that in order to set computers to work with real-world problems, they would have to develop methods to make computers "loosen up."

One technique, suggested by Herbert Simon, a founder of the science of artificial intelligence, was to write programs that used heuristics, or rules of thumb, to find satisfactory, if not optimal, solutions. One such heuristic embodied in the General Problem Solver, a program that Simon wrote along with his colleague Allan Newell, was means-ends analysis. The program compares the current state with the goal, or ending state, and then looks for ways to lessen the differences between the two. Simon called the process of looking for nonoptimal but achievable solutions "satisficing." Simon and Newell used the General Problem Solver to find theorems and solve problems in symbolic logic.

Another approach to making computers behave more realistically is to use what mathematician Lotfi Zadeh calls "fuzzy logic." Traditional logic assigns entities to classes. We might say, for example, "Ralph is short," meaning that Ralph belongs to the class of short people, or that one of the elements in the set "short people" is Ralph. The problem with such statements is that shortness is not a discrete, either/or characteristic. In fact, shortness is a fuzzy, or analog, concept. Is a 5'6" man short? How about a 5'5" man? a 5'4" man? At what point does shortness set in? Fuzzy logic addresses such problems by making use of partial membership in sets, describing people of different heights, for example, as being 95% tall, 90% tall, 85% tall, and so on. This technique enables computers to continue to calculate precisely, which is what they are designed to do, while dealing with a fuzzy, imprecise concept. The fuzzy logic developed by Zadeh and others has been applied to many difficult real-world problems, from choosing moves in computerized chess to designing parts for automobiles that respond appropriately in uncertain situations, such as brakes that "sense" the slipperiness of the road.

Future Trends in Operating Systems

Although no one can predict the future with certainty, computer operating systems will continue to evolve in specific directions already emerging today. Tomorrow's OS will be integrated directly into the task being performed rather than the user needing to employ a generic choice like Windows, MAC-OS, or Linux. Since many predict that the Internet, and not individual desktop PCs, will gain much more importance in the future, new user interfaces, including the one now being developed by Microsoft called .Net technology, will employ a range of links that connect directly to World Wide Web services such as financial information, entertainment options, or news venues. Web pages will be so interlinked, in fact, that they can "talk" to each other, allowing the user to locate multiple layers of information or perform actions such as researching and booking a train trip in Spain with just one click rather than having to visit many sites. Such future operating systems can be cus-

tomized to the user's specific needs. Their speed will be greatly increased to take advantage of ever-faster CPUs and data buses. Virtual reality and three-dimensional application support will also be improved, and their growth will be significant.

Figure 3-14: How Wireless Devices Work

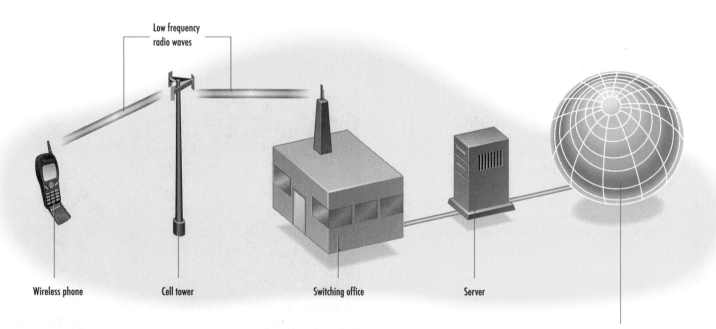

Low frequency radio waves

Wireless phone   Cell tower   Switching office   Server

Internet

Also in the future, small-capacity operating systems will be embedded in hundreds of everyday products. Wireless communication devices (see Figure 3-14) such as cell phones, pocket and handheld computers, palm-sized media screens, and even watch bands will provide complete Internet, computing, e-mail, and video services to create an "information everywhere" society.

Embedded computers will operate every function in wired "smart houses," from regulating the temperature to making coffee, through a centralized programmable system. Computers will routinely be installed in new cars to control auto functions as well as provide Internet access and e-mail on the road. In fact, perhaps the greatest change we can look forward to soon is the disappearance of the bulky desktop computer altogether. Control systems will be so transparent in all of our homes and offices that we will not even be aware that computers are at work behind the scenes in our daily lives.

Chapter
SUMMARY

A computer's operating system is its most important piece of software. The OS controls all of the operations of the CPU, allowing it to coordinate and use all of the hardware and software available on the system. Among its many tasks, the OS creates the user interface, controls peripheral devices, enables communications links to networks, provides for system security, manages files, and coordinates multitasking activities. Operating systems were developed in the 1970s. In 1980, IBM and Microsoft combined to release IBM computers running the DOS operating system, which were used by millions.

Two types of user interfaces have evolved along with computers. DOS is a command-line interface in which users must type certain cryptic commands to perform operations. Command-line interfaces were ideal for early computers, but have many limitations today. A second type of interface, graphical user interface or GUI, is based on visual graphics and is much easier to use and more intuitive. The GUI was first used by Apple in 1983. Microsoft introduced its own version of a GUI in 1985 with its Windows software. Microsoft's earliest GUIs merely provided a shell that converted graphical choices into DOS-equivalent commands, but with Windows 95 it released the first fully integrative GUI program.

Today, most personal and business computers use one of the Microsoft family of operating systems. There are, however, other competitors on the market with small but significant followings such as MAC-OS, UNIX, Linux, NeXT Step, and JavaOS. In the future, operating systems will no doubt continue to evolve for enhanced speed, ease-of-use, and efficiency. The clear trend today is for computers to become increasingly embedded in hundreds of products consumers use every day, invisible to all except those who look for them.

Key terms are presented here in the order in which they are cited in the text. A complete list of key terms in the text, in alphabetical order with definitions, can be found in the Glossary at the end of the book.

Changes, *Challenges,* and C H O I C E S

CONFIGURING KNOWLEDGE

Multiple Choice Questions
Choose the best answer from those provided.

1. The software that controls all aspects of a computer is called the _____.
   a. control unit
   b. operating system
   c. ALU
   d. CPU
   e. primary program

2. The part of the operating system that resides in secondary storage is made ready for operation by a process called _____.
   a. processing
   b. start-up
   c. calling
   d. strapping
   e. booting

3. A user of an operating system can create organizational tools called _____ to manage files.
   a. disks
   b. drives
   c. folders
   d. drawers
   e. pointers

4. An OS performs all of the following actions except _____.
   a. creating a user interface
   b. managing files
   c. coordinating all hardware and software operations
   d. negotiating Internet provider service costs
   e. providing system security

5. The operating system capability that permits more than one program to be running simultaneously is called _____.
   a. multitasking
   b. simultaneous processing
   c. multi-string
   d. binary processing
   e. multicycle

6. A computer _____ can be defined as a set of instructions for manipulating data.
   a. monitor
   b. program
   c. byte
   d. hardware device
   e. interface

7. In a command-line interface environment, a _____ tells the computer where to locate a document in storage.
   a. pathname
   b. binary code
   c. file
   d. pull-down menu
   e. shell

8. A program that works with the operating system to perform tasks such as virus protection is called a(n) _____.
   a. accessory program
   b. utility program
   c. auxiliary program
   d. ancillary program
   e. operating program

9. A GUI is based on _____ rather than character-based command lines.
   a. DOS
   b. subdirectories
   c. multitasking
   d. visual graphics
   e. wizards

10. A computer that has Windows 2000 installed can be referred to as a(n) _____.
    a. MS platform
    b. MAC platform
    c. OS platform
    d. Windows platform
    e. User platform

11. The Microsoft _____ operating system is for small computer applications such as PCAs or automobiles.
    a. Windows 3
    b. Windows CE
    c. Windows 95/98
    d. Windows NT
    e. Windows 2000

12. Microsoft Windows NT has recently been superseded by the upgrade versions Windows 2000 Professional, Windows 2000 Server/Advanced Server, and _____.
    a. HPC
    b. NeXT Step
    c. Macintosh OS 8
    d. Datacenter Server
    e. JavaOS

13. Approximately _____ of all computers today use some version of the Microsoft family of GUIs.
    a. 40%
    b. 75%
    c. 90%
    d. 100%
    e. 25%

14. Today's GUIs feature all of the following except _____.
    a. icons
    b. dialog boxes
    c. personal digital assistants
    d. shortcuts
    e. pull-down menus

15. Future developments in operating systems will most likely include all of the following except _____.
   a. more direct integration with tasks performed
   b. increased speed
   c. customization to users' needs
   d. improved virtual reality capabilities
   e. increased computer visibility

True or False?

Rewrite each false item to make it a true statement.

1. Software applications can be run on GUI systems without the need for an operating system.
2. The booting process loads part of the operating system from disk storage into RAM memory.
3. Users can organize file storage on a computer hard disk by creating electronic folders and subfolders.
4. The multitasking capability of modern systems makes it possible to run more than one software program simultaneously.
5. A user interface refers to the way in which a computer interacts with a human user.
6. Virus protection is a type of utility program that can be installed onto a computer by system users.
7. Microsoft's Windows 3.0 and the Linux operating systems are similar in that they both use a shell to create a graphical user interface.
8. A computer that uses any Windows version can be referred to as a multi-application platform.
9. The Microsoft Windows CE operating system can only be used on the largest capacity computers.
10. Command-line interfaces such as DOS limit file names to 14 characters.
11. Software that can be freely shared among users is said to be in the public domain.
12. The first company to introduce a GUI was Apple.
13. A shortcut is a feature of a GUI that presents an icon that acts as a proxy for a file or program.
14. JavaOS is a single-platform operating system.
15. Of the Windows 2000 versions, Windows 2000 Me is the OS designed for businesses and schools.

TECHNOLOGY IN CONTEXT

Prepare to discuss each of the following questions, drawing upon the material presented in this chapter as well as your own experience and additional information you may have researched on your own.

1. What makes a graphical user interface simpler to learn and to use than a command-line interface?
2. Compare and contrast the two major user interfaces, command-line and GUI. Cite the advantages and/or disadvantages of each.
3. Personal computers have introduced millions of people to the concept of an interface. The same concept can be applied to many other designed objects. For example, one can speak of the user interface of an automatic coffee brewing machine or of a videotape player. What characteristics, in general, does a good human/machine interface have?
4. Discuss some of the predicted future trends in the evolution of operating systems. Where are they headed, and why?
5. Explain why Microsoft Corporation has been charged with antitrust violation and

how and why such a trial may influence the software market of the future.

DEVELOPING MINDSHARE

1. Locate a person who has used both a command-line user interface and a graphical user interface. (If you cannot locate a source to interview, research the information using traditional print resources as well as online resources.) Ask the user to identify the best features of each interface. Are there any command-line interface features that are more efficient than their GUI counterparts?
2. Visit a computer store, look through computer magazines, or use other resources to research the new features of the most recent Windows upgrade, Microsoft 2000 Millennium. For the home user, how exactly does it improve on Windows 98?
3. Research more fully other current OS systems such as Macintosh OS 8, Linux, NeXT Step, and JavaOS. What are their system requirements and features? What type of users are most likely to choose them?
4. Use magazines such as *TIME*, *Newsweek*, or computer magazines to research the current status of the Justice Department's antitrust lawsuit against Microsoft. Do you agree with the initial findings of fact? Write a paper defending your position.
5. Locate types of consumer products currently on the market that contain hidden operating systems such as Microsoft CE. Research future directions in this technology. What applications do you foresee in 5 or 10 years?

THINK TANK

The Reality Interface presented at the beginning of the chapter projects a wireless Internet access future in which people can send e-mail, buy products, and talk on the phone from a single handheld device similar to a mobile phone or personal digital assistant. Imagine the day when this type of communication and activity is available to everyone—anytime, anywhere. Think of this scenario within the context of the different economies of the world, particularly the wealthy nations such as the United States in contrast with poorer countries. Is there a way to make mobile Internet access available to everyone within a poor country? Is there a need to? How should a government spend its resources if infrastructure needs such as transportation and housing compete with the need for global communication capabilities? Will market demand eliminate the need for difficult policy decisions by government leaders? In other words, will people choose to spend their money on global communication access, therefore building a need, creating competition among providers, and driving the cost of services downward so they are affordable?

Team Challenge: Develop a multipart presentation that addresses the questions raised above. Consider using PowerPoint slides and other visual aids to make your project stimulating and interesting. Or, you might address the questions using the format of a futuristic news report. Be creative as well as thoughtful.

Answers to Configuring Knowledge Questions

Multiple Choice: 1 – b; 2 – e; 3 – c; 4 – d; 5 – a; 6 – b; 7 – a; 8 – b; 9 – d; 10 – d; 11 – b; 12 – d; 13 – c; 14 – c; 15 – e **True-False:** 1 – F; 2 – T; 3 – T; 4 – T; 5 – T; 6 – T; 7 – T; 8 – F; 9 – F; 10 – F; 11 – T; 12 – T; 13 – T; 14 – F; 15 - F

Bob Frankston (standing) and Dan Bricklin (c. 1982), creators of VisiCalc and co-founders of Software Arts, Inc.

Reality
INTERFACE
PCs Enter the Workforce

Although we can hardly imagine the business world without computers today, computer use in the workplace was actually slow to catch on. Many managers doubted that computers could be effective tools in the work environment. Some considered the computer no more than a passing fad. For businesses to adopt PCs as work tools and invest the large sums of money needed to furnish computer systems, the computer had to prove its worth in enhancing productivity. This goal was realized with the development of an innovative software program, the electronic spreadsheet, that changed the direction of personal computing. In 1979, Dan Bricklin and Bob Frankston created **VisiCalc**, an electronic spreadsheet for the Apple II. In 1981, VisiCalc was released on the new IBM PCs. The tremendous power of these automatic error-free calculations tools prompted businesses to deploy computers for the first time as planning devices and as aids for **decision support systems (DSS)**. The new spreadsheet applications quickly canceled all doubts about the PC's usefulness in the workplace, and IBM's personal computer loaded with Lotus 1-2-3 soon became the industry standard. As millions of these computers and spreadsheet packages were sold, numerous competitors and clones in both hardware and software also entered the market. The fierce competition that ensued is now part of computing history.

4 SOFTWARE:
PRODUCTIVITY
Applications

OBJECTIVES

After reading this chapter, you will be able to. . .

➤ Explain the productivity benefits of each category of application software

➤ Chart the growth of word processing software in terms of processing power and enhanced functions

➤ Illustrate how the processing power of spreadsheet applications has impacted business systems and accounting functions

➤ Describe how database technology changes how we store, retrieve, and access information

➤ Identify the applications of presentation software and personal information managers

➤ List various types of creativity software and explain how each type is used

➤ State your understanding of multimedia software and give examples of how multimedia will improve information presentations at home, in schools, and at work

KENSINGTON TURBORING

The Basics of Applications Software

As you learned in Chapter 3, the instructions that run on a computer are called software. A piece of software, also known as a computer program, or simply a program, is written in a computer programming language such as COBOL, C++, Java, Linux, or UNIX. There are basically two types of software, operating systems (see Chapter 3) and applications, which carry out specific functions for users.

Applications software turns computer systems into useful tools. A computer user today is confronted with a dizzying array of commercial software choices, as a trip to a local computer store will quickly demonstrate. But in general, applications software can be grouped into a number of broad processing categories, such as words, numbers, graphics, databases, and specialized communications. The primary programs for manipulating text, or written materials, are word processing and desktop publishing programs. Numeric data is most often processed by spreadsheet software. Graphics software can create, edit, and present virtually any kind of picture or image. Database software is designed to process large amounts of statistical or text information efficiently in order to yield useful information. This chapter explores these and other common types of software applications.

While the intent and design of computer applications programs vary, they share a number of common features. For one thing, all software is written to work with a specific operating system. In fact, many of the icons, commands, and tools that appear in a particular software program are actually derived from the operating system. The applications designed to run on Microsoft Windows, for example, include the same graphical user interface (GUI) used in the operating system. A

KEY Terms

decision support systems (DSS)
System of hardware and software that models the reality of a problem to assist a manager in making decisions.

applications software Computer programs for carrying out specific functions not related to the operation of the computer itself.

EXPANSION CARD

Buying Software

Before purchasing a particular software program, you need to consider a number of factors:

- System requirements: At a minimum, check to see what operating system it requires, the amount of hard-disk space needed for installation, and the amount of RAM memory necessary for its use. These compatibility factors should be clearly printed on the outside of the software package.
- Program features and ease of use: Make sure the program does all that you want it to do, and that it is simple enough to use immediately but powerful enough to provide additional capabilities as your familiarity with the program increases. There can be severe restrictions on the return policies for software packages that have been opened.
- Quality of documentation, or instructions for use: The **documentation** should be easy to follow and available in printed form. Or, as is more common today, the software should include a step-by-step tutorial feature built into the program.
- Licensing agreement: Make sure you understand and agree with the **licensing agreement**, a set of terms to which you consent for using the program.

Most firms identify successive software versions by adding a numerical suffix to the software's name, such as Windows 3.0, Windows 3.1, and Windows 3.11. Typically the higher the version number, the newer the application. Microsoft began dating its versions with Windows 95, and has since released Windows 98 and Windows 2000. When a new version of an application becomes available, registered users are often offered the **upgrade**, or newly released version, at a reduced price. Software is typically sold with a **limited warranty** that guarantees replacement of a defective disk or CD-ROM for a specific period of time while disclaiming any responsibility for lost data.

Software manufacturers protect their product by **copyrighting** it. Typically, a software license specifies how many people may use the software and the number of computers on which the software may be installed. Often, it also explains how many backup copies, if any, the user can legally make. The license may require the user to register the copy of software with the manufacturer, similar to the way an owner obtains a title as proof of legal ownership for an automobile. Making unauthorized copies of copyrighted commercial software or using it in other ways that violate the licensing agreement is called **software piracy** and is against the law.

familiarity with the Windows GUI thus makes learning a new application much easier and faster. This carry-over factor is just one of the reasons that GUI operating systems and applications have become so popular in recent years.

Processing Words

Word processors are the most widely used of all software programs. In the early 1970s, when computers advanced enough to allow for the editing of documents before printing, their usefulness quickly became apparent. Almost overnight, computer word processing antiquated the typewriter, which had been a standard in business for more than a hundred years. Although typewriters were efficient tools, they did not offer an easy way to make multiple copies of a document or to correct errors. Carbon paper was awkward to use, and the manual erasing of mistakes was a tedious, often messy process.

The first computerized word processors were stand-alone machines dedicated to the single purpose of word processing. By the 1980s, software was written to perform the same word processing functions on personal computers and, as a result, dedicated word processing machines all but disappeared.

Milestones in Word Processing Software Development

As word processing technology developed, so did printing technology. A drawback to early word processing output was the poor quality of dot-matrix printers. As ink-jet and laser technologies were developed, printers began to have the ability to produce letter-perfect output. Early word processing programs also had limited editing capabilities, and users were unable to place text and images on the screen exactly as they would appear on the hard copy. Instead, they had to use a separate desktop publishing program to arrange both text and images creatively for newsletters or other printed materials. With the development of the Windows operating system, limited text and image manipulation began to be included directly into word processing software, a concept known as **"What You See Is What You Get" (WYSIWYG).**

When Windows 3.0 adopted **TrueType** as a format for text style selection, it became possible for the first time to have virtually limitless control over the look of any document. A document could be edited, and all of the special effects such as underlining, boldface, and bullets would be printed exactly as they appeared on the screen. Today's word processing software can produce professional quality documents limited only by the user's creativity (see Figure 4-1). The distinction between word processing and desktop publishing programs has thus begun to blur somewhat.

A recent—and timely—addition to today's word processing software is the ability to create Web pages. In fact, any document that can be created by a word processor can be saved as a **Hypertext**

WYSIWYG Acronym taken from "What You See Is What You Get," which means that the view on screen is exactly how it will appear when printed.

SULLIVAN TRAVELS

782 North 23rd Street
Portland, Maine 01232

Open House

Thursday, April 5, 2001

9:00 a.m. - 8:30 p.m.

Stop by and check out our new offices!
Sign up for a drawing for a free cruise!

Figure 4-1: Sample Announcement Created in Microsoft Word

Markup Language (HTML) document to create a Web page (see Figure 4-2). During the save process, HTML "tags" are automatically added to the document so that it can then be recognized by Web browser software. (See Chapter 6 for a more complete discussion of HTML documents and the creation of Web sites.)

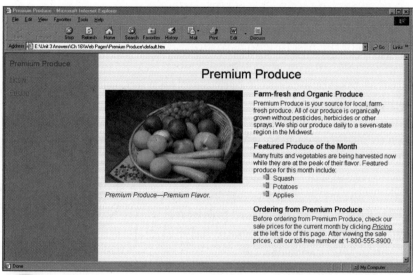

Figure 4-2: Example of Web Page Created in Microsoft Word

Word Processing Steps

With word processing software, users can create nearly any type of document, from letters and essays to research reports, marketing brochures, and newsletters. Regardless of the document type, the steps to create it are essentially the same:

Hypertext Markup Language (HTML) Programming language used to create documents that make up the World Wide Web.

1. Enter text.
2. Edit the text.
3. Format the text.
4. Proofread the document.
5. Save the document.
6. Print the document.

Although each software manufacturer uses different commands and instructions,

all word processing programs perform these tasks in a similar manner. This makes it very easy to transfer skills from one program to another. The toolbars for two of today's most popular word processing programs appear in Figure 4-3.

Entering Text

As the user enters text, word wrap and other software features automate the process of creating a document. For example, when the user reaches the end of a line, the text wraps around to the next line automatically (on an old-fashioned typewriter, the typist had to manually return the carriage, or print mechanism, to the next line). The user simply continues to enter text and presses the Enter key only when moving to a new paragraph.

Editing Text

Few, if any, writers produce polished text in the first draft. Even experienced authors must rework text several times before it is satisfactory. With word processing software, the writer can revise and edit using commands that automatically copy, cut, or paste single words or entire paragraphs. A built-in thesaurus can propose alternative word choices, and the Find/Replace command can locate specified words and replace them with others. Many of these common editing tasks are performed easily with the click of mouse.

Formatting Text

One of the most powerful features of current word processing programs is their ability to format, or change the appearance of, text. Two popular programs, Microsoft Word and Corel WordPerfect, offer formatting features at the word, line, paragraph, page, and document levels. For example, at the word level both

Microsoft Word 2000

Corel WordPerfect 9

Figure 4-3: Toolbars of Two Popular Word Processing Programs

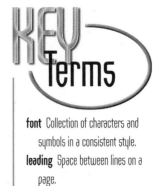

programs offer several **font** and typeface choices, such as Times New Roman, the default font, or Arial in regular, bold, and italic style. Fonts can be scaled to a desired size, specified in numbers of points with 72 points equaling an inch (see Figure 4-4 for a sample of fonts and typefaces). The font can be changed for **leading** and for **kerning.** From individual words and lines to the entire document, the **alignment** (right, left, or justified) of text and the amount of space left before and after paragraphs can be changed. Document formatting commands allow a user to specify the form of the document as a whole. For example, the user can format the text in columns, insert page numbers or other **headers** or **footers** on each page, or change the page size and the width of margins.

Proofreading the Document

One of the last steps in producing a document is checking the text for accuracy. Word processing programs streamline this time-consuming process by providing spelling and grammar checkers that highlight possible errors (Figure 4-5 shows the spell checker being used in a document). Some versions of these checkers perform these actions in real time, that is, at the same time the text is being entered. The spell checker does not, however, eliminate the need for manual proofreading. Some mistakes can be actual words, and therefore not recognized by the checker as errors. Dictionaries of various languages are also available on word processing programs. Most programs, in fact, allow the user to create a personal dictionary, or customized list of words, against which spelling can be checked.

Saving the Document

After the user creates a document, he should save it on the computer's hard disk or on a removable floppy diskette. Especially valuable documents should be stored on both media. The more important the data is to the user, the greater the

need for redundant backup in case of damage to one or another of the media.

Printing the Document

Today's computer systems support a wide variety of printers. Most computers have a dedicated printer attached to them for immediate delivery of as many hard copies of a document as desired. Networked computers often share resources such as expensive laser printers. With their increasingly wide range of desktop publishing capabilities, contemporary word processing programs can produce color documents, photographs, and other creative designs if the printer supports it.

KEY Terms

font Collection of characters and symbols in a consistent style.

leading Space between lines on a page.

kerning Space between letters in a word or sentence.

alignment Position of text on a page, either side-to-side or top-to-bottom.

8-point Arial
12-point Arial
18-point Arial
24-point Arial

Tahoma regular	Times New Roman regular
Tahoma bold	**Times New Roman bold**
Tahoma italic	*Times New Roman italic*
Tahoma bold italic	***Times New Roman bold italic***

 Figure 4-4: Sample of Font Styles and Sizes Offered in Microsoft Word 2000

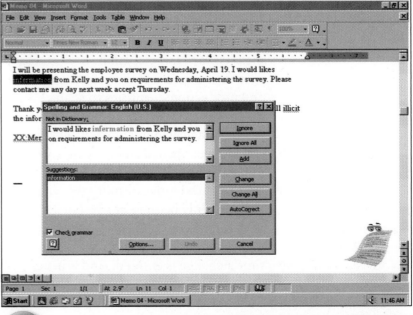

 Figure 4-5: Microsoft Word Document Being Spell Checked

Processing Numbers

The rapid and accurate processing of numbers is perhaps the most important contribution that the computer has made to the business world. While word processing has, in a sense, merely improved on documents produced with typewriters, no counterpart for number processing existed prior to the computer. Adding machines and calculators can produce accurate results for the data entered, but they cannot automatically recalculate results if any number is changed. Before computers were available, accountants and financial analysts manually wrote cost and quantity figures on paper spreadsheets, large sheets filled with many columns and rows of boxes. If the analyst wished to change any number, she erased certain figures and recalculated all affected totals, a very time-consuming and tedious process. Such changing and recalculating variable quantities to view their impact is called the **what-if factor,** and it takes place regularly in the business world. A business planner, for example, might need to evaluate various possible manufacturing costs and production quantities to achieve a desired profit margin and the break-even point. The development of the electronic spreadsheet opened an entire new world of opportunity in numeric analysis. The time involved in performing the what-if task suddenly became much shorter because the electronic spreadsheet automatically recalculates all of the sums each time a change is entered. And it never makes a mistake: when entered correctly, **formulas** will always return accurate results even as individual figures are manipulated.

Using Spreadsheets in Business

A spreadsheet program, then, can convert numeric data into useful information for informed managerial decision making, an area of business referred to as **management information systems (MIS).** One aspect of MIS uses computer-based models to simulate a decision. A manager fills in a spreadsheet to create a model of the actual business situation. The user then enters variables into the model and manipulates them to evaluate their impacts on the desired outcome. This type of analysis is commonly called decision support systems (DSS). Such modeling is invaluable in helping managers improve their analysis and make timely decisions.

Another major use of electronic spreadsheets in business is for statistical analysis. The predefined functions built into a spreadsheet make simple work of the most complicated statistical calculations. For example, spreadsheets can average a series of numbers such as salaries, production costs, or sales. In addition, they can display the highest and lowest values, or the number that occurs most often. The results of the calculations can be presented as a numerical summary or in a pictorial graphic called a **chart.** Pictures are often much easier to grasp, and a graphical chart can transform numerical results into visual illustrations of trends, variations, and other data that might be overlooked in a numerical summary. A sales chart, for instance, can be constructed with the time period displayed on the horizontal axis and the sales totals on the vertical. Viewing the graph from left to right as time moves forward will reveal upward or downward trends that may not be as apparent by merely reviewing the numbers. Different charting options, such as line charts, bar graphs, and pie charts, are available so users can match the type of information with the most appropriate chart style (see Figure 4-6).

KEY Terms

management information systems (MIS) Use of computer-based models that provide a flow of information from everyday actions to assist decision makers in carrying out their tasks.

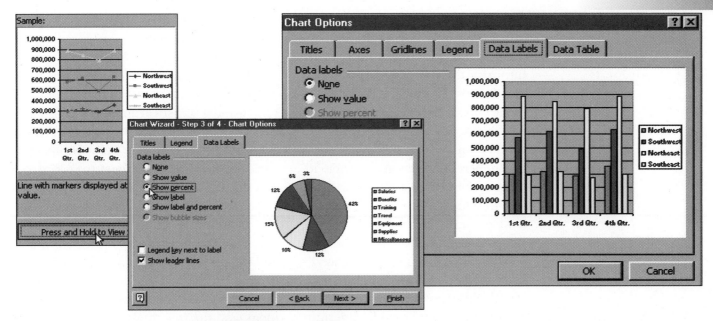

How Spreadsheets Work

Lotus 1-2-3 and Microsoft Excel are two of the more popular spreadsheet programs on the market. Though they compete with each other, they use similar structures and offer parallel features. The rows and columns of the spreadsheet are made up of **cells**, each of which has a particular location, or **cell address**. The cell address consists of a letter designating the column and the number of the row that the data occupies on the spreadsheet. A typical spreadsheet has 256 lettered columns and 65,536 numbered rows. The first cell is called A1 with the "A" representing the first column, and the "1" representing the row number. Figure 4-7 shows the structure of a Microsoft Excel 2000 worksheet.

Types of Cell Entries

Four types of entries can be made into cells: numeric, **alphanumeric**, formulas, and **functions.**

- **Numeric Entries:** Numbers do not change; they remain constant in value. On a spreadsheet, numeric constants are entered into a "constants area" where they can be manipulated. Results can then

Figure 4-6: Line, Pie, and Bar Charts

be observed in a "calculations area." Some examples of numeric constants include interest rates, discount percentages, commission rates, postage rates, sales tax percentage, and hourly wage rates.

- **Alphanumeric Entries:** Entries that include all text, or numbers that are not to be calculated, are called

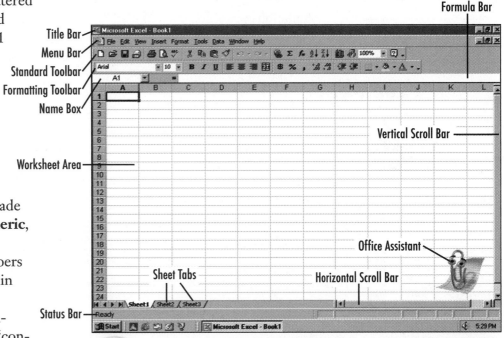

Figure 4-7: Microsoft Excel 2000 Worksheet

alphanumeric entries. This type of data can be sorted or its appearance changed, but the contents cannot be automatically altered as a result of calculations. Examples of alphanumeric entries include names, addresses, social security numbers, and phone numbers.

- **Formulas:** Formulas are mathematical equations, from addition to division to standard deviation. Formulas can be entered into cells and can incorporate amounts from other cells. A formula can add, subtract, multiply, or divide any combination of cell addresses. As in mathematics, parentheses can be used to determine a specific order of calculation. Figure 4-8 illustrates some typical spreadsheet entries.

- **Functions:** All spreadsheets include a great quantity of mathematical, statistical, financial, and other types of programmed calculations. Since there are no keys on the computer keyboard designated for calculating functions such as sum, average, count, square root, and others, predefined program functions in the spreadsheet application make these calculations possible.

functions Programmed capabilities included in a software package to ease the performance of complex actions or calculations such as mathematical, statistical, or financial measures.

Performing Three-Dimensional Statistical Analysis

Even though they are two-dimensional, electronic spreadsheets can make three-dimensional statistical analysis a possibility. For example, a sales manager can keep track of the performance of his company's stores by using a spreadsheet to record and summarize sales results. For each store, the manager uses a two-dimensional spreadsheet. Each store's spreadsheet lists the departments across the columns and the products in the rows down the side. In this format, the column totals will indicate the performance of each department, and the row totals will show the product summaries. Then, a summary sheet showing the grand total of all of the stores is created by adding together the figures in the same cell addresses on all of the sheets.

For instance, the third product in the second department on each of the separate spreadsheets shows the sales for that particular store. By transferring all of the numbers from this same cell address from all of the spreadsheets onto the summary sheet and then totaling them, the grand total of the product sold in that department in all locations can be determined. This kind of calculation effectively adds a third-dimensional capability to the analysis. The maximum number of spreadsheets that can be used depends on the amount of memory in the user's computer, although it would take an extremely large amount of data to exceed the capabilities of modern spreadsheet software packages.

After a spreadsheet is constructed, it should be tested for accuracy and to determine if the model achieves the expected results. Then, it can be saved for later analysis. Electronic spreadsheets have truly revolutionized the important aspect of planning and prediction in the business world. The power of automatic recalculation with no chance for error provides users with a priceless analytical tool that dramatically saves time and effort.

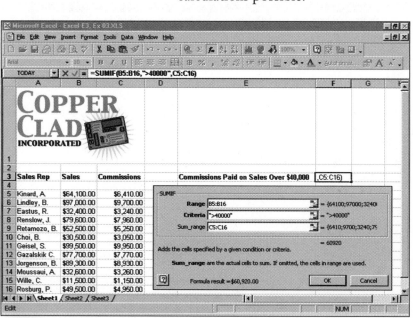

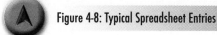

Figure 4-8: Typical Spreadsheet Entries

EXPANSION CARD

Should I buy individual applications or a suite?

While buying a new computer is a major investment, purchasing software can also be quite expensive. Consumers have two major options: 1) they can buy individual software applications, or 2) they can purchase software suites, packages that contain complete, full-featured versions of several software programs. These suites of software can save money and have the particular advantage of being designed to be used together, making it possible to exchange files among the programs. Suites usually include a word processing, spreadsheet, and graphics presentation program, and some also include a database program. Common software suites include Microsoft Office, WordPerfect Office, and Lotus SmartSuite.

A variation of the suite option is a works program. A **works program** is a single computer program that combines scaled-down versions of several different applications, typically a word processor, a spreadsheet, a database program, and a graphics program. Works programs have fewer features and are less sophisticated than the corresponding applications included in a software suite. Works programs also often use a file format that is not compatible with other software, making the interchange of data between users difficult. ClarisWorks and Microsoft Works are examples of such combined programs. Works programs are ideal for occasional computer users with limited computing requirements who do not need or want all of the features of full-scale individual programs. If regular file sharing with others is a necessity, however, they are probably not a good choice.

Before purchasing software, it is a good idea to evaluate it carefully (see the guidelines offered in the Feature Box called "Buying Software"). Some software manufacturers offer limited-use evaluation copies or limited-capability demo versions of their products. In most cases, however, you will need to research the software on your own. The reviews of new software in computer magazines such as *Byte, PC Week, PC World, Computer Shopper,* or *MacWorld* can prove helpful. Reviews can also be found on the Internet, although you should check to make sure such sites come from reliable unbiased sources. You can also visit a computer store to try out the product. In purchasing software, one important consideration is the program others are using with whom you will need to interact. For example, if your business or school has adopted Microsoft Office Professional, your work will be simplified by purchasing the same product for home use. If you can, take advantage of the discounted prices many software manufacturers offer college students. These discounts can be substantial. Microsoft Office Professional sells for around $200 in college bookstores, for example, which is well below its usual consumer retail cost.

Database Programs

Database programs, or **database management systems (DBMS),** are software for storing, organizing, and manipulating large amounts of information. A database is a collection of information that is accessible by computer. Such a collection can be as simple as an electronic address book or as complicated as a collection of all of the records that make up the U.S. Census. Many businesses and organizations, such as banks, colleges, hospitals, and government agencies, make extensive use of database programs. Besides text entries, the newest database software can also handle such data types as sounds, images, video, and animations. A college

student's file record, for example, can now include a digital photograph of the student, and a hardware store parts inventory can include an image of the item described or an animation demonstrating its use. Microsoft Access and Corel Paradox are two popular database programs used in business and industry.

Elements of a Database Table

At the core of every database is one or more sets of information collected in tables. A **table** consists of rows, called **records,** and columns, called **fields,** as shown in Figure 4-9. When multiple tables have at least one field in common,

KEY Terms

database management systems (DBMS) Software programs that efficiently store, organize, and manipulate large amounts of information.

relational field Field that appears in common in multiple tables in a database, allowing tables to be linked.

data warehousing Data files stored for future examination for reasons unrelated to their original creation.

data mining Examination of current or warehoused data to discover potentially useful new information.

they are said to be relational; that is, a relationship exists between the data in the various tables that can be joined. Reports can be generated that combine information from linked tables, thus eliminating the need for redundant records. For example, a student's name, address, and phone number might be needed for a college registrar's files as well as by the college business office, security office, health office, and individual instructors. Multiple copies of the same information could be saved and errors in copying information avoided if each of these offices or individuals had access to a single database of this information. By using a student ID number as a **relational field**, or an item shared in common, authorized users who need access to the student's information can retrieve it.

Find. This feature allows the user to locate specific information in a table by looking up a number or specified piece of text, such as a name or an address.

Query. A more complicated search than using the Find command can be done by means of a **query**. Such searches are accomplished by querying the database using **SQL (Structured Query Language)** or **QBE (Query By Example).** Using one of these query methods, for instance, a college dean can generate a report for each term of the names, addresses, and grade point averages of students who earn Dean's List recognition. The query is created to extract this specific information from the database, and the same query can be saved to be run for every future term.

Links. So-called **relational database programs** allow users to link tables in significant ways. Reports can then be created that combine information from linked tables.

Output. Output from a database can take a wide variety of formats. Printed reports of information are one kind of output. Mailing labels are also easy to create through **mail merge,** a feature that collects the data from one file and layout information from another and combines them in a third, merged document to create labels and form letters. Using mail merge, personally addressed form letters can be created, such as those from a college development office requesting donations from alumni.

Each row is one record in the table

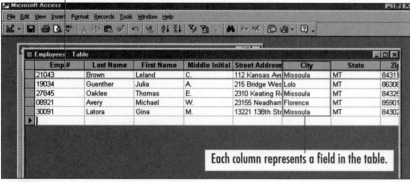

Each column represents a field in the table.

Figure 4-9: Microsoft Access Database Table

Common Features of Database Programs

Features commonly found in database programs include the following:

- **Sort.** This feature allows the user to sort, or arrange, records in many different ways with the touch of a button. Each user of the database can rearrange information in a way that is most useful for his or her purpose. For example, student information could be sorted by age, hometown, ethnicity, grade point average, parking ticket violations, and so on. Different arrangements, or views, can be easily stored.

New Uses of Databases

Databases can be extremely valuable resources in businesses and organizations. Even when no longer immediately useful, data files can be stored for future examination by a strategy called **data warehousing.** They may even be queried later on for reasons unrelated to their original creation. The activity referred to as **data mining** examines current or warehoused data to discover potentially useful new information. An auto manufacturer who has a financing subsidiary, for example, might examine a database of paid-off accounts to create a new database of potential car-buying customers to whom he can send brand-loyalty discounts. A credit card issuer might review an accounts database for potential consumers of additional services that his firm can offer. Moreover, many companies sell database information to other companies for revenue; even some colleges sell student name lists to potential credit card issuers.

Other Business-Related Software

Several kinds of software have been developed for specialized use in business and commercial interactions. A few of them are described below.

Project Management Software

A popular business application is **project management software** such as Microsoft Project. This category of software enables users to collaboratively plan and track projects and deliver the results in any format that the business needs. This includes the creation of timing bar charts (also known as Gantt charts), as well as calendars, status reports, materials reports, and numerous other planning and reporting tools. Much of this software is accessible over the Internet, supporting two-way communication that can also be used offline. The use of project management software improves work team productivity, increases the effective use of the project's data, and extends its benefits across the entire organization.

Presentation Software

Presentation software allows a user to create presentations that combine text, numbers, graphics, sounds, and movies. Such programs are commonly used by sales representatives for making pitches to customers, by trainers and other educators for creating educational graphics, and by business people in general for creating materials to present their ideas at meetings. Presentation software makes it possible for a user to alter a presentation for different audiences, to include in one presentation materials created by several programs (such as word processors, graphics programs, and page layout programs), and to output a presentation in one of more of many different formats (such as 35mm slides, transparencies, or

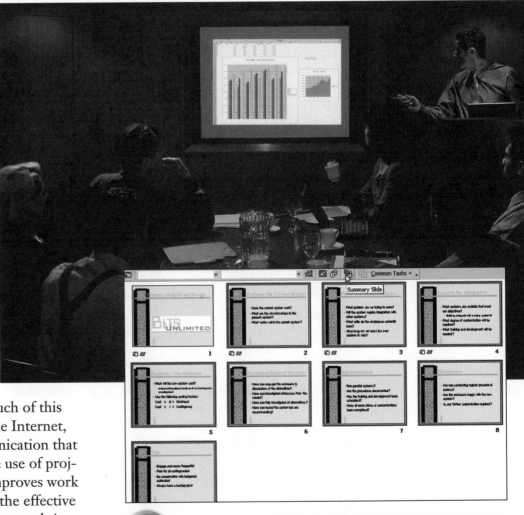

Figure 4-10: Individual Slides in a PowerPoint Slide Show

hard-copy handouts). A presentation created by presentation software and run on a portable computer can be projected onto a screen using a projection device attached to the computer. One of the most widely used presentation programs is Microsoft PowerPoint. An example of a slide show created in PowerPoint is shown in Figure 4-10.

Personal Information Managers

Personal information managers (PIMs) are programs that offer the same calendar and address book functions that one might find in a pocket calendar. Some widely used personal information managers include Lotus Organizer, Microsoft Outlook, ACT, and Info Select. Although the various PIMs differ, most offer similar characteristics and features, such as a range of scheduling options, including scheduling of rooms, resources, and events; an alarm clock; a to-do list; an address book; and the option of viewing the calendar in various views, such as by day, by week, or by month.

Money Management Programs

A wide variety of money management programs are now available for personal computers. These vary from simple checkbook balancing programs to complex accounting packages appropriate for medium-sized corporations. The program Microsoft Money often comes already loaded on many new personal computers. The most widely used of all money management programs, however, is Quicken, which allows the user to work in an environment that simulates a checkbook register. This program allows individuals and small businesses to reconcile monthly bank statements, print checks, and assign disbursements to par-

ticular categories. Although designed as a personal check register program, Quicken can be used by small businesses to manage budgets, track expenditures, and provide reports.

Tax software has greatly enhanced the speed and accuracy of the complex annual tax process. Programs such as TurboTax or MacinTax come in federal and state versions that allow the user to download, complete, and file all necessary forms. Data from Quicken can be directly imported into a tax preparation program. As the user enters the information on each form, the program performs calculations, analyzes the amount due, and automatically transfers certain totals and other necessary numbers between forms.

Creativity Software

One of the most exciting features of modern computing is the ability to create and manipulate pictures and graphics. In fact, since its inception, the computer has grown from a specialized device for doing computation into an unparalleled tool for creative expression for amateurs and professionals alike. With today's creativity software, a user can sketch and paint; touch up photographs; create animated cartoons; construct virtual reality worlds; edit a film; compose and play a musical piece; record and listen to a song or lecture; and design and lay out the text, photographs, and illustrations for a newsletter or brochure.

Graphics Software

One popular type of creativity software, graphics software, was created in 1963 by Ivan Sutherland, a graduate student at the

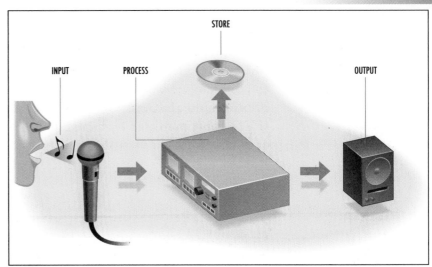

Figure 4-11: Image Created in Adobe Illustrator

Massachusetts Institute of Technology (MIT). Sutherland's Sketchpad used a light pen to draw simple lines on a screen. In the early days of personal computing, software developers created two types of programs for producing computer graphics. **Bitmap-** or **raster image-based graphics** programs, commonly called painting programs, allowed users to create pictures by changing the pixels on the screen from white to black. As discussed in Chapter 2, an image on a monitor or printer is made up of tiny bits of print, called pixels. Bitmaps are stored collections of information about the color and intensity of each pixel. Painting programs were used by those who wished to produce graphics with irregular shapes. **Object-** or **vector-based graphics** programs, commonly called drawing programs, allowed users to construct pictures by creating, editing, and combining mathematically defined geometric shapes. Drawing programs were generally used by those who needed to produce regular geometric shapes, such as pie charts, bar graphs, and figures. Eventually, color versions of both painting and drawing programs were developed.

Painting and Drawing Programs

Today, the output quality and range of features of graphics software are far superior to those of early programs. In addition, distinctions between painting and drawing programs have blurred considerably because high-end drawing programs such as CorelDraw!, Canvas, and Adobe Illustrator contain both drawing and painting features. Relatively simple painting and drawing programs are still available, such as Windows Draw, MacDraw Pro, Microsoft Paint, and Paintbrush. Some of the many features of contemporary painting and drawing programs include a variety of paintbrush tools in different shapes and sizes; an eyedropper tool that allows users to import color from one part of an image to another;

tools for cropping, rotating, flipping, or resizing an image; tools for blending colors; 3-D effects, such as wrapping textures, text, and images around objects; and rulers, grids, compasses, and other tools for accurate measurements. Figure 4-11 shows an image drawn with Adobe Illustrator.

File Formats for Graphics Programs

These days, it is common to create graphics in one program and then use them or edit them in another program. For example, a computer artist might create a painting in Adobe Illustrator and then place it in a page layout program such as PageMaker. Or, a graphics designer might scan a photograph using Adobe PhotoShop and then use it in a PowerPoint slide presentation. Almost all graphics programs enable users to save files in a **native format,** or one that is read by that application. In addition, however, there are a number of **standard graphics file formats** in which graphics can be saved to be used in other applications. Saving a graphic in a standard file format is called **exporting** the graphic. Placing a graphic in a standard file format into another document or file is called **importing** the graphic. Some commonly

native format Instructions that enable users to save files so they can be read by the application in which they were created.

standard graphics file format Standard set of instructions that enable users to save files so they can be read by many applications.

used standard graphics file formats include **Encapsulated PostScript (EPS)** for vector-based graphics; **BitMap**, or **BMP**, for bitmap graphics on IBM PCs and compatibles; and **Joint Photographic Experts Group**, or **JPEG**, for compressed bitmap graphics, or files that have been made smaller for storage.

Other Graphics Programs

Raster image-editing programs have evolved considerably since the days of the early painting programs. High-end raster image-editing programs such as Adobe PhotoShop and Corel Photo House are commonly used today for editing digitized photographs. A **digitized photograph** is a photograph that has been stored as a raster image, or collection of black, white, or colored pixels. By using a photo manipulation or image-editing program, a user can touch up a photograph, move objects within the photograph, add objects, combine photographs with other photos or artwork, incorporate text within photos, change color hue and intensity, and much, much more. Photographs and other images thus manipulated can then

be saved and exported into a page layout program for incorporation into newsletters, brochures, advertising layouts, or books.

Editable digital photographs can be obtained in many ways, including scanning a photographic print or slide; taking photographs with a conventional camera and having a development house transfer them to disk or CD-ROM; or using a digital camera that contains no film but rather captures images in digital format.

Other common graphics programs include 3-D modeling programs and computer-aided design, or CAD, programs. Most painting and drawing programs create two-dimensional images. A **3-D modeling program,** such as Ray Dream Designer, 3-D Studio, MacroModel, or Strata StudioPro, is used to create images that give the illusion of being three-dimensional and that can be rotated or viewed from different angles (see Figure 4-12 for an example). Such programs are commonly used to create graphics for motion video animations, technical illustrations, and environments for multimedia applications such as computer games. The 1995 movie *Toy Story* was the first completely computer-animated motion picture, making extensive use of 3-D graphics.

Computer-aided design, or CAD, programs such as AutoCAD, DenebaCAD, and CorelCAD, enable engineers, architects, product designers, and others to produce precise technical drawings and blueprints. CAD programs have several features not found in other drawing programs that make them especially suited to technical work, such as the ability to give extremely precise measurements, to calculate such quantities as area and volume, and to generate dimensions, or notes, showing the measurements of objects in drawings. Drawings from CAD programs are often output to plotters, special kinds of printers that use pens to create images on very large sheets of paper.

Key Terms

Joint Photographic Experts Group (JPEG) Format for saving and transferring files that compresses the data; created by a group within the International Standards Organization.

3-D modeling program Software used to create images that give the illusion of being three-dimensional and can be rotated or viewed from different angles.

Figure 4-12: Example of Image Created in a 3-D Modeling Program

Page Layout Software

A **page layout program** such as Adobe PageMaker or Quark XPress enables its user to combine text and graphics to produce finished, publication-quality layouts. The process of producing such layouts on personal computers, known as desktop publishing, has revolutionized the publishing and advertising industries. With a desktop publishing program, a designer creates a template in the page layout program that contains **boilerplate** page layouts and style sheets. These are specifications for recurring elements such as headings and basic text. A manuscript produced in a word processing program is then imported into the page layout program. Next, styles are applied to the various text elements, including font size, font style, color, alignments, and column width. Boxes for artwork and photographs are added, and the images are ported into them. After copyediting and proofreading, the user prints the finished page layout. Desktop publishing programs have vastly simplified the old-fashioned printing process of typesetting, making corrections, and combining text and art. Such programs have brought the power of a publisher's design and typesetting departments to the desktops of individual computer users. Today, it is common for people to use these programs to produce their own fliers, posters, greeting cards, brochures, and newsletters. Figure 4-13 shows a brochure created in a desktop publishing program.

Multimedia Software

Software that uses some combination of speech, text, still graphics, animation, moving pictures, and sound is known as multimedia. Today, multimedia elements are often incorporated into ordinary documents, into business and education presentations, and into pages placed on the World Wide Web. Many software programs today allow a user to incorporate

multimedia elements. For example, it is usually possible to embed speech annotations, graphics, and video clips into word processing programs or into slide shows prepared in presentation programs. The Adobe Acrobat program, for example, allows a user to create platform-independent documents, known as **PDF** documents, that contain text, graphics, video, and sound in the Quicktime video format. **Web authoring software** allows users to incorporate multimedia elements into pages to be posted on the World Wide Web. It is also possible to create stand-alone multimedia products using **multimedia authoring software** such as Macromedia Director, Quark Imedia, and mTropolis. Content for a multimedia work can come from many different sources. Text can be prepared in a word processing program. Graphics can be cre-

boilerplate Component of a page layout software program that includes standardized specifications for recurring elements.

PDF Format for file creation and transfer (Portable Document File) that enables a document to appear identical on any computer, no matter what platform is being used; viewable with Adobe Acrobat software.

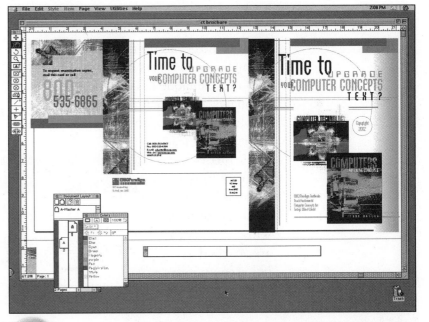

Figure 4-13: Brochure Designed and Created with a Desktop Publishing Program

ated in painting, drawing, or 3-D modeling programs, taken from clip art or stock sources, or produced by traditional means and scanned and edited in a graphics program. Many **sound capture and editing programs,** such as SoundEdit, are available for capturing and editing sounds.

Video digitizing cards allow a user to capture and digitize video images and sounds from such sources as television, videotape recorders, and camcorders. **Video editing software,** such as Adobe Premier, VideoVision MI, and Avid Cinema, allows the user to edit sound and video and output it in various digital formats, such as QuickTime, Motion Picture Experts Group (MPEG), and Video for Windows.

Digital video recordings are multimedia presentations that permit the mixing of multiple images much like music combines different microphones or recording cuts. As the United States continues its conversion to digital television broadcasting and as digital photography becomes more affordable, more personal computer users will be able to create and edit graphical media in much the same way as some enjoy collecting photographs today.

MIDI Software

Popular music has been dominated by digital audio synthesizers for many years, but now the technique has come to the home computer. Software programs such as Finale and Digital Orchestrator Plus are available that teach music theory and compose music scores using electronic keyboards. These keyboards are attached to home computers using a standard connection called a **musical instrument digital interface (MIDI).** MIDI files are collections of instructions that re-create a specific sound at a particular time and at a certain volume. As you

learned in Chapter 2, any analog sound can be scaled into a digital audio form for storage as binary numbers. By using MIDI software, a user effectively turns the computer into a music composition and recording machine. A composition played on a keyboard can be recorded and output as printed sheet music, as shown in Figure 4-14. The same file can also replay the music on the same keyboard on which it was recorded and include any edited changes or special effects. With sound editing software, digital music files can be modified and mixed, and special effects such as echoes can be incorporated.

Games Software

Many thousands of games are available for personal computers, including traditional games such as tic-tac-toe, solitaire, poker, chess, darts, Parcheesi, and Go. Some games, such as Microsoft's Solitaire and Apple's Puzzle, are bundled with operating systems. The high speed and excellent multimedia capabilities of contemporary computers have made possible superb simulation games, including many versions of auto racing, flight, and golfing simulators, and multimedia, arcade-style

musical instrument digital interface (MIDI) Standard connection through which musical instruments such as keyboards can be attached to computers.

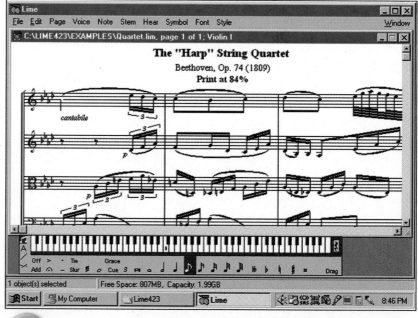

 Figure 4-14: Sheet Music Created and Printed Using MIDI Software

games with video or virtual environments, such as Tetris, Myst, Warcraft II, SimAnt, SimCity, Unreal Tournament, Tomb Raider, and Mech Warrior 2.

Freeware and Shareware

Not all software is created by commercial firms. Some software is produced by independent programmers who distribute their work as freeware or shareware on disks or through a bulletin board service, an online service, or the Internet. Typically, users can download such software directly to their personal computers. A **freeware** program is software that can be copied and distributed at no cost. While such a program may be distributed without restriction or payment to its

KEY Terms

MP3 Data compression standard for music file creation.

Secure Digital Music Initiative (SDMI) Technology that allows no more than three copies to be made of a music file for personal use.

INNOVATIONS
The Changing Face of the Music Industry

A new data compression standard is rapidly altering the recorded music industry. The standard, called **MP3**, resulted from the work of the Moving Pictures Experts Group (MPEG) of the International Standards Organization (ISO). With MP3-compliant software, digital recorded music distributed on CDs containing tens of megabytes of data can be compressed into just a few megabytes for storage on a computer. These MP3 files can be arranged in any order or transferred to other users by e-mail or over Web sites. Users have been exchanging MP3 files on the Web for a number of years, and new download sites are growing daily. Portable MP3 players now make it possible to load MP3 selections into stand-alone units that can be reprogrammed and the play list reordered at will. Music artists who have not been able to secure recording company contracts are thrilled with the opportunity to reach listeners through this means, bypassing traditional publishing channels. Others claim that the high cost of CDs is driving users to share music in this way. In fact, in May 2000 the five largest recording companies settled a price-gouging case with the Federal Trade Commission; essentially, they admitted that American consumers have been overcharged for CDs more than $480 million since 1997. It is, therefore, no surprise that during the past two years since the development of MP3, sales of CDs have decreased by 4% within five miles of college campuses. College students frequently use school facilities to download huge numbers of MP3 files.

MP3 technology also opens up a whole array of issues in piracy and copyright infringement for the music industry. One MP3 leader, Napster.com (see Figure 4-15), has been the object of lawsuits by music industry associations as well as by such artists as Metallica and Dr. Dre. A recent log of just one of Napster's more than 100 servers showed that over 800,000 files were transferred by users in a single week. Napster has thus been forced to sever the accounts of many thousands of members who were guilty of copyright infringement on Metallica's music. However, Napster has formed an alliance with the global media company Bertelsmann, owner of BMG music, as a first stage in transforming itself into a membership-based service. Obviously, the music publishing industry wants to protect its investments; therefore, a consortium of some 160 record labels, device manufacturers, and software makers have created the **Secure Digital Music Initiative (SDMI).** SDMI-compliant technology allows for no more than three copies to be made of a music file for personal use. Music files that use SDMI will have embedded digital codes that will limit its recording and downloading capability. SDMI is now on the market, and the music industry is gearing up for full-scale digital music sales over Web links.

Although SDMI sounds like the answer to copyright infringement issues in the music industry, it is worthwhile to note that similar technology has been tried by the video industry to eliminate the illegal duplication of videotapes. Tapes continue to be duplicated illegally, however, because as soon as a technique to block copying is in place, another technique is created to override it. Clearly, the matter of piracy with MP3 will remain a concern for the music industry for some time to come.

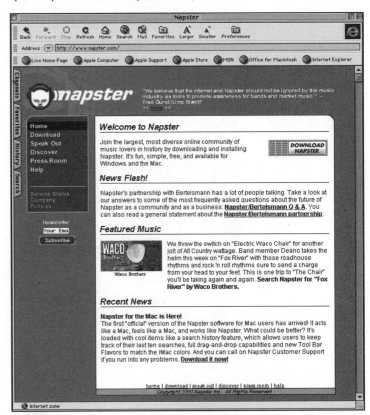

Figure 4-15: Napster's Web Site

shareware Software that can be freely copied and distributed, but for which the author retains the copyright.

author, the author retains the copyright and the program may not be altered or sold without permission. **Shareware,** like freeware, can be freely copied and distributed, and the author holds the copyright. Shareware differs from freeware in what its author expects after users try the program. If users decide not to continue using the program, they are usually obligated by the shareware agreement that comes with the program to remove it from their hard drive after a specified period of time (thirty days, for example). On the other hand, if a user likes the program, the shareware agreement asks the user to send its creator a small amount of money, often in exchange for an upgraded version and sometimes more detailed documentation. Essentially, then, the author of shareware grants a temporary license allowing use of the software for a limited period of time. Shareware commonly operates on the honor system. Besides freeware and shareware, other software in the public domain such as games and utility applications are also available through Web sites, electronic bulletin boards, and person-to-person contact. Typically, this software is not under copyright protection and there is no enforcement of author's rights.

EXPANSION CARD

Groupware in Today's Collaborative Work Environment

Collaboration in the workplace is greatly valued today. By pooling individual skills, a work team benefits from the expertise of each of its members. A well-designed work team is comprised of individuals whose talents complement one another in the effort to solve a company problem or achieve a company goal. In many instances, however, achieving teamwork is difficult due to the fact that not all members can be in the same location for meetings. Groupware, or collaborative software, provides a solution to that problem. Groupware users use standard Internet communication techniques to work on the same project simultaneously whether at the office, at home, or on the road—no matter where they are physically located in the world.

Consultation firms, financial planners, legal and medical professionals, and thousands of other business workers rely on groupware to work effectively and efficiently with others. Groupware is especially useful in situations where teamwork is critical or where decisions must be executed sequentially and are based upon information housed in a common file location. One such groupware software package, Lotus Notes, includes e-mail, networking, scheduling, and database components. Notes makes it possible for participants to conduct a split-screen real-time dialog with each other no matter where they are located. It also allows participants to interface with shared databases that are relevant to the conversation taking place or decisions being debated.

With groupware, workers can consult common files, share ideas, consider others' input, and evaluate solutions. Moreover, specialists from around the world can be consulted and brought into the conversation at a fraction of the cost it would take to arrange an actual visit for that person to the particular firm. Groupware can also reduce paper consumption and processing costs. In the insurance industry, for example, the same software that is used to enter a claim is also used by the adjuster to authorize its payment and by accounts payable personnel to record their activities. As a result, there is never a missing paper file or a bottleneck where paperwork is held up before being passed on to another desk. In the future, the growing networked economy will no doubt rely even more heavily on groupware as employee travel and home office work make on-site collaboration and office meetings increasingly obsolete.

Tomorrow's Applications Software

Like everything else in the computer industry, software programs will continue to undergo rapid development. In the future, we can expect them to be more automated and less visible, even as the computers they empower become more and more embedded in the numerous activities of daily life. The way humans interface with software will also change. A dramatic leap forward in interface design occurred when command-based computing was replaced by the now-familiar virtual desktop interface used by Macintosh and Windows computers. Research is now working on an even easier design, one in which users will be able to communicate with software by speech. Communication with the computer will thus be as simple as talking with another person. Such voice recognition software or speech processing software, while still in early stages of development, has tremendous potential for translating languages, converting speech into text, and converting text into speech. All over the world today, programmers, linguists, engineers, and cognitive scientists are working together to advance this technology.

If today's trend continues, **software convergence** will also increase in the future. In the past, to produce a company newsletter, the worker often used a half-dozen or more separate programs—a word processor, a spell checker, a scanning program, a photo editor, a spreadsheet, and a page layout program. Today, a worker can perform most of these tasks with a single program, and future programs will converge tasks to an even greater degree. The rapid growth of the Internet has also made **platform-independent software** for networks increasingly necessary. This is software that can be run on any machine at any time. When different kinds of computers are connected by a network, users need to be able to create documents that can be read on any platform—supercomputers, minicomputers, workstations, PCs, handheld devices, and others. In the future, operating systems will merge with browsers, and browsers will handle platform-independent pages containing every conceivable type of application, from word processing to rendering of 3-D virtual environments. In other words, the whole idea of separate applications running on separate platforms will soon become obsolete.

Key Terms

software convergence Industry trend toward combining features of multiple software packages into a single program.

platform-independent software Software that can be run on any kind of computer at any time, used for creating documents that can be read on any platform.

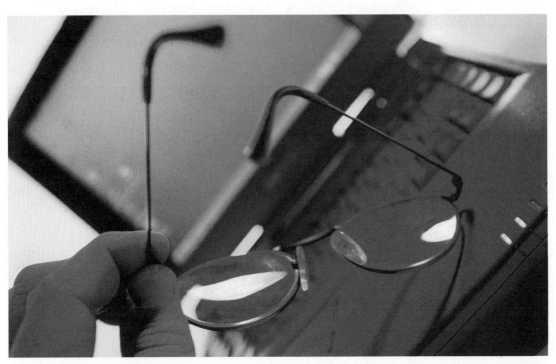

KEY Terms

intelligent agents (bots) Small programs that can be sent on searches to locate desired information and then deliver it to the user on demand or on a schedule.

application service provider (ASP) Firm that makes software available for rental or lease over the Internet.

A new software trend in retailing is designed to read customers' minds and help direct the future of consumer purchasing. So-called **customer management software** helps retailers learn exactly what their customers want and will purchase even before the products exist. The software can be used to track customers' past purchases, create customer profiles, and even analyze customers' online activity. It can ask direct questions of customers as to their shopping preferences. This software provides a resource of customer information that a business can mine to create products and market them to an audience that is guaranteed to be receptive.

As computer processors improve in capacity, many more software programs will involve multimedia and virtual reality simulations, enhancing the way we view and comprehend information. Already, virtual reality is widely used for diverse purposes, to provide airline pilots with a visual map of a runway obscured with fog or to train army troops to maneuver in places that they have not yet visited. Virtual reality has tremendous potential for recreation and entertainment, for product development, for city planning, and for education. While such software will be able to do an astonishing variety of creative and practical tasks, it will also become increasingly accessible to the everyday user and no longer be reserved for specialists or computer "techies."

Future software applications will make extensive use of **intelligent agents**. These agents, sometimes called **bots** (an abbreviated form of *robots*), are small programs that a user can send on searches to locate the desired information and to

deliver it to that person's desktop or mailbox. The domain to be searched can be specified to be a computer, a specific network, or the Internet as a whole. The agent freely roams the search domain to return the requested information. The use of these agents not only simplifies the search process, but also provides a means to deal with the ever-growing mountain of information that is accumulating at a startling rate. The many search engines available on the Internet work in a similar way, but they are restricted to their programmed settings. Software agents, on the other hand, search the entire Internet including search engines for the desired data. (Search engines and intelligent agents are discussed in more detail in Chapter 6.)

One of the hottest new trends is the movement toward renting or leasing software over the Internet. Companies that make software available for rental are called **application service providers (ASPs).** Instead of buying and installing a software application, a user logs onto the product's Web site, rents the program for a fee, and uses it. An ASP thus allows employees and others to use a much wider and diverse range of software than they otherwise would if they or their business had to purchase and install each separate software package. We can expect to hear much more about ASPs in the near future.

INNOVATIONS

Computers Go Racing

Computers process data into information. As we have seen, this function enables business managers to improve the quality of their decision making. But the information systems concept can extend beyond business to many other areas of work and play, including to motor sports. In designing, tuning up, and setting up racing equipment, engineers and mechanics must examine data from prior performances to make decisions that will improve the next effort's results. Each racing organization has its own rules for the use of data collection technology. For cost reasons, some organizations limit the use of computers. For example, drag racing professional competitors in the National Hot Rod Association (NHRA) record all of their runs on a computer, but NASCAR stock-car racing teams use them only in closed testing. Whenever World Formula 1 racers are on the track, computers relay real-time telemetry back to team engineers in the garage and to engine specialists who may be at a factory on the other side of the world. An amazing array of data can be collected regarding engine speed and temperatures, oil and fuel consumption, electrical voltage, and much more. Mechanics analyze this information to make changes to the setup of a racecar to improve its next performance. Advanced systems can even record tire air pressure to determine if one is going flat. They can also measure the amount of time the driver has a foot on the brakes. These multi-channel computers gather data at up to 100 samples per second. Continuous recording can last for up to two hours. Today's racing competitors understand that part of their success is based on this high-tech computer data.

Such advanced racing data has the additional advantage of helping design tomorrow's automobiles. All cars manufactured today include devices that are the product of racing heritage, including ignition control, fuel injection systems, and traction control devices. Vehicles with multi-valve overhead cam engines to reduce environment-damaging pollution also have their origins in motor sports. While skilled automobile mechanics show little sign of disappearing anytime soon, such mechanics rely increasingly less on muscle and deft hands than on computer knowledge to keep automobiles running smoothly. Perhaps someday the Indianapolis 500 will commence with the command, "Ladies and gentlemen, start your engines—and your computers!"

Chapter
SUMMARY

Applications software turns computer systems into useful tools. Today, numerous types of software programs are available for every conceivable business, educational, or creative use. This chapter has explored some of the more common broad categories of software. For the average user, word processing is the most familiar of all software programs. In general, processing words involves six basic steps, each one of which is made easy by word processing functions: entering text, editing text, formatting text, proofreading the document, saving the document, and printing the document. Today's word processing software also includes many enhanced features for document design such as font selection, automatic bulleting of lists, and other formatting options that were previously available only in desktop publishing programs.

A second major type of software programs is electronic spreadsheets. The invention of these powerful recalculation tools has truly revolutionized the business world. Spreadsheets are used in businesses and organizations for decision making and statistical analysis. The user enters data into cells and then can change variables; the spreadsheet program recalculates using formulas and standard equations, and the user analyzes the results.

Another important category of software is database software. Database programs store, organize, and manipulate large amounts of information. Database tables consist of records and fields, and reports can be generated that combine data from linked fields to produce the precise information the user requests. Some commands used in database searches include sort, find, and query.

Other types of software frequently used in business include:

- Project management software applications, which assist business users with scheduling and communications activities that enhance a firm's productivity and efficiency.
- Presentation software, used to create engaging slide shows and multimedia presentations.
- Personal information managers, programs that offer organizing tools such as calendars and address books to users.
- Money management programs, which include everything from simple checkbook balancing, to small business accounts management, to tax management.

Recently, major development has taken place in the category of creativity software, and this trend will certainly continue in the near future. Today's graphic software allows both experts and amateurs alike to unleash their creativity. Very simple to very advanced programs exist, including drawing programs, painting programs, 3-D modeling programs, CAD programs, and photo-editing programs. Page layout programs allow a user to produce professional-looking brochures and fliers by combining and manipulating text and graphics. Multimedia software uses some combination of speech, text, graphics, animation, motion pictures, and sound. Such software is increasingly accessible to the average computer user.

The trend toward renting software over the Internet from application service providers (ASPs) is one of the most significant recent changes in business software use.

Key terms are presented here in the order in which they are cited in the text. A complete list of key terms in the text, in alphabetical order with definitions, can be found in the Glossary at the end of the book.

CONFIGURING KNOWLEDGE

Multiple Choice Questions
Choose the best answer from those provided.

1. Today's word processing programs allow users to save files in _____, the language used on the Web.
   a. DSS
   b. HTML
   c. DBMs
   d. JPEG
   e. CAD

2. All of the following features that help in editing, formatting, and proofreading text can be found on today's word processing programs except:
   a. spelling and grammar checkers
   b. boldfacing and italicizing
   c. creating columns
   d. cut, copy, paste commands
   e. querying

3. A WYSIWYG-capable software that allows a user to mix multiple text and graphics files into a print-ready layout is called a _____ package.
   a. word processor
   b. postscript
   c. spreadsheet
   d. desktop publishing
   e. print master

4. When a spreadsheet is used as a decision support application in which some variables are changed to observe the impact on an objective, the process is called _____.
   a. data mining
   b. objective analysis
   c. trial and error
   d. data warehousing
   e. what-if analysis

5. _____ may be entered into a spreadsheet cell in order to perform arithmetic operations that involve the contents of other cells.
   a. formulas
   b. functions
   c. text
   d. numeric data
   e. prefixes

6. The final results of the analysis performed by a spreadsheet can be pictorially presented as bars, lines, or pie wedges by using a feature called _____.
   a. macros
   b. modeling
   c. projection
   d. interpolation
   e. charts

7. The inexpensive computer application that includes limited features of several types of software is called a(n) _____.
   a. suite package
   b. integrated software package
   c. works package
   d. shareware package
   e. groupware package

8. A musician who wishes to connect a synthesizer keyboard to a computer to create a new score would make use of a _____ connection.
   a. serial
   b. parallel
   c. MINI
   d. MIDI
   e. MAXI

9. The type of software that is available for no charge and comes with no obligation of the user to the creator is called _____ .
   a. groupware
   b. shareware
   c. net ware
   d. freeware
   e. project ware

10. Authorized users from several different departments within an organization can access common database information through use of a(n) _____ such as an employee ID number.
    a. relational field
    b. common key
    c. alphanumeric entry
    d. primary key
    e. database management system

11. The technique that enables a firm to review a database to discover new business opportunities is called _____.
    a. milking the data
    b. data mining
    c. data stretching
    d. table sifting
    e. data recovery

12. Users who wish to produce regular geometric shapes, such as pie charts, bar graphs, and others, typically choose a(n) _____ program.
    a. painting
    b. drawing
    c. image editing
    d. computer-aided design
    e. 3-D modeling

13. Saving a graphic in a standard file format is called _____ the graphic.
    a. importing
    b. tabling
    c. capturing
    d. exporting
    e. reserving

14. _____ is the name given to producing professional-style page layouts of publications material such as brochures and fliers on personal computers.
    a. multimedia authoring programs
    b. boilerplate
    c. CAD programs
    d. image editing
    e. desktop publishing

15. While the future of software is still unknown, many predict that development will continue in all of the following areas, except_____.
    a. intelligent agents
    b. platform-independent software
    c. customer management software
    d. stand-alone word processors
    e. voice recognition software

True or False?

Rewrite each false item to make it a true statement.

1. All software programs are written to perform with certain operating systems, and some of their commands and icons derive from those operating systems.
2. Today's word processing programs combine some features formerly available only on desktop publishing programs.
3. Word processing software programs can create attractive documents, but they cannot be published to the World Wide Web without using special Internet software.
4. A spreadsheet's cells use the letter of each column and the number of each row to create addresses that identify their location.
5. A formula can be entered into a cell of a spreadsheet to perform arithmetic operations using the contents of other cells.
6. Electronic spreadsheets can only produce two-dimensional statistical analysis.
7. A software "works" program and a software "suite" are essentially the same thing.
8. Some contemporary database programs can also handle such data types as sound and animation.
9. A user must query a database by using SQL.
10. Although tax programs are helpful in filing taxes, a user cannot obtain tax forms on them.
11. Using image-editing software, a user can touch up, add to, or otherwise manipulate photographs.
12. MIDI is the acronym used by marketing strategists to refer to medium-sized computers.
13. Shareware software lets individuals work together on projects from multiple locations over a network.
14. Data warehousing refers to storage centers where large-capacity computers are stored.
15. APS technology opens up new legal issues in software piracy and copyright infringement.

TECHNOLOGY IN CONTEXT

Prepare to discuss each of the following questions, drawing upon the material presented in this chapter as well as additional information you may have researched on your own.

1. How are freeware, shareware, and commercial software similar? How are they different?
2. What characteristics make one software program better than another? What characteristics make one program a good buy and another not a good buy?
3. Describe the power of automatic recalculation in electronic spreadsheets. Explain how spreadsheets could be used in a home-building business.
4. This chapter has presented information on some of the most common types of software. What other types are you familiar with and what are their capabilities and features? Which is your favorite program, and why? What direction do you think software will take in the future?
5. Why might it be advisable for a company to use site licensing? networkable versions of software? software suites?

DEVELOPING MINDSHARE

1. Check the system capabilities of a personal computer to which you have access and determine its processor, memory size, hard-drive free space, and video adapter type so that you are ready to shop for software. Either go to a computer store or to a Web site and check out the system requirements for: a) a word processor, b) a spreadsheet, and c) a graphics or multimedia program. Is your system deficient in any of the requirements? Which ones? Research the cost of upgrading your equipment and detail the results of your research in a written report.

2. Check advertising in magazines or the online sites of the following software manufacturers to compare the features and capabilities of their suites of programs. Create a table that compares the newest releases of Microsoft Office Professional, Lotus SmartSuite, and Corel WordPerfect Office. In the table, list the features that you prefer. Finally, identify the program that best meets your needs, citing the reasons for your choice.

3. Check your local store or go online to discover the portable music devices that play MP3 files. Find Web sources to examine the quantity and variety of free downloadable music. Also check library archives or Web news stories for the copyright infringement implications of MP3 technology. Is this a case of pure music piracy—stealing intellectual property from authors—or is it a free-speech issue on the Web? Carefully examine both sides of the issue and then state your opinion and defend it.

4. Locate and read several new software reviews in computer magazines or on the Internet. Also, find several articles that discuss current and future trends in software development. Write a report explaining these latest developments and what they may imply about the future of computing.

5. Search for shareware online. Create a table that displays all the categories of software you can locate for personal use without charge.

THINK TANK

Philippe Kahn, a French immigrant who founded Borland International in the 1980s and grew it into the world's third-largest software company, has recently started a new company that may revolutionize the sending of images on the Internet. Called LightSurf, the company has developed a tiny nickel-sized camera that snaps onto a cell phone and, with the click of a button, sends a photo directly to the Web, to an e-mail file, or to a site for printing as a traditional photo. As of fall 2000, the LightSurf camera works only on specific brands of cell phones and only on one cellular network. But Kahn and his staff are confident this new wireless technology will one day be in the hands of everyone.

Teamwork Challenge: Kahn envisions using the LightSurf technology to deter crime. Can you imagine how this might work? What other kinds of applications for this technology can you brainstorm? Every new technology seems to have a downside. What might be the downside of the LightSurf camera technology? With your team members, create either an oral presentation, with visuals, or a written report that discusses your ideas.

Answers to Configuring Knowledge Questions

Multiple Choice: 1 – b; 2 – e; 3 – d; 4 – e; 5 – a; 6 – e; 7 – c ; 8 – d; 9 – d, 10 – a; 11 – b; 12 – b; 13 – d; 14 – e; 15 – d **True-False:** 1 – T; 2 – T; 3 – F; 4 – T; 5 – T; 6 – F; 7 – F; 8 – T; 9 – F; 10 – F; 11 – T; 12 – F; 13 – F; 14 – F; 15 – F

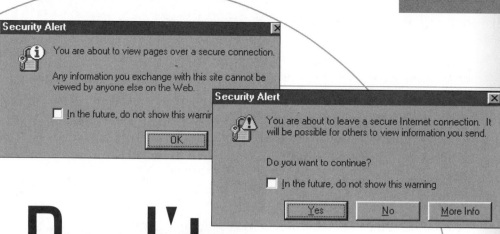

Reality
INTERFACE

Privacy on the Net: At Home and at Work

One of the greatest concerns with the rapid growth of the Internet is the matter of privacy. Issues concerning Internet privacy and security are numerous. Many fear, for instance, that the use of user-monitoring software will lead to an invasion of personal privacy or the theft of personal information. The Internet, after all, practically invites unscrupulous individuals to use open network connections as a gateway to virtual robbery. Web sites frequently monitor how often users visit them and the specific information for which they look. Without thinking much about it, users tend to enter personal information such as their names, addresses, consumer preferences, and even credit card numbers. In turn, many Web site providers sell this information to others who can then pitch to users products based on the profiles created from the information the users have supplied. With good reason, many firms worry that their competitors can obtain access to important customer or business information, and that such information will be used to gain an advantage in the marketplace.

In order to protect their interests, some companies place restrictive limits on system access. By doing this, they hope to maintain the integrity of their networks and the information they post. However, some businesses have also discovered that a networked computer makes an excellent electronic "spy" with which to observe the actions of employees. A company's system can be programmed to monitor and record all actions performed at every individual workstation on the network, including all Internet activity, e-mail content, and downtime when the computer is not in use. In addition, some systems have inexpensive video cameras normally used for teleconferencing that can be periodically scanned to observe the actions of workers without their knowledge. While most people would agree that this human monitoring is unethical, the courts have ruled that computer transactions on an organization's system belong to that firm and do not represent an invasion of personal privacy. The bottom line for individuals using the Web and especially for employees working on company computer systems is be cautious! Your boss may be watching you. In the work environment, even a single inappropriate or off-color e-mail comment from one employee to another is officially the property of the company and may cost the employee his or her job.

5 Understanding Networks and COMPUTER SECURITY ISSUES

OBJECTIVES

After reading this chapter, you will be able to. . .

➤ Define the hardware, software, and connecting media required for creating a network

➤ Differentiate among types of network configurations

➤ Distinguish among the kinds of connections necessary for a computer network

➤ Explain the protocols involved in sending and receiving data

➤ Describe the requirements and the methods of maintaining privacy and security in network communication

What Is a Network?

A network is a group of computers that are linked together so that information can be exchanged between them. Through the use of networks, productivity in the workplace and among individual users can be greatly enhanced. Networks vary enormously, from simple interoffice systems that connect a few personal computers and a printer to complex global systems that connect thousands of machines of different kinds, from laptops to supercomputers. To create a network, the proper hardware, software, and connecting media need to be configured so that a **communications channel** is forged between individual computers.

The resources shared on networks may take the form of hardware, software, data and information, or the talents of the persons who use the system. It is, for example, quite common for laser printers, scanners, and other expensive hardware to be shared through networks in both offices and homes. Networked versions of software programs save on the cost of installation, and they allow users to share documents. Users also can transfer files to each other through a "Transfer" directory and folders set up on the network server for each person. Many employees also use the network server to store backups for important data files on their hard drives. Another significant benefit to network users is the ability to pool knowledge and skills, thereby gaining a synergy in decision making without needing to be in the same place at the same time.

Despite its many benefits, the creation of a network is not without risk, however. Networked hardware can be attacked by fire, theft, misuse, or sabotage from internal or external sources. Networked software can be damaged either intentionally or unintentionally, causing a disruption in communication or a shutdown of the entire system. Misuse of software can, in addition, expose a company to libel from copyright licensing violations. Data files can be pilfered from the outside or deliberately corrupted by disgruntled employees. Given these hazards and their significant implications for a business, it is imperative that companies implement and monitor protections of the network before problems arise, not after.

Types of Networks

A network that connects computers that are close to one another (for example, on the same floor, within the same building, or in an adjacent building) is known as a **local area network,** or **LAN.** Typically, computers connected in a LAN share one or more printers, storage devices, or other hardware such as scanners. A network that spans a larger area and connects two or more LANs is known as a **wide area network,** or **WAN** (see Figure 5-1). A company might use a WAN, for example, to communicate between a manufacturing facility in one part of a city and corporate headquarters in another. Similarly, a bank with widespread national branch offices and instant-banking terminals would probably use a WAN to link its resources. Governments, universities, and large corporations typically use WANs to share data between separate networks.

Intranets, Extranets, and the Internet

A network that uses a particular type of connecting software within a single organization is sometimes referred to as an **intranet.** By contrast, an **extranet** connects an entity to one or more private external networks. For example, a retail firm may permit an outside supplier to have access to its sales records to ensure a timely flow of inventory to avoid the possibility of losing potential sales.

Over the past few years, many thousands of networks around the globe have

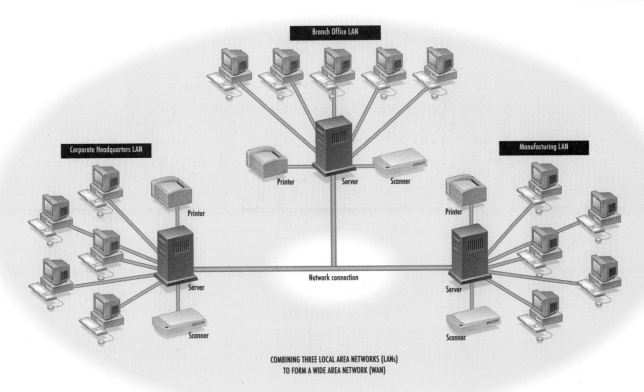

Branch Office LAN

Corporate Headquarters LAN

Manufacturing LAN

Printer

Server

Scanner

Printer

Server

Network connection

Printer

Server

Scanner

Scanner

COMBINING THREE LOCAL AREA NETWORKS (LANs)
TO FORM A WIDE AREA NETWORK (WAN)

Figure 5-1: Computers
in a LAN share hardware;
two or more LANs are connected to form a WAN

been connected to one another in a vast system known as the Internet (see Chapter 6). Almost overnight, the dream of a worldwide system of connections among computers has become a reality. One part of the Internet that has become especially popular is the **World Wide Web,** or simply **the Web,** which consists of computers and storage devices on which people place **hypertext documents,** written in the code language HTML. To view hypertext documents on the World Wide Web, one uses a kind of software known as a **browser.**

Peer-to-Peer and Client-Server Networks

One way to classify networks is by the nature of the relationship among the individual computers, or **nodes,** on the network (see Figure 5-2). In a small setting of up to approximately ten computers, files and printers can be shared using a **peer-to-peer network.** A **peer** is a

member of the workgroup with whom resources are to be shared. In a peer-to-peer network, the controls for the network and the program software must be installed on all of the linked computers, but any peripheral devices need to be connected to only one location. For example, by using peer-to-peer networking in a small medical practice facility, staff can access patients' records, insurance information, and the appointment calendar from any computer in the office. They can thus answer a patient's e-mail question at any computer terminal, reducing the need to be at a specific workstation for a specific task. A second type of network, a **client-server network,** organizes the nodes or **client** computers of the network so that they are served by one or more **file servers** that control all of the major functions of the network. Servers themselves become clients when they are linked to other servers to form an even larger network.

World Wide Web (the Web)
Part of the Internet that consists of linked documents that can display text, graphical, audio and video content.
browser Software used to view hypertext documents on the World Wide Web.

PEER-TO-PEER NETWORK

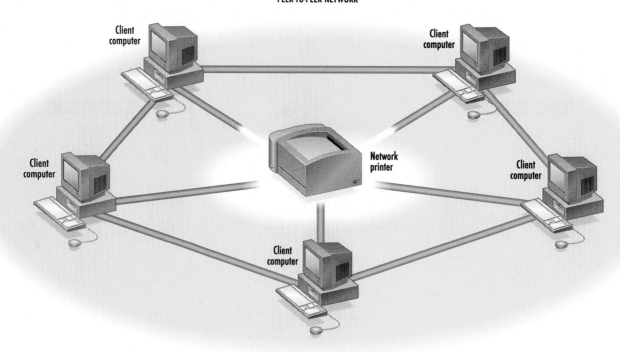

CLIENT-SERVER NETWORK

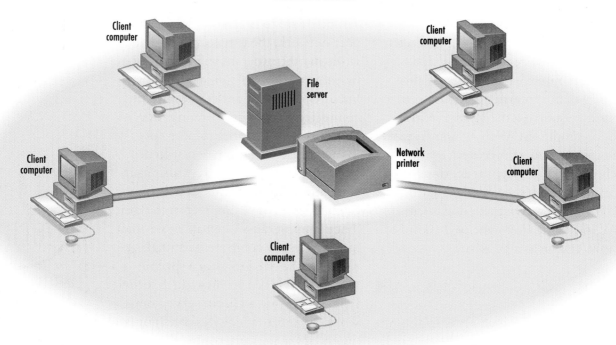

Figure 5-2: Peer-to-Peer and Client-Server Network Configurations

Connectivity Hardware

Setting up a computer network generally requires special forms of connectivity hardware. The point of entry of the connectivity hardware to the computer is called the communications port. Typically, connectivity hardware includes a **network interface card (NIC),** which is placed into an expansion slot within the CPU case and provides a port to which the network cabling can be attached. The most common method for connecting computers is with modems and telephone lines. A **modem (Mo**dulation-**DEM**odulation device) is a computer peripheral that converts the digital output signals of a computer into analog signals to be sent by telephone lines, a process called **modulation.** The reverse process, translating analog signals from a telephone line into digital signals that a computer can process, is called **demodulation.**

Modems serve many purposes (see Figure 5-3). They enable people to gain remote access to other computers, to transfer files, to send e-mail and faxes, and to access online services, bulletin boards, and the Internet. A modem may be either internal, a card placed into a slot in the CPU case, or external, a device with its own case that sits outside the computer. A **fax modem,** external or internal, can send and receive faxes as well as other data. A **cable modem** provides Internet access using high-speed TV cable connections instead of telephone lines. Cable modems make possible the connection to coaxial cable media (see the discussion below) that is broad enough to carry multiple television channels and also to enable **cable access television (CATV)** companies to become Internet service providers.

Bandwidth and Communications Media

In a network, the number of bits that can be transferred in a given second over a given medium is known as **bandwidth.** Analog transfers are measured in the number of cycles per second, or **hertz (Hz),** while digital data is measured in **bits per second (bps).** The broader the bandwidth, the larger the capacity to carry data in network connections.

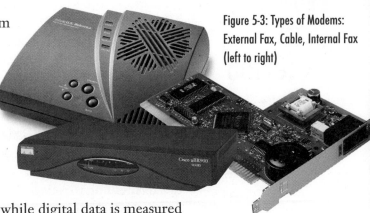

Figure 5-3: Types of Modems: External Fax, Cable, Internal Fax (left to right)

Enormous changes are currently taking place throughout the developed world as individual homes and businesses are connected to outside networks by media of sufficient bandwidth to carry all of the different kinds of information that people have received in the past by other means. High-quality voice, music, and video transmissions require, respectively, bandwidths of 64Kbps, 1.2Mbps, and 45Mbps (see Table 5-1). A high-bandwidth network pipeline, sufficient for such transmissions, is known as a **broadband** medium. A number of different media are used to transmit signals over networks. These media include twisted-pair cable, coaxial cable, fiber-optic cable, and wireless media (the atmosphere).

Table 5-1: Measurement of Bandwidth

Abbreviation	Term	Meaning
54Kbps	54 kilobits per second	54 thousand bits per second
30Mbps	30 megabits per second	30 million bits per second
1Gbps	1 gigabit per second	1 billion bits per second
1Tbps	1 terabit per second	1 trillion bits per second

Twisted-Pair Cable

The electronic pathway or communications channel between any two hardware devices may be made of wire, it may be an optical medium, or it may be a wireless form. The simplest and most common of

Key Terms

modem Device that converts digital output signals of a computer into analog signals to be sent by telephone or other communication lines.

bandwidth Measure of the number of bits of data that can be transferred in a given second over a medium in a network.

broadband High-bandwidth network pipeline sufficient to carry extremely large data transmissions.

coaxial cable Communication medium commonly used for cable television connections, in telephone networks, and in some computer networks.

fiber-optic cable Communications medium made from a string of glass or high-quality plastic, used to transmit beams of light carrying data.

these media forms is called a **twisted-pair cable,** or telephone wire (see Figure 5-4). The term *twisted pair* is an anachronism, harkening back to the days when telephone lines consisted of wires wrapped around one another. Today, such cables typically consist of two parallel copper wires, each individually wrapped in plastic and bound together by another plastic casing. Some of these cables have additional insulation called **shielding** to reduce the likelihood that line interference or noise will corrupt the signal. As a result, in networking applications the **shielded twisted-pair (STP)** cable is often preferred over standard twisted-pair cable.

Standard telephone lines are known as **switched networks** because each loca-tion has a number that is used to connect to the system on an as-needed basis. The network, therefore, is not connected all of the time, but is accessible by dialing into a host location.

Coaxial Cable

Coaxial cable is a medium commonly used for VCR and cable television connections, in telephone networks, and in some computer networks (see Figure 5-5). A coaxial cable consists of concentric parts, namely, from the inside out: a copper wire, a sheath of insulation, a wire mesh that both conducts and shields against interference, and an outside coating. Because of its insulation, coaxial cable is much better shielded from interference than is twisted-pair cable, and it can carry its signal a greater distance and at a faster transfer rate. Some versions of coaxial cable can even carry multiple signals concurrently.

Fiber-Optic Cable

Twisted-pair and coaxial cable both contain copper conductors and are used to transmit electronic signals—streams of electrons. **Fiber-optic cable,** on the other hand, is a string of glass used to transmit **photons**—beams of light (see Figure 5-6). A fiber-optic cable contains a very pure central glass filament surrounded by a more refractive material known as **cladding.** Digital electronic pulses at one end of the cable are transmitted by light pulses by a laser or a light-emitting diode. These pulses travel along the fiber and are kept in place by the cladding, which works like a mirror, bouncing the light back to the fiber. At the other end, a photodetector transforms the light pulses back into electrical pulses. Although fiber-optic cable is more expensive and difficult to install than other media, its advantages (see the "Fiber-Optics at the Speed of Light" Expansion Card) have caused its use to grow tremendously in recent years in all data and telecommunications applications.

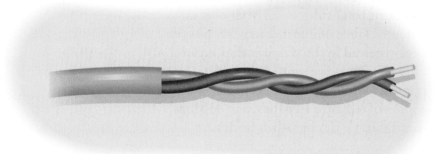

Figure 5-4: Twisted-Pair Cable

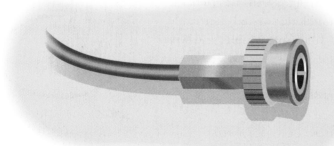

Figure 5-5: Coaxial Cable

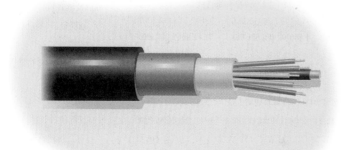

Figure 5-6: Fiber-Optic Cable

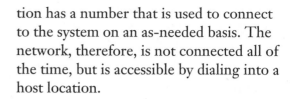

EXPANSION CARD

Fiber Optics at the Speed of Light

The invention of the fiber-optic cable has completely changed the telecommunications industry. After years of research, the breakthrough in developing this technology was the identification of a way to transmit light impulses without significant deterioration of the signal. In 1970, Robert D. Maurer, Donald B. Keck, and Peter C. Schultz, researchers at Corning Glass, designed the first optical fiber with signal deterioration low enough to be used for numerous practical applications. Fiber optics works by the use of laser beams that move at the speed of light and send pulses through the fiber-optic pathway to the receiver at the opposite end.

Today, optical fiber is the foundation for global multimedia telecommunications. More than 90% of U.S. long-distance communications traffic is currently carried on fiber-optic cable, and much of the backbone of the Internet is created from it. One of the major advantages of fiber-optic cable is its very high bandwidth. This bandwidth can support extremely fast high-volume data transfers. One fiber the width of a human hair can carry many thousands of voice and data-transfer sessions simultaneously. Researchers are continuing to develop even faster and more reliable transfers. Fiber-optic cable also has other advantages. Fiber-optic light impulses are impervious to corruption by other nearby media and, as a result, the signal is virtually immune to noise distortion. Made of glass or plastic, fiber-optic cable is not subject to corrosion from water or other substances. Fiber-optic cable also offers a measure of security because it is extremely difficult to intercept a digital-optical signal.

Fiber-optic cable was initially used by large telecommunications firms such as AT&T and Sprint. However, because installation is now easier than before due to technological advances, fiber-optic cable has recently become more widely used in other high-traffic corridors of communications in business and research environments. The pioneering work of Maurer, Keck, and Schultz has hastened the day that broadband data transmission will be available to everyone, bringing motion video and other multimedia applications directly into our homes.

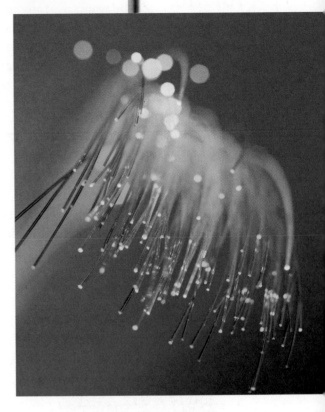

ISDN, or Integrated Services Digital Network

The backbone of today's telephone network is digital and makes use of fiber-optic cables, but the lines that run into homes and businesses are still, for the most part, old-fashioned analog telephone lines. One alternative to such **Plain Old Telephone Service**, or **POTS**, is an **Integrated Services Digital Network**, or **ISDN**, line. An ISDN is specially installed by a telephone company, and a user pays a monthly fee. Unlike a standard telephone line, an ISDN line is digital and thus provides a completely digital pipeline from the home or business and across the telephone network. ISDN connections provide faster file transfers and Internet downloads, and can support better quality images in videoconferencing and online video broadcasts.

Wireless Media

Another way to connect computers and other electronic devices is to send electromagnetic signals through the air or through empty space. Such **wireless communication** makes use of data encoded as electromagnetic signals such as radio waves, microwaves, or infrared light. **Radio frequencies (RF)** are used for many types of wireless communications, including radio and television broadcasts, private two-way communications for businesses and governments, portable telephones and communicators, and some wireless keyboards. Frequencies are assigned by the Federal Communications Commission (FCC) to ensure compliance with international telecommunications agreements. To use a frequency channel, one must have the appropriate sending and receiving

devices. Networks can be created by using this same wireless media for channels. As discussed previously, among the fastest-growing areas of telecommunications today are the fully digital **personal communications services (PCSs).** These devices, such as the Palm Pilot, are capable of a wide range of communications, including Internet connections, e-mail, voice mail, and cellular phone transmission. Most PCS services use earth-based cellular towers to broadcast the signal to the receiver from the nearest location. These towers hand off the signal to another transmitter as the user moves from cell to cell. In many of these networks, intermediate transmissions may be made by **microwave** for faster and more accurate distribution.

Wireless transmission over short distances can also be accomplished by **infrared (IR)** technologies that carry digital signals on light waves beyond the visible spectrum in line-of-sight applications. Wireless keyboards, mouse pointers, printers, and digital camera picture downloads often use this form of data transfer.

To send data over many hundreds of thousands of miles, companies and governments make use of transmission towers and communications satellites. A **geosynchronous communications satellite** (see Figure 5-8) orbits the earth at the equator at an altitude of 22,300 miles and travels at a speed that allows it to remain in a constant position to the earth. Three such satellites are sufficient to provide continuous telephone, television, and data communications to the entire globe. Earth-based parabolic antennas are used

Figure 5-7: Palm Pilot and Cellular Telephone are Internet-Enabled PCS Devices

to transmit signals to and receive signals from communications satellites. PCS systems and other more traditional networks use this technology to make their networks accessible from anywhere in the world. For instance, banking and financial systems can access information from any linked computer in real time from any location around the globe. See Table 5-2 for a comparison of the speeds available in various modes of transmission.

Figure 5-8: A Geosynchronous Communications Satellite

Table 5-2: Various Media Speeds of Data Transmission

Channel Type	Speed of Transmission*	Distance	Cost
Twisted-pair cable	1–128Mbps	Up to 300 ft.	Low
Coaxial cable	Up to 200Mbps	500–2,500 ft.	Moderate
Fiber-optic cable	100Mbps to 2Gbps	Up to 25 miles	High
Wireless broadcast radio waves	Up to 4Mbps	Wide variation	High
Wireless microwave radio waves	45Mbps	Wide variation	High
Wireless communications satellite	50Mbps	N/A	High
Wireless cellular radio waves	9,600bps–14.4Kbps	Up to 5 miles	High
Wireless infrared light waves	1–4Mbps	Up to 500 ft.	Moderate

*Measured in data bits per second

T-1 and T-3 Lines

To establish a network, a medium needs to be selected that is appropriate for the network's expected use. In most homes, connected time to a network is limited. Thus, the most efficient choice for home use is probably a switched network connection

EXPANSION CARD

Only Broadband Networks in Your Future?

Broadband transmission has many advantages. It has the ability to send multiple signals and a large volume of data. It can also transmit a range of data types, including audio, video, and other multimedia, and it can do so concurrently, at great speed, in both directions. Because of its power, large telecommunications companies use broadband to provide services to satellite-linked firms, television networks, and similar high-volume users. Cable television companies have likewise chosen broadband connections to service the increased number of channels they offer. Most cable firms, in fact, have recently set about replacing their baseband one-way networks with digital systems that will support many hundreds of channels using optical fiber and broadband coaxial cables. With more than 100 million American homes now wired for cable television, the delivery of Internet access seemed like a logical service extension for cable companies. Therefore, some have begun to offer Internet service at a nominal cost and at transfer speeds from 10 to 100 times faster than the 56K modems in use today over normal telephone lines.

In response to this Internet service competition, some telephone companies have started to offer **digital subscriber lines (DSLs).** DSLs are broadband connections that operate at a reduced cost, since the digital signal can be sent through the same twisted-pair telephone wires that are already installed in homes. Normally, twisted-pair wires use baseband transmission and thus can send only one signal at a time. DSL lines, on the other hand, employ multiple-signal broadband technology through the same wires and eliminate the need to rebuild the cable infrastructure. One of the more popular forms of DSL is an **asymmetric digital subscriber line (ADSL).** ADSLs support a faster download speed when receiving data than when uploading or sending data. A disadvantage of ADSLs is that they have a limited transfer range. They must be within a certain limited distance of the telephone company sending station or data may be lost or compromised. If a longer transmission distance is needed, **symmetric digital subscriber lines (SDSLs)** can be installed. All DSL forms require special DSL modems to make the network connection.

Competition between cable service providers and DSLs will no doubt continue for some time. Both technologies are developing rapidly, and access speeds are rising constantly as the fiber-optic network expands. Users are increasingly demanding extremely fast, high-quality, and reliable computer connections. Whether through cable or telephone wires, broadband will provide the medium for these powerful linkages in the future.

that uses twisted-pair telephone lines. If a user requires continual connected time, however, dedicated digital transmission lines are available for lease from local telephone service providers. Very high volumes of data transfer may require an even faster medium to meet the network's needs. Therefore, local telephone companies also lease **T-carrier lines** that have extremely high capacity and speeds. These special digital lines have the capability of **multiplexing,** or supporting numerous phone lines over a single carrier. For example, a T-1 line carries 24 separate signals concurrently at a combined transfer rate of 1.544Mbps. T-1 lines are widely used by businesses, educational institutions, and some Internet service providers for Internet connections. A T-3 line is even more powerful. Essentially equal to 28 T-1

lines, a T-3 line provides a combined transfer rate of 43Mbps. T-3 lines are generally used by very large organizations and telephone companies. They also form part of the primary connections of the Internet.

Network Topologies

The physical arrangement of computers connected in a network is called a **network topology,** or **architecture**. Three types of topologies are common today: linear bus, star, and ring.

Linear Bus Topology

Connecting all of the nodes to a single primary cable called a bus creates a **linear bus network** (Figure 5-9). Each node has

KEY Terms

digital subscriber line (DSL) Broadband communication line that operates economically by using existing copper wire connections.

linear bus network Network with all of its parts connected to a single primary cable connection.

a **transceiver,** a device that sends messages along the bus in either direction. As a message passes each node, that node checks the message for its address. If a node finds its address in a message, it then reads the data, checks for errors in the transmission, and sends a message to the sender of the data acknowledging that it was received. Computers can be added to or taken from a bus network without any disruption in normal activity since they all share the same data path. But several problems may occur with a linear bus network. One is when two or more nodes send messages at the same time. This creates an interference pattern, and when one of the nodes on the network detects this pattern, it jams the network, stopping all transmissions. Nodes that are sending messages must then wait and resend, a process that is repeated until a message gets through without being blocked. Another problem with a linear bus network is that a broken connection along the bus can bring down the entire network.

Star Topology

Another topology, a **star network,** is a configuration that resembles the hub and spokes of a wheel (Figure 5-10). Each of the nodes is connected to the central system, or hub, by its own path. The hub acts as a switching station, reading the addresses of messages sent by the nodes and routing the messages accordingly.

This arrangement can be an improvement over the linear bus topology because the hub can prevent data collisions and because the rest of the network can remain operational when a given node's connection to the network is broken. But a failure of the hub computer shuts down the entire network's functions.

Ring Topology

A third common network topology, a **ring network,** is so named because a connecting cable forms a closed circle, or ring, through all of the networked computers (Figure 5-11). In the popular ring topology developed by IBM and known as a **token-ring network,** a **token,** which is a code indicating that the network is clear, circulates continuously around the network until a given node sends a message. When a node sends a message, it intercepts the token, changes it to indicate that the network is in use, and attaches a message that includes data, error-checking codes, and the address of the node that is to receive the message. The message passes around the circular path until it reaches its address. The node that receives the message copies it and then passes it back along the path until it reaches the sender. The sender then removes the message from the network and changes the token back to its original state to indicate that the network is clear again. Like a star network, a token-ring

LINEAR BUS NETWORK

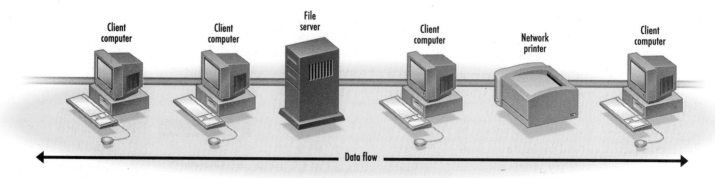

Client computer Client computer File server Client computer Network printer Client computer

Data flow

Figure 5-9: Linear Bus Topology

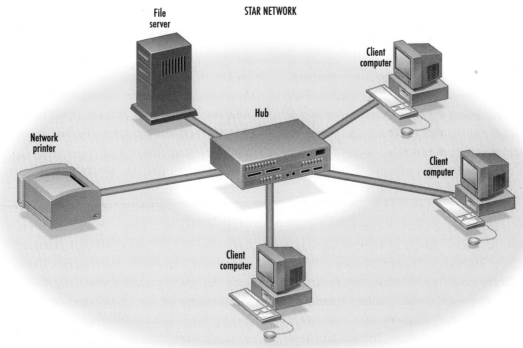

Figure 5-10: Star Topology

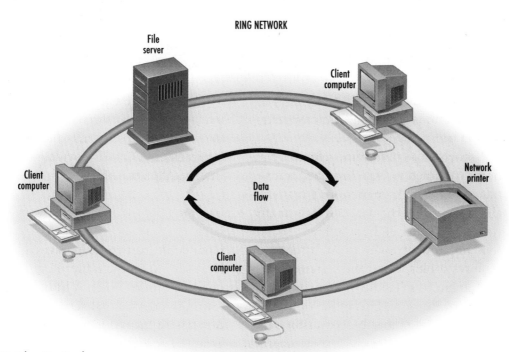

Figure 5-11: Token-Ring Topology

network avoids data collisions, but like a linear bus network, it will go down if a single connection is broken.

Protocols

No matter what media type is chosen for data transfer, it must follow a set of pro-cedures, or **protocol,** for the network system to function. A matching protocol requires that both the sending and receiving systems use compatible binary interpretation, the same speeds of trans-mission, and other identical functions so that communication can occur. Protocols specify other characteristics of data trans-mission as well. For example, data can

Ethernet Simple local area network form that uses linear bus topology and a wide variety of media.

packets Small sections into which a message is broken in order to facilitate efficient transfer of data.

flow along transmission lines in three different ways. A **simplex transmission** flows the data in one direction only. An example of a simplex transition is the connection between a temperature sensor and a computer-controlled heat and air conditioning system. Once the temperature sensor sends the signal to increase or decrease temperature to the system, there is no need for this information to flow from the computer back to the sensor again. A **half-duplex transmission** permits the data to flow in both directions, but the users must alternate in their usage. Half-duplex transmission is frequently employed in two-way radio systems where the communicants must take turns speaking. They cannot talk to each other at the same time. In **full-duplex transmission,** the data flows in both directions concurrently. Standard telephones operate by full-duplex transmission, where both parties talking at once can still be heard. Full-duplex transmission lines are the most costly of these means of transmission, and they are used in applications with significant amounts of data transfers.

Protocols also determine whether data flows are timed for synchronized transmission or not. **Asynchronous transmission** means that the data can flow at any time from either end of the line. **Synchronous transmission,** by contrast, requires sophisticated and expensive equipment to schedule the synchronized timing of the flow. This mode of transmission has the capacity to transfer data at faster speeds and with greater accuracy.

Types of Communications Protocols

As discussed above, networks have certain communications protocols that dictate the manner in which data is transmitted. The protocol establishes the manner in which a message is fragmented, the routing information it needs to reach the receiver, and the method used to recombine the data at the opposite end. The most widely used network protocol is **Ethernet**, which is a simple LAN form that uses a linear bus topology. **Ethernet networks** can use any type of connecting media. The standard transfer rate of 10Mbps is adequate for smaller LANs, and faster ethernet protocols up to 1,000Mbps are available for higher volume applications.

For ring networks, a token-ring protocol is used. As mentioned, ring networks require the connected computers to pass along a special signal, or token, to indicate each computer's turn for transfers. The computer with the token is the only one that can send or receive data. Advantages of the token-ring protocol are that it avoids data collisions and operates at fairly high speeds, either 4 or 16Mbps. A disadvantage is that it is relatively expensive. A token-ring protocol can also be used with star topology. Yet another type of protocol, a **transmission control protocol/Internet protocol (TCP/IP),** was developed for use with the ARPANET (see Chapter 6). TCP/IP manages data transfers by breaking messages into small sections called **packets** for transfer. TCP/IP is widely used for Internet data transfers.

Additional Networking Hardware

Connecting networks involves additional hardware to merge multiple signals into one (see Figure 5-12). A **hub,** or concentrator, is a device that serves as the location where the individual connections to a group of computers are centralized for further routing and for sharing of information. As data travels over distances in a channel, the quality of the transmission progressively deteriorates. It is necessary, therefore, to frequently enhance the signal to keep it accurate and strong enough to continue transmission. The device that performs this function is called a **repeater.** Repeaters are used throughout networks where it is necessary to maintain the integrity of the data transmission.

INNOVATORS

Robert Metcalfe and the Invention of Ethernet

Born in Brooklyn, raised on Long Island, and educated at MIT and at Harvard (where he received a PhD in computer science), Robert M. Metcalfe earned fame and fortune as the inventor of the world's most widely used networking system, Ethernet. Metcalfe conceived of Ethernet in 1973 while working at the Xerox Palo Alto Research Center (Xerox PARC), which was also the birthplace of the graphical user interface, of WYSIWYG computing, and of the pointing device known as the mouse. For a while, Metcalfe taught at Stanford University, but in 1979 he left to found 3Com Corporation, of Santa Clara, California, the leading manufacturer of Ethernet adapter cards and other equipment. Metcalfe's invention made him a multimillionaire. Today, Metcalfe is a respected and often controversial computer columnist for IDG's *Infoworld* magazine. In this column, called "From the Ether," Metcalfe predicted a collapse of the Internet due to excessive traffic. While such a collapse has not yet occurred, many people do experience excessive delays when using the Internet; most observers agree that network backbone upgrades are necessary. Metcalfe is also widely known for what is called **Metcalfe's law**, which states that the value of a network increases exponentially with the number of machines (and users) connected to it.

In creating a LAN, multiple hubs can be linked together by using a repeater. LANs can also be linked by the use of another piece of hardware called a **bridge** if the protocols for each of the local networks are the same. If the protocols for the two LANs are different, however, the appropriate connector is known as a **gateway.** Another device called a **router** can connect multiple networks regardless of the protocols used. These smart devices route the data being sent to the fastest channel that will reach the objective. Routers have the capability to send data along any transmission path should the preferred alternative be crowded or incapacitated. For this reason, routers are a foundational element in the creation of the Internet.

Connectivity Software

In order for a networked system to share data, common **communications software** must be installed. This software manages the transmission of all data and information that flows between the linked computers. It also manages the dialing function on connections that use switched telephone lines or the instructions to connect to a network interface card. Moreover, communications software typically includes the capacity to do file transfers, emulate terminals as though connected to a larger computer system, and provide support for access to the Internet. This software is often included in computer operating systems. It may

Figure 5-12: Examples of Networking Hardware: Gateway, Router, and Hub (left to right)

computer virus Small program with buried code that is sent to computers with the intent to do damage to hardware or software.

also be provided by the manufacturer of communications hardware devices, such as the modem.

Whatever communications software is used, it must work under the direction and control of the **network operating system (NOS)**. The NOS takes overall responsibility for how the network communicates. It performs all of the administrative and file management activities necessary to coordinate the individual computers or nodes that are connected in the network. If printers are connected to the network, their output scheduling and prioritizing is also managed by the NOS. In addition, the NOS is responsible for maintaining data security and the integrity of network access. Popular network operating systems include Windows NT, Unix, and Windows 2000 Server.

Security and Privacy Issues

Computers and networks have become a vital part of our personal and business lives. Because of their importance in our world today, protecting systems and networks is an ever-increasing and costly priority. Computer crime is on the rise, and law enforcement agencies have created special units with expertise in detecting and preventing its spread.

Computers can be damaged or their integrity compromised in numerous ways. Hardware can be damaged by fire, theft, intentional destruction, or unauthorized use. Software can be corrupted by user ignorance or error, or by sabotage. Data can be stolen, erased, or modified. Networked systems are especially vulnerable to attacks from computer viruses. A **computer virus** is a bit of code that is buried within a computer program or data. Like a biological virus, it is transferred from host to host by contact. When a person loads software contaminated by a virus onto his or her computer or downloads virus-infected software or data over a network, then his or her computer can become

infected. Viruses are created by programmers, sometimes as naïve pranks, but often with the intent to do damage. Viruses can do many different things. Some make innumerable copies of themselves, clogging and choking storage devices. Some erase storage devices, destroying programs and data. Some display messages or graphics. Some simply corrupt programs or operating systems and cause them to crash. In spring 2000, attacks from the so-called "Melissa" and "I Love You" viruses in over 22 countries around the world caused nearly $20 billion of data damage and lost productivity time. Since viruses represent a significant danger to a network, it is imperative that systems have a wall of defenses in place before a virus strikes.

Federal and State Laws

Deploying hardware-damaging viruses is a crime. Federal and state laws make illegal the hacking into and tampering with computers regardless of the reason. Prosecutions of these crimes are often highly publicized in order to serve as a deterrent to others. David L. Smith, the creator of the Melissa virus, for example, was tracked down within days and convicted with the assistance of engineers from America Online (AOL) and others. He entered guilty pleas to both federal and state charges, and his case represents a significant prosecution of a virus-related computer crime in the United States. More minor attacks may also do harm to networks, but may not have criminal implications. The truth is that all business and organization networks are constantly exposed to the risk of unethical or destructive behavior by authorized users. Yet, placing limits on system use or supervising the network too rigidly can undermine employee trust, restrict creativity, and foster an unhealthy work environment. A fine line exists between trusting employees and being prepared for computer catastrophe, and this line is an important topic of discussion in workplace management today.

EXPANSION CARD

Who Owns Your Personal Data?

As data management tools, computers are unsurpassed. However, controversy has arisen concerning a computer's ability to store and report private information about individuals. Much of this controversy revolves around issues of the invasions of privacy that can occur when Internet content providers capture and store information such as names, addresses, phone numbers, and e-mail addresses from the persons who visit their Web sites. Many businesses do in fact collect this information and sell it to others. This is by no means a new phenomenon. In fact, credit bureaus maintained such personal records manually for many years before moving to computer database systems.

Today, however, the number of information reporting companies has grown enormously. An entire industry has evolved around the capture, classification, and distribution of consumer personal data, characteristics, and preferences. The growth in the use of personal computers and online data distribution has made this information more accessible than ever before. The question for you as a consumer is this: Does the sale of the personal information you enter into a computer constitute an invasion of your privacy?

One major problem with tracking consumer information is inaccuracy. An indictment of credit-reporting companies, for example, centers around rampant inaccuracies in their reports. Numerous independently conducted studies have revealed widespread errors in these firms' files. Recently, consumer protection laws have been passed in an attempt to allow consumers to correct errors discovered in their reports. While credit bureaus have some detractors, the services they perform are essential for the prudent administration of lending programs. If credit bureaus attempted to survey all Americans to obtain a list of personal credit and payment histories to verify their records, they would, no doubt, get a less than adequate response.

A possible solution to the dilemma is for people to acknowledge that their personal data is owned by themselves and not by a reporting company. Each person could then subscribe to a credit bureau and pay the firm as needed to provide information to inquiries about his or her credit history. When a person wished to buy a new home or car, for example, the loan officer would ask the individual for the name of the credit bureau to which he or she subscribes so that the credit history could be examined. A loan would not be given if the individual had failed to subscribe to a credit bureau. This solution has several advantages. It not only removes the cost burden from the lenders and places it on the borrowers, but it also makes individuals take a vested interest in maintaining the accuracy of their credit histories. Furthermore, if individuals are considered to own information about themselves, the practice of selling personal information could be limited or curtailed altogether. Because this solution represents a major shift from the way we think about, value, and manage personal information today, however, it could only be implemented slowly and over a longer period of time, if at all.

Protecting Computer and Network Systems

Personal computer users and network administrators have at hand a wide array of methods to guard against computer crime. Some methods of control are applied to the computer, others to its network and data, and still others to the human interface. **Access controls** can be programmed into the computer to guard against unauthorized use. Typically, these controls include an **identification** section that determines if the user is recognized or not, and an **authentication** step to ascertain if the user making the request is actually the one who is authorized to do so. **Passwords** are usually included in these and other entry steps. Passwords need to be changed often, and they should be placed in as many gateways as necessary to guard against inappropriate entry. Simple passwords such as a bank's 4-digit PIN number are very easy to duplicate by a serious hacker. Unauthorized entry, however, can be significantly more complicated if a password is longer and contains a combination of both letters and numbers. Though users sometimes consider passwords a nuisance, it is good to remember that they serve a vital gatekeeping purpose.

Encryption

Another possible risk to system integrity occurs when data and information are being transferred over networks. In this case, using an **encryption** process, one that converts data into an indecipherable

KEY Terms

encryption Process that converts data into an indecipherable code to protect sensitive information during transfer.

COMPUTERS IN

GOVERNMENT

With the participation of San Francisco's FBI Computer Intrusion Squad, the Computer Security Institute (CSI) performs an annual "Computer Crime and Security Survey." The survey's objective is to heighten security awareness among users and assess the scope of computer crime in the United States. According to the 2000 survey, 90% of respondents, primarily large businesses and governments, reported detecting computer security breaches over the past twelve months. Seventy percent reported serious problems, such as the theft of proprietary information, financial fraud, system penetration from the outside, and sabotage of data or networks. Omitted from the survey were the more common problems, including viruses, laptop theft, or employee misuse of the Internet. In addition, 74% of the respondents acknowledged financial losses due to computer security issues, but only 42% were willing or able to quantify losses. These losses, reported by 273 respondents, totaled more than $265 million. This amount far exceeds the average dollar loss over the previous three years of around $120 million. Furthermore, losses in eight of the twelve problem areas reported reflected totals in excess of any previous report. Some 61 respondents reported losses due to the sabotage of data or networks, for a total of $27 million. The most serious losses, however, occurred in the theft of proprietary information ($66 million) and financial fraud ($56 million). Sixty percent of respondents reported that the sources of attacks came through Internet linkages.

As this last statistic shows, we are in the midst of an increasing volume of criminal activity on the Internet, threatening networked individuals and firms alike. In an attempt to combat this activity, the FBI has established a Web site, the Internet Fraud Complaint Center (http://www.ifccfbi.gov/). The purpose of this site is to collect reports of illegal activity on the Web. Periodically, the FBI releases statistical information about these findings.

Today, electronic crime is easier to carry out than ever before. While helpful, governmental regulations and law enforcement cannot be counted on fully to protect computer network systems. Network users must be vigilant, and they must take seriously any signs of computer or data compromise.

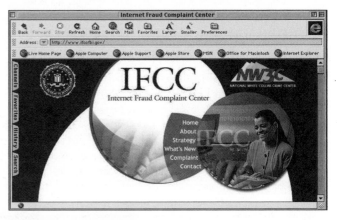

code, can protect sensitive information during the transfer process. At the receiving end, the recipient then **decrypts** the code using a previously received **encryption key.** Several methods for encryption are in widespread use. However, the U.S. government is concerned about encryption, fearing that subversive information may be transferred that they are unable to capture and understand. For its part, the government argues that it is in the best interest of the public that networks are monitored for such subversive elements. But widespread resistance to governmental controls in the name of the right to free speech has thus far kept regulations against encryption from being enacted.

Firewalls

To prevent others from tapping illegally into their networks, businesses and other organizations use specially designed hardware and software, known as **firewalls,** to limit access to their intranets and extranets. A firewall may consist of a single computer with numerous connections to the outside world via modems and connections to publicly accessible materials on the company intranet, but a single connection to secure parts of the intranet, one that is closely monitored and protected by various means. Access through a firewall might be obtained, for example, only by means of the intervention of a human operator or by means of a complex exchange of passwords or keys.

Virus Protection Software

Computer viruses transferred to a system from any source such as e-mail, file transfers, or floppy disks can destroy vital files and shut down the network very quickly. All computers, therefore, should use some type of **virus protection software** (see Figure 5-13). These products check for unusual activity, such as rewriting bits of operating system code, and either prevent such activity outright or provide warnings through dialog boxes. Virus protection software must be updated frequently to keep pace with new viruses. More than 10,000 viruses have appeared so far, and about six new ones are created every day. All data files should, in addition, be **backed up** at regular intervals.

While most servers and personal computers have virus protection software installed, a recent survey shows that infections continue to grow. The infection rate in 1999 was nearly double that of the previous year, which in turn was four times the 1997 rate. The survey indicated that the average recovery time was twenty-four hours for cases in which twenty-five or more computers were infected. The average loss per incident, including employee downtime, was $1,750. Several firms reported losses as high as $100,000 for a single virus infection event. Total losses in 1999 approached an astonishing $15 billion.

Information systems researchers cite poor virus protection budgets and a lack of support as primary factors in these losses. One low-cost way to reduce exposure to virus attacks is merely to be careful when opening e-mail from unknown sources, since many viruses attack by spreading through e-mail.

Audit-Control Software

Audit-control software is another form of software security protection. This software keeps a running log of all computer transactions and provides periodic reports that can be analyzed for unusual activity. For example, take the case of a college professor who related his computer access ID and password to his assistant and was overheard by a passing student. The student enters the system illegally and logs many hours of usage. If audit-control software were in place, the next month's report would show excessive activity and possibly contrast with the usual lighter use of the professor. While such audits will not catch all unauthorized usage, they can be helpful as another layer of security defense.

Physical Protections

Some security controls are directed toward the protection of the physical system. Secure doors and an identification card system can be installed to control access to the computer hardware. As in the case of internal intrusion, frequently changed passwords can provide a dual check on the entrant. In addition, **biometric scanning devices** can be used with card systems to prove that the person on the ID is the one making entry (see Figure 5-14). Different types of biometric scan-

biometric scanning device
Access-control hardware designed to recognize a characteristic of an authorized human user, such as the eye, finger, or thumbprint.

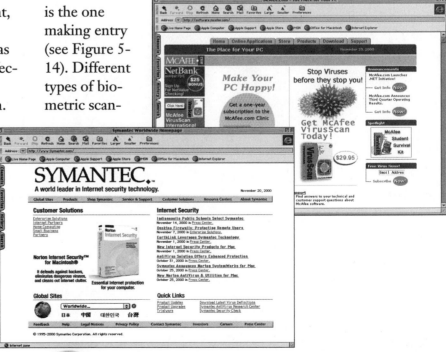

 Figure 5-13: A number of companies manufacture virus protection software.

ners are available, including scanners for finger or thumbprint detection, hand geometry, or retinal scans of the eye. However, even with the most sophisticated security systems in place, physical systems are often accessed by intruders and their contents compromised. Those computer networks that permit dial-in access for authorized users are particularly vulnerable to hackers who work to locate a legitimate ID and password. A possible solution for this hacker problem is the creation of a **callback system.** When a user dials into the system and is identified, the computer hangs up and dials back a previously provided phone number that is known to belong to the authorized user. Since a hacker's phone connection would not be on record, the break-in attempt would be terminated.

KEY Terms

surge protector Hardware that protects computer circuits from extraordinary and damaging surges in electrical current.

Electrical Surge Protection

Another source of damage to hardware are extraordinary surges in electrical current. In North America, standard electric current flows at approximately 120 volts of alternating current. Some normal variation occurs. However, if the flow drops significantly below 120 volts, computer data can be lost. If, on the other hand, the flow surges above 120 volts, it is likely to burn out system circuitry and cause damage to the hardware. **Surge protectors** (see Figure 5-15) are a good guard against such electrical **spikes.** But the best protection for a system is an **uninterruptible power supply (UPS)** that maintains the flow of current from its batteries for a period of time after a loss of power. This device also has circuitry to reduce the likelihood of spike damage to the protected hardware.

The Future of Networking

Researchers are hard at work developing many new technologies that will make network transmission more efficient and reliable. On the wish list for tomorrow's networks is the ability to see, hear, and touch computer-generated images that are transmitted nearly instantaneously over networks. Online shopping for an automobile will include a virtual-reality test drive with you in control behind the wheel. A virtual-reality trip to a famous museum anywhere in the world will allow you to view, circle around, and touch a great work of sculpture while listening to a museum guide explain it. A central computer will control all of your home appliances and a central calendar all of your appointments, and you will control both with your voice. Broadband networks are rapidly being constructed to manage the size of these data transmissions.

Recent developments promise to bring broadband services into homes and small businesses very soon. Already, in cities

Figure 5-14: A Biometric Scanning Device for Fingerprint Identification

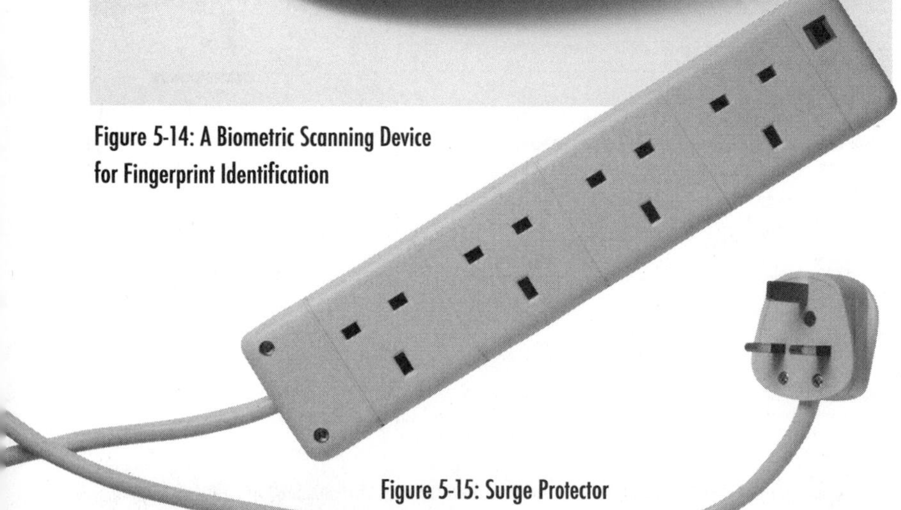

Figure 5-15: Surge Protector

throughout the United States, people can have cable modem hookups installed for low monthly fees. Such hookups can deliver data at 30Mbps, and low-orbit satellite systems promise to deliver broadband wireless connections worldwide within the decade. Large communications and computer companies are jockeying for position to deliver content for new broadband global networks, and governments around the world are beginning to see the creation of information infrastructures as essential to their national security and economic growth.

DSL connections will soon be used by more and more Internet service providers. An even faster form of DSL, the so-called **very high rate DSL (VDSL),** is beginning to compete with other broadband connectivity forms. The **asynchronous transfer mode (ATM)** can carry voice, data, multimedia, and motion video at very high transfer speeds. Currently, telephone companies and large-scale networks are using ATM at transfer speeds up to 622Mbps. This transmission method could become the Internet standard in the future. Worldwide, the predicted rapid conversion of telephone systems from analog to digital, and from copper wire to fiber-optical networks, will create an all-digital **optical network** that will result in communication channels with incredible speed and the capability to transfer all voice, data, and video connections with perfect sound and graphical reproduction.

Another future trend is the expected continued growth of wireless networked personal communication devices. In order to serve this expanded use, network administrators have proposed a new radio frequency specification called **Bluetooth.** Bluetooth will let portable devices communicate by way of an embedded transceiver. These devices will use transmitted radio frequencies to connect to cellular phone systems and other hardware directly, thereby bypassing other Internet gateways.

KEY Terms

optical network All-digital fiber-optic network that will result in communication channels with incredible speed and superior accuracy.

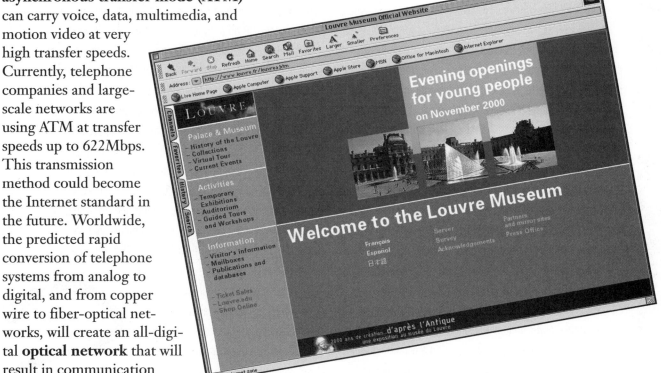

Chapter
SUMMARY

Computers can be connected in networks to share information, hardware, and human resources. Networks vary from several computers connected to a printer, to complex worldwide systems of thousands of computers. In a small setting, LANs are typically created using either a simple peer-to-peer network or a more capable client-server arrangement. WANS are networks that cover larger areas and are often used by businesses with offices around the country or around the world. Setting up a network requires special connectivity hardware such as a network interface card or a modem. The communications channel between hardware devices can be made of copper wire or fiber-optic cable, or it may be a wireless form. While new technologies such as ISDN allow network transmissions to use twisted-pair cable, optical fiber is increasingly replacing POTS due to its very high bandwidth and extreme speeds. Competition between providers of broadband fiber-optical cable and digital subscriber lines will likely continue in the near future.

Network topologies may take several forms. Among the most common today are linear bus, star, and ring architectures. Protocols specify the procedures for data transmission. Data can flow along transmission lines in one of three ways. In a simplex transmission, data flows in one direction; in a half-duplex transmission, data flows in both directions, but users must alternate in use; and in a full duplex transmission, data flows both directions concurrently. Asynchronous transmission means that either channel end can send data at any time without special timing requirements, and synchronous transmission means that computers must be synchronized for timing of data signals before transmission. This method of transmission is faster and more accurate, although more costly. The most widely used network protocol is Ethernet, which is a simple LAN form that uses linear bus typology.

In some networks, multiple signals are merged into one using additional hardware such as a hub, a repeater, a bridge, a gateway, and a router. A hub serves as the location where individual connections to a group of computers are centralized. Repeaters are used to boost a data signal if deterioration occurs due to the length of the transmission. LANs can be connected to one another by a bridge if the protocols are the same or by a gateway if they are not. A router connects multiple networks, routing data being sent to the fastest channel that will reach the target.

Networks are able to perform their tasks under the control of communications software, which manages the transmission of all data and information that flows between linked computers. The network operating system has the overall responsibility for how data flows will occur. It performs all of the administrative and file-management activities, handles any necessary printer or other peripheral coordination, and manages access security.

Networks are vulnerable to damage to their hardware, software, and data. One of the most destructive forms of data compromise are viruses, which have the potential to cause massive shutdowns of worldwide systems and cost billions of dollars in lost data and productivity. Computers are also vulnerable to attacks by unauthorized users. While individuals can and should establish a plan to back up their data regularly, install virus protection software, and change their access password frequently, businesses and organizations need to have an appropriate firewall system in place to guard against computer sabotage.

Key terms are presented here in the order in which they are cited in the text. A complete list of key terms in the text, in alphabetical order with definitions, can be found in the Glossary at the end of the book.

communications channel (p. 112)
local area network (LAN) (p. 112)
wide area network (WAN) (p. 112)
intranet (p. 112)
extranet (p. 112)
World Wide Web (the Web) (p. 113)
hypertext documents (p. 113)
browser (p. 113)
nodes (p. 113)
peer-to-peer network (p. 113)
peer (p. 113)
client-server network (p. 113)
client (p. 113)
file server (p. 113)
network interface card (NIC) (p. 115)
modem (p. 115)
modulation (p. 115)
demodulation (p. 115)
fax modem (p. 115)
cable modem (p. 115)
cable access television (CATV) (p. 115)
bandwidth (p. 115)
hertz (Hz) (p. 115)
bits per second (bps) (p. 115)
broadband (p. 115)
twisted-pair cable (p. 116)
shielding (p. 116)
shielded twisted-pair (STP) (p. 116)
switched network (p. 116)
coaxial cable (p. 116)
fiber-optical cable (p. 116)
photons (p. 116)
cladding (p. 116)
Plain Old Telephone Service (POTS) (p. 117)
Integrated Services Digital Network (ISDN) (p. 117)
wireless communication (p. 117)
radio frequencies (RF) (p. 117)

personal communications services (PCS) (p. 118)
microwave (p. 118)
infrared (IR) (p. 118)
geosynchronous communications satellite (p. 118)
digital subscriber line (DSL) (p. 119)
asymmetric digital subscriber line (ADSL) (p. 119)
symmetric digital subscriber line (SDSL) (p. 119)
T-carrier lines (p. 119)
multiplexing (p. 119)
network topology or architecture (p. 119)
linear bus network (p. 119)
transceiver (p. 120)
star network (p. 120)
ring network (p. 120)
token-ring network (p. 120)
token (p. 120)
protocol (p. 121)
simplex transmission (p. 122)
half-duplex transmission (p. 122)
full-duplex transmission (p. 122)
asynchronous transmission (p. 122)
synchronous transmission (p. 122)
Ethernet (p. 122)
Ethernet network (p. 122)
transmission control protocol/Internet protocol (TCP/IP) (p. 122)
packets (p. 122)
hub (p. 122)
repeater (p. 122)
Metcalfe's law (p. 123)
bridge (p. 123)
gateway (p. 123)
router (p. 123)
communications software (p. 123)

network operating system (NOS) (p. 124)
computer virus (p. 124)
access controls (p. 125)
identification (p. 125)
authentication (p. 125)
password (p. 125)
encryption (p. 125)
decrypt (p. 126)
encryption key (p. 126)
firewall (p. 126)
virus protection software (p. 127)
backed up (p. 127)
audit-control software (p. 127)
biometric scanning device (p. 127)
callback system (p. 128)
surge protector (p. 128)
spikes (p. 128)
uninterruptible power supply (UPS) (p. 128)
very high rate DSL (VDSL) (p. 129)
asynchronous transfer mode (ATM) (p. 129)
optical network (p. 129)
Bluetooth (p. 129)

Changes, *Challenges,* and CHOICES

CONFIGURING KNOWLEDGE

Multiple Choice Questions

Choose the best answer from those provided.

1. The forging of hardware, software, and connecting media that are necessary to enable data transfers between computers is called a(n) _____.
   a. broadband connection
   b. communications channel
   c. communications pipeline
   d. intranet
   e. extranet

2. A(n) _____ can easily be created in a home or office environment to permit two or more computers to share an expensive printer.
   a. WAN
   b. extranet
   c. client-server network
   d. PAN
   e. LAN

3. A(n) _____ organizes the nodes of the network so each is served by one or more file servers that control all of the major functions in the network.
   a. peer-to-peer network
   b. extranet
   c. client-server network
   d. ethernet
   e. WAN

4. XYZ Credit Card Co. wants its offices in each of the 50 states to have access to all customer records regardless of the issuing location. Their needs would be best served by the creation of a(n) _____.
   a. extranet
   b. LAN
   c. peer-to-peer network
   d. WAN
   e. PAN

5. When a company uses Internet technology to create a network for use *exclusively* within the firm it is called a(n) _____.
   a. intranet
   b. extranet
   c. WAN
   d. peer-to-peer network
   e. internet

6. A type of connectivity hardware called a _____ located on the CPU case provides a port to which cabling is attached.
   a. router
   b. hub
   c. gateway
   d. network interface card
   e. repeater

7. By using a switched network connected to a _____, a user can connect to a network on an as-needed basis.
   a. router
   b. T-carrier
   c. repeater
   d. gateway
   e. modem

8. The simplest media form used in the creation of a network is a _____, or telephone wire.
   a. fiber-optic cable
   b. coaxial cable
   c. twisted-pair cable
   d. infrared unit
   e. microwave unit

9. Personal communications devices that have Internet access typically use _____ network media.
   a. coaxial
   b. radio frequencies
   c. shielded
   d. fiber-optics
   e. infrared

10. A satellite that circles the earth at a speed that makes continuous communication links with the earth possible is called a(n) _____ communications satellite.
    a. earthsynch
    b. geodesic
    c. hypersync
    d. nonsynchronized
    e. geosynchronous

11. _____ is the network term used for the number of bits that can be transferred in a given second over a given medium.
    a. baseband
    b. broadband
    c. bandwidth
    d. bus speed
    e. hertz

12. T-carrier lines have the capability of _____; that is, they can support numerous phone lines over a single carrier.
    a. multiplexing
    b. networking
    c. infrared
    d. baseband
    e. routing

13. Fiber-optic cable and DSL connections that can be used to create high-bandwidth networks are known as a(n) _____ system.
    a. baseband
    b. synchronous
    c. asynchronous
    d. multiplexed
    e. broadband

14. The communications medium that supports a higher download speed than upload speed is called a(n) _____.
    a. symmetric digital subscriber line   d. broadband line
    b. asymmetric digital subscriber line   e. multiplexed line
    c. baseband line

15. The transfer connection used in regular telephone service that permits data to flow in both directions simultaneously is called _____ transmission.
    a. full-duplex   d. multiplexed
    b. tele-plex   e. half-duplex
    c. simplex

16. The data transfer connection that sends messages in each direction but not at the same time, such as in two-way radio transmission, is called a _____ transmission.
    a. full-duplex   d. half-duplex
    b. simplex   e. multiplex
    c. tele-plex

17. The networking hardware that enhances a data signal that is deteriorating due to the distance traveled is called a _____.
    a. booster   d. bridge
    b. repeater   e. hub
    c. router

18. The software that ultimately is responsible for all of the operations of the network is called the _____.
    a. system controller   d. network operating system
    b. communications system   e. system operator
    c. ethernet system

19. Connecting all of the computers to a single primary cable creates a _____ network topology.
    a. ring   d. hub
    b. linear bus   e. star
    c. wheel

20. A security application that monitors all of the activities of a computer is called _____.
    a. the network operating system   d. the journal
    b. communications software   e. the registry
    c. audit-control software

True or False?
Rewrite each false item to make it a true statement.

1. In a network, the communications channel between hardware devices must be made out of either wire or optical media.
2. Each of the computers on a network is known as a node.
3. A network that is accessible to authorized users outside an organization is called an extranet.

4. A NIC is required to connect a modem to a telephone line.
5. Fiber-optic cable uses light impulses to create a broadband network that has the capacity to transmit enormous amounts of data.
6. Coaxial cable is better shielded from interference than twisted-pair cable.
7. Communication transmissions can only occur over relatively short distances when using infrared technology.
8. Bandwidth is the measure of transmission speed that a communication channel can support.
9. A regular telephone system is an example of a switched network.
10. Multiplexing enables simplex transmission networks to function as full-duplex.
11. Installing digital subscriber lines (DSLs) means running broadband-capable media where the network is to be connected.
12. Coaxial cable is the foundation for worldwide multimedia telecommunications today.
13. A connection from a burglar alarm sensor to a computer is an ideal application for a network simplex transmission.
14. A star network is a topology in which each node is connected to every other node by means of a path.
15. A bridge is hardware used to connect local area networks that do not use the same protocols.
16. In a token-ring topology, a token circulates around the network and intercepts and delivers messages sent by individual nodes.
17. Ethernet connections are simple linear bus LANs.
18. A computer virus is a bit of code that is transferred from host to host in a variety of ways.
19. Access controls typically include authentication steps such as entering names and passwords.
20. A firewall is a concrete wall installed around a network server to protect it from fire damage.

TECHNOLOGY IN CONTEXT

Prepare to discuss each of the following questions, drawing upon the material presented in this chapter as well as additional information you may have researched on your own.

1. Think of a computer network you are familiar with, such as one in your office, home, or school. Describe how human and physical resources are shared in that network. What efficiencies and cost savings might result from that network? What other resources could be shared? In what ways do you think the network could be improved?
2. Are there types of businesses and organizations that should *not* install networks? If so, why?
3. What are the advantages in using twisted-pair wire for ADSL applications? How might the advantages of these high-speed data communications lines outweigh the costs?
4. What kinds of ethical guidelines apply to employees on a company network? For example, should they feel free to look at files in other employees' folders on a network server? Is it possible for one employee to sabotage another employee's work?

5. Identify a computer network or computer center in your office or school. Describe the security measures that are in place to protect the facility, including physical protections. What are the potential weaknesses in the system that might be vulnerable to sabotage? What recommendations would you suggest for improvement?

DEVELOPING MINDSHARE

1. Identify a local area network that you can examine. What network topology is being used? Is the network connected to the Internet? What kind of cable is connecting the network? Do the network users have any complaints about its operation? Can you make any suggestions for its improvement?

2. Visit an electronics store or use the Internet to find some of the new portable devices that are connected to Internet resources with wireless media. Compare the prices and capabilities of these wireless systems with their wired counterparts. What features do you believe would be the most useful for you?

3. Find out if DSL service is available where you live. Compare the features and costs from each of the competitors. Which service would you choose, and why? Also, use your library or consult recent computer journals to read about and report on current advances in DSL technology.

4. What security access controls restrict your own ability to be served by networks of which you are a part? For example, bank ATM cards use a PIN number; computers at work or school use passwords; and student or business facilities use ID cards. How well do these systems work? Are their protections adequate? Have you known any person who tried to fool the system and gain unauthorized use? Did he or she succeed? What suggestions for security improvements would you make?

5. Examine the communications channels with which you interact in your personal life. For example, explore your computer networks, telephone company, business transactions, library, school, and so on. If possible, identify the information that is retained about you on the networks. Is there an opportunity for the data to be compromised? Can you identify any situations where information about you has been shared or sold? Is this activity unethical? Why, or why not?

THINK TANK

George Orwell's landmark novel *1984*, published in 1949, described a world in which "Big Brother" had his eye on members of society. Orwell predicted a world in which personal privacy was subrogated to some "greater purpose." But the year 1984 came and went, and few people then saw much evidence of widespread spying. By 1999, however, the Mel Gibson movie *Conspiracy Theory* echoed the anxiety that many people share. Today, many of our financial activities are electronically transacted. Records of these transactions identify the location where each purchase is made and list every item that is bought. In many states, fingerprints are routinely taken during banking transactions and when people apply for a driver's license. Security cameras are located in nearly every store and public building. Our offices and schools have installed computers that observe and report human activity. Conceivably, all of these computer networks make possible near-constant observation of the public activities of every person in the nation. In fact, it is for this reason that modern types of outlaws, so-called "survivalists," declare war on computer network systems. They insist that the government uses such systems to curtail individual rights and suppress Americans' freedoms.

Teamwork Challenge: Prepare a group report or present a team debate that addresses the following issues: Given the widespread use of networks in businesses, colleges, government, and organizations of all types, do you consider eavesdropping and monitoring of individuals' communications an invasion of privacy? At what point should the government's need to be alert to subversive elements encroach upon an individual's civil liberties? Organizations need to be alert to the actions of their members, but at what point does observation become unethical? What suggestions would you recommend to improve the situation? What do you believe the end result will be? What can computer professionals do to ensure society of proper and ethical use of networked systems? What can individuals do to be more aware of how their private lives are being recorded by others? Should the Bill of Rights be updated to include clauses about network privacy issues?

Answers to Configuring Knowledge Questions

Multiple Choice: 1 – b; 2 – e; 3 – c; 4 – d; 5 – a; 6 – d; 7 – e; 8 – c; 9 – b; 10 – e; 11 – c; 12 – a; 13 – e; 14 – b, 15 – a; 16 – d; 17 – b; 18 – d; 19 – b; 20 – c
True-False: 1 – F; 2 – T; 3 – T; 4 – F; 5 – T; 6 – T; 7 – T; 8 – F; 9 – T; 10 – F; 11 – F; 12 – F; 13 – T; 14 – F, 15 – F; 16 – T; 17 – T; 18 – T; 19 – T; 20 – F

Reality

INTERFACE

The First Amendment and the World Wide Web

The first amendment to the U.S. Constitution guarantees every American the right to free speech. But this free speech is not without some limitations. You are not permitted to scream "fire" in a crowded theater, for instance, so as to purposely cause a panic and potentially hurt those who attempt to flee to safety. The age of the Internet brings with it new challenges to the limits of free speech. Advocates are now attempting to convince the government to limit Internet access so that objectionable language and subject matter are removed to prevent their viewing by children and others who are offended by such material. While Congress enacted the Communications Decency Act in 1996 to establish such restrictions, the U.S. Supreme Court ruled this law unconstitutional in 1998. In that same year, another law, the Child Online Protection Act, was passed, but it too was ruled unconstitutional the following year. These decisions confirm that, at least up to now, free speech on the Internet is a protected right under the U.S. Constitution.

However, the Constitution does not protect the right of an individual who uses any form of media to harm another person. Court cases are now being heard against persons who cause harm to others by malicious activity on computers, including the spreading of viruses. Computer users also need to remember that U.S. law is not enforceable elsewhere in the world. Persons from other countries may post questionable material to the Web, and what is acceptable in one culture may not be in another. As more individuals use the World Wide Web, the exposure to new ideas and cultural differences will add to the debate surrounding limitations on Internet content. But until an acceptable resolution is established, users need to be aware that the price we pay for the privilege of free speech means that just about anything can be seen and heard on the Internet—for better or worse.

6 Understanding the INTERNET

OBJECTIVES

After reading this chapter, you will be able to. . .

➤ Explain the significance of the Internet and the World Wide Web in terms of connectivity and shared access to information

➤ Describe the basic structure of the Internet and how the Internet functions

➤ Define the World Wide Web and distinguish among its rich components

➤ Describe the various modes of communicating over the Internet

➤ Examine Internet security and ethics issues and debate solutions for each of the problems

The Internet and the World Wide Web

The emergence of the Internet and the World Wide Web (WWW) marks a dramatic change in our society today that rivals the introduction of such technological milestones as the telephone, radio, and television. One can only imagine the amazement of early telephone and radio pioneers as they experienced human voices coming through wires or through the air for the first time. In adding pictures to accompany sound, television provided an amazing sensory display. Looking back at these inventions, we have to remind ourselves that for their time they were complete innovations. As with the introduction of any radical new technology, some people rushed to adopt them and others scoffed at and condemned them. Yet as time progressed, even the critics came to regard these devices as common household items and even necessities of daily life.

We are living today through a similar time of momentous technological breakthroughs and the exciting, but often difficult, adjustment to such rapid change. In less than a decade, the advent of the World Wide Web has completely revolutionized the worlds of telecommunications, business, and entertainment. Many companies are now strategically realigning themselves to take advantage of the emerging electronic-commerce (e-commerce) economy. Web site addressees are included in most advertising today, and the level of business being transacted over the Internet is growing at a dizzying pace (see Figure 6-1 for examples of some popular e-commerce sites). The way we work, communicate, entertain ourselves, and carry on our daily activities is being transformed before our eyes through the use of the World Wide Web. There is little question that very soon the Web will be as indispensable to our lives as the telephone, radio, and television.

Figure 6-1: Commerce on the Web

The Development of the Internet

Where and when did the Internet begin? The Internet traces its origins to a Cold War era technology project, called **ARPANET**, initiated by the Pentagon's Advanced Research Projects Agency

(ARPA). This project sought to create a network that would permit collaborative work on research projects and would not be disrupted by the failure of any one site, especially through nuclear attack. The theory was that if a centralized computer had control of all communications activities, it could easily become a target for subversive action. Therefore, ARPANET's technicians gave the network a noncentralized, weblike design to ensure that if one or several network computers or connections were destroyed by nuclear explosions, the remaining computers on the Net would still be able to communicate with one another. In technical terms, the network thus had a peer-to-peer topology.

Made operational in 1969, ARPANET originally consisted of four linked **host computers** at four different California and Utah research institutions. By 1984, the number of ARPANET networked systems had grown to more than 1,000 host computers. Other networks were also connected to ARPANET, effectively merging their resources. For example, the **National Science Foundation (NSF)** connected its network of supercomputers, called the **NSFNet**, in 1986. This early network of networks soon became known as the Internet. The high-speed data connections of the NSFNet, called the **backbone**, provided the primary linkage of the emerging Internet. This backbone can be compared to a major highway with numerous small roads feeding cars into it for high-speed transit. The NSFNet backbone handled the majority of the data transfers, called **traffic**, on the early Internet. However, NSF removed itself from the Internet in 1995 to return to being a private research network. Since that time, backbone services have been provided by a variety of private firms. These private firms, such as telephone companies, cable television services, communication satellite operators, and government agencies, connect more than 150 million users today. The Internet is now

comprised of all of these independent entities who are collaborating to establish standards and objectives. There is, therefore, no single "owner" of the Internet or controlling central authority. Rather, advisory organizations exist whose charge it is to facilitate the communications necessary to address changes and concerns in the Internet's operations. See Table 6-1 for a list of these organizations.

Entity	Membership	Activities
World Wide Web Consortium (W3C)	Private commercial and educational institutions	Oversees research and development of the World Wide Web; sets many Web standards.
Internet Society (ISOC)	Private and public organizations, nonprofit entities, foundations, governments, and individual persons	Coordinates the INET annual conference; publishes the *Internet Society News*; oversees the maintenance, development, and use of the Internet and the specialized boards that establish Internet standards.
Internet Network Information Center (InterNIC)	National Science Foundation, Network Solutions, Inc., AT&T, and General Atomics	Registers and maintains domain names and IP addresses.
Internet Engineering and Planning Group (IEPG)	Internet Service Providers	Coordinates technical issues of the Internet.

Table 6-1: Internet Advisory Organizations

Internet Basics

Any firm, school, or organization can establish a network of computers to facilitate data exchange. To further expand user outreach, networks can also be linked to one another. The Internet, often referred to simply as the Net, is a very large and continually growing network of networks. The major components of today's Internet include:
- e-mail for communications
- newsgroups for sharing information about a topic
- chat rooms for written or oral conversation
- mailing lists for information distribution
- World Wide Web to share information in multiple medias.

To be connected to the Internet, a user needs to have a computer or personal

backbone High-speed data connections that provide the primary linkages of the Internet.

digital assistant (PDA); a modem or cable modem; a telephone line or cable connection; telecommunications software (either **Point-to-Point Protocol [PPP]** or **Serial Line Internet Protocol [SLIP]**; and a Web browser. Once the appropriate hardware and software are in place, a user needs to set up an account with a local area network service, an **online service** such as America Online (AOL) or CompuServe (see Figure 6-2), or with an Internet Service Provider (ISP).

lease high-speed data lines from their local telephone companies. These lines are connected directly to the Internet. Individuals and small businesses can choose between dial-up access or the newer data transfer lines that are connected all of the time. ISPs that provide dial-up service use a local telephone number called a **point of presence** (**POP**) for access. A computer's modem dials the number to establish connection. National ISPs generally provide their users with many hundreds of local numbers around the country to avoid long-distance charges. Some firms even provide toll-free numbers for service, but they may also charge fees per minute of access time used. As can be imagined, long-distance and other toll call charges can quickly mount up when a user is connected to the Internet. However, newer high-speed data transfer technology does not require dial-up connections. As discussed in Chapter 5, Integrated Services Digital Networks (ISDNs), cable television broadband services, and digital subscriber lines (DSLs) are now providing connections that are extremely fast and are on-line all of the time. Selecting a connecting service is thus a balancing act between its cost and the user's needs. Faster and more capable services, as expected, carry a higher price tag.

Figure 6-2: America Online and CompuServe Promotional Sites

Numerous ISPs now exist. For a relatively small fee, usually a monthly flat rate, an ISP gives its subscribers telecommunications software and a local telephone number that they can call to connect to the ISP's Internet access point, or gateway. ISPs vary in their offerings, although most provide access to the Internet only. By contrast, online services provide Internet access as well as a specific package of content (news, stock quotations, electronic magazines, and so on), usually at higher subscription rates.

Making the Connection

The method of connecting to the Internet depends upon the level of service needed. Local area networks typically

How the Internet Works

The Internet is a system of network linkages that uses the client-server model of organization (see Chapter 5). In this type of organization, each individual workstation in a network is called a client in the system, and access to one another is effected through another computer that is known as the server. Servers become clients when they are linked to other servers until a high-speed data line connects the final one directly to the Internet backbone. When data is sent over the Internet, it is broken into small parts

INNOUATORS

Tim Berners-Lee: Inventor of the World Wide Web

Tim Berners-Lee created the World Wide Web while working independently on a networking program. Physicist Berners-Lee graduated in 1976 with a degree in physics at Oxford University's Queen's College. While working for the Centre Européen pour la Recherche Nucléaire (CERN) in Geneva, Switzerland, he developed a computer program for his own use that he called *Enquire*. His objective was to be able to store random associations between disparate things. Although this concept is a normal function of the human brain, it was then new to computer networks. Berners-Lee succeeded in his project. The Enquire program stored not only text, but also random associations in the form of hyperlinks that linked the desired materials. Enquire was never published, but by 1989 Berners-Lee had proposed a universal system that would let all people everywhere participate in the development of a new "web" of knowledge. The World Wide Web was launched at CERN in December 1990. It grew so dramatically in a few years that changes were soon needed to support its growth. In 1994, Berners-Lee became director of the **World Wide Web Consortium (W3C)**, located at the Massachusetts Institute of Technology (MIT). Composed of more than 300 private firms and public organizations, this consortium oversees issues concerning the development of the World Wide Web and serves to channel its growth in ways that will allow it to reach its full potential.

called packets. Every packet carries a part of the data, the addresses of the sender and the intended recipient, and the placement order needed to re-create the original message. These multiple pieces of data are transferred into the Internet, where they may travel over quite different paths to reach their objective. In a process called **packet switching**, routers along the way determine the fastest available pathway to reach the desired recipient. Once arriving at the recipient, the packets are reassembled to re-create the original message. Internet communication is made possible by the use of a common set of instructions that all computers can recognize, Transmission Control Protocol/Internet Protocol (TCP/IP). This communications protocol is included as a set-up option in most operating systems. Every computer network on the Internet has an assigned number called an **IP address** ("IP" stands for "Internet Protocol"). IP addresses are made up of clusters of numbers from 0 to 255 divided by periods. For example, 168.28.223.11 is the IP address for Georgia Perimeter College, the professional home of these authors (see Figure 6-3). The first num-

ber identifies the network, and the last number specifies a particular computer.

Memorizing these numbers-only addresses, however, would be difficult. Therefore, the Internet also accepts text names called **domain names** that replace the numeric address. Each domain name contains a **top-level domain** or **domain suffix** abbreviation that indicates the type

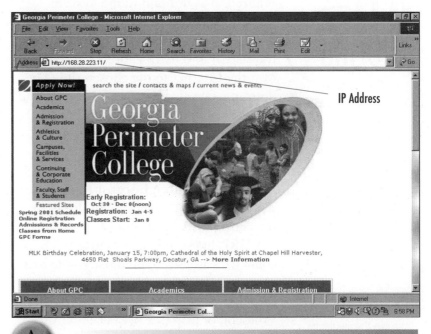

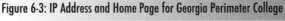

Figure 6-3: IP Address and Home Page for Georgia Perimeter College

of organization that is operating the site. Table 6-2 shows the types of top-level domains that are currently available for the Web. Anticipating the continued rapid growth of the Internet, technicians are currently implementing an enhanced IP address system that will be able to accommodate many times more users and domain names. It should also provide for improved transaction security.

Top-Level Domain Abbreviation	Organization Type
com	Organizations engaged in commerce, business entities
edu	Educational institutions
gov	Governmental units at any level
int	International
mil	Military organizations
net	Network providers
org	Nonprofit organizations
Newer additions (as of November 16, 2000)	
aero	Air-transport industry
biz	Businesses or other firms
coop	Nonprofit cooperatives
info	Information services (unrestricted use)
museum	Museums
name	Personal Web sites
pro	Accountants, lawyers, and physicians

Table 6-2: Top-Level Domain Designations

KEY Terms

Uniform Resource Locator (URL) Combination of necessary Internet routing information that enables a specific Web site to be located.

Hypertext Transfer Protocol (HTTP) Set of data creation and transfer instructions used to support the World Wide Web.

hyperlink Link in a Web document that enables immediate jumping to other Web sites with the simple click of a mouse.

All domain names are stored in the **domain name system (DNS)** on Internet computers. These servers are referred to as **domain name system servers (DNS servers)**. Anytime a domain name is used, a DNS server must translate it into its IP address for routing over the Internet to the chosen site. The domain name also carries a **country code** for international locations (see Table 6-3). When a person uses the Internet for browsing the World Wide Web, the domain name becomes a part of the **Uniform Resource Locator (URL)** for the desired site. A typical URL looks like this: http://www.emcp.com.

A URL has several parts separated by a colon (:), slashes (/), and dots(.). The first part of a URL is the protocol, which in the above example is Hypertext Transfer Protocol, or http (see below). After the protocol comes format information, such as www for Web pages. The next part of a

URL is the domain name and identifies the person, organization, server, or topic. Finally, following a dot, comes the top-level domain that identifies the type of organization.

Country Code Abbreviation	Country
au	Australia
ax	Antarctica
ca	Canada
cn	China
de	Germany
dk	Denmark
fr	France
jp	Japan
mx	Mexico
nl	Netherlands
pr	Puerto Rico
ru	Russian Federation
es	Spain
se	Sweden
uk	United Kingdom
us	United States

Table 6-3: Domain Country Code Abbreviations

The World Wide Web

The development of the Internet communications methodology called **Hypertext Transfer Protocol (HTTP)** led to the development of the World Wide Web, a new way of using the Internet. People often use the terms *Net* and *Web* interchangeably. There is, however, a difference. Strictly speaking, the Internet is a system of computers, storage devices, and connections, along with the software that allows people to use these connections. The Web, in contrast, is the total collection of information available on that portion of the Internet that contains linked HTML documents. The Web is thus only one of the many services that are available on the Internet. The primary advantages of the Web are its use of an attractive and user-friendly graphical user interface and its use of **hyperlinks**, links that enable immediate jumping to other Web sites with the simple click of a mouse (see Figure 6-4). The Web's ease of use and its wide-scale commercialization have made it the Internet's fastest growing component.

Navigating the Web

A Web site is made up of one or more **Web pages** on a computer that is networked into the Internet backbone. A user can find a Web site by typing its complete URL address into the location box (see, for example, Figure 6-5). The first page that appears upon transferring to the Web site is called the **home page**. The software that allows even novice users to explore the Web with ease is called a browser. A browser interprets HTML code, provides a graphical interface, and permits users to browse, or visit, sites on the Net using hypertext links. Currently, Microsoft Internet Explorer and Netscape Communicator are the dominant browsers in use (Figure 6-6). Basic versions of each are available as no-charge downloads from the firms' respective Web sites. Moving from place to place on the Web is called **surfing** the Web, a term suggesting speed, excitement, and continual motion through the sea of information one finds there.

Search Engines

To find information on the World Wide Web, one can simply open a browser and type into a location box the complete URL for the site one wishes to visit. Often, however, a user will not know in advance what Web site he or she seeks. New Web users, or **newbies**, often ask for a directory of sites in order to find information. In fact, early in the Web's development, some publishers did print guides that attempted to map the Internet's growing resources. By the time the guide was published, however, its content was already sorely out of date. This problem of an Internet directory has been solved by the use of **online searches**. Online searches are conducted by programs called **search engines**, which find information

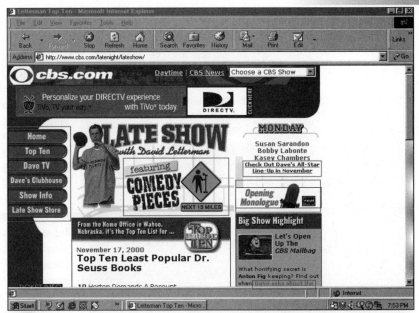

Figure 6-4: A Web Site with Numerous Hyperlinks (outlined in red)

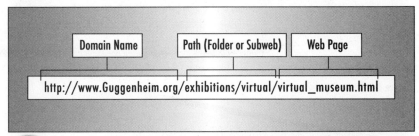

Figure 6-5: Components of a URL

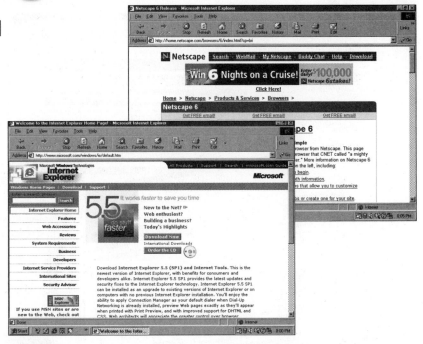

Figure 6-6: Internet Explorer and Netscape Communicator

EXPANSION CARD

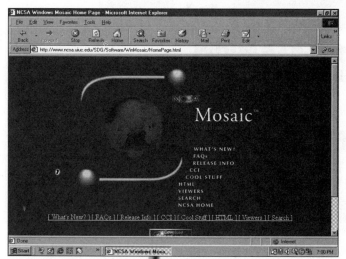

The first graphical Internet browser that gained wide distribution was called **Mosaic.** Mosaic was first envisioned by Marc Andreessen, a part-time worker at the National Center for Supercomputing Applications (NCSA). Andreessen's job was to write programs in UNIX for supercomputer applications. His work required that he become thoroughly familiar with the Internet, which at the time was primarily a text-only network. Andreessen envisioned developing a browser software application that would take advantage of the capabilities of the Hypertext Markup Language developed by Tim Berners-Lee in Europe. With his friend Eric Bina, Andreessen created Mosaic in about three months. Introduced in 1993, it allowed persons with little or no computer knowledge to browse the Internet. NCSA widely distributed Mosaic as a free download. Though primitive in its capability, this browser marked the beginning of the World Wide Web as we know it today.

After graduating from college, Andreessen and Jim Clark of Silicon Graphics launched a new computer software company called Netscape to capitalize on the work previously done at NCSA and to produce a browser that would compete with Mosaic. The result of that effort is the popular browser Netscape Navigator. At about the same time, Microsoft released its Internet Explorer browser, and competition between the two browsers began. Today Microsoft Internet Explorer is the most widely used browser, followed closely by Netscape Communicator. While other browsers exist, use of the Web is dominated by these applications.

Figure 6-7: Some Popular Search Engines

based on key words typed into a query box (see Figure 6-7). Suppose, for example, that a person wants to find information on inline skating. She can simply open a browser, call up a search engine, and type the words *inline skates* at the engine's search prompt to find sites dealing with the subject. Some search engines scour the entire Web for content while others look in the contents of their own directory of locations. Some popular search engines today include Yahoo!, Alta Vista, Lycos, Excite, Ask Jeeves, and HotBot (a longer list, with URLs, is provided in

Table 6-4). Search engines are constantly being updated to maintain their levels of currency, and all of them do a good job of helping users find information on the Web.

Search Engine	URL
AltaVista	www.altavista.com
Ask Jeeves	www.askjeeves.com
Excite	www.excite.com
Google	www.google.com
HotBot	www.hotbot.com
InfoSeek	www.infoseek.com
iWon	www.iwon.com
Lycos	www.lycos.com
Northern Light	www.northernlight.com
Yahoo!	www.yahoo.com

Table 6-4: Common Search Engines

Web Site Content

One of the most exciting aspects of the World Wide Web is its capacity to deliver colorful text, graphics, animations, audio, video, and virtual-reality experiences. Newer browser software includes the capability to deliver much of this multimedia Web content. Older browsers can be updated to receive the latest technology, although some Web content files will still require a **plug-in application,** also called a **helper application.** Plug-ins are small programs that enhance the capabilities of the browser software (see, for example, Figure 6-8).

A Web site that uses a plug-in generally includes a link to the location from which a personal copy of the plug-in can be downloaded at no charge. See Table 6-5 for a list of popular plug-ins.

Helper Plug-In Application	Description/Activity	Web URL
Acrobat Reader	Permits viewing, printing, and navigation of files that are transferred in Portable Document Format (PDF)	www.adobe.com
Cosmo Player	Virtual Reality Viewer for 3D and VRML applications	cosmosoftware.com
Flash Player	Animation, music, and other sounds that dramatically enhance Web site	www.macromedia.com
QuickTime Player	View movie, animation, music, and some virtual-reality files	www.apple.com
RealPlayer	Streaming video and audio in Near CD quality sound and TV quality picture	www.real.com
Shockwave	View dynamic interactive graphics, multimedia, and streaming audio	www.macromedia.com

Table 6-5: Plug-in Applications

Web Graphics

Any graphic or text object on a Web page can be made into a link to any other page in the same Web site or any other location around the world. The creation of these links is part of the Web site authoring process and its maintenance. Responsibility for this and other Web site tasks are often assigned to a single person or team of persons called the **Webmaster.** The design of a Web site and its ongoing maintenance are time-consuming, yet important marketing aspects for any business or

Figure 6-8: RealPlayer Provides Streaming Video and Audio

search engine Internet application that will find information on the Web based upon key words typed into a query box.

organization. An attractive and user-friendly Web site will entice visitors to return. Some Web designers build in an **attractor**, or **hook**, to draw return visits. These attractors may be games, chat rooms, information not readily available elsewhere, or stunning visual images (see Figure 6-9).

Figure 6-9: Various Attractors in Web Sites

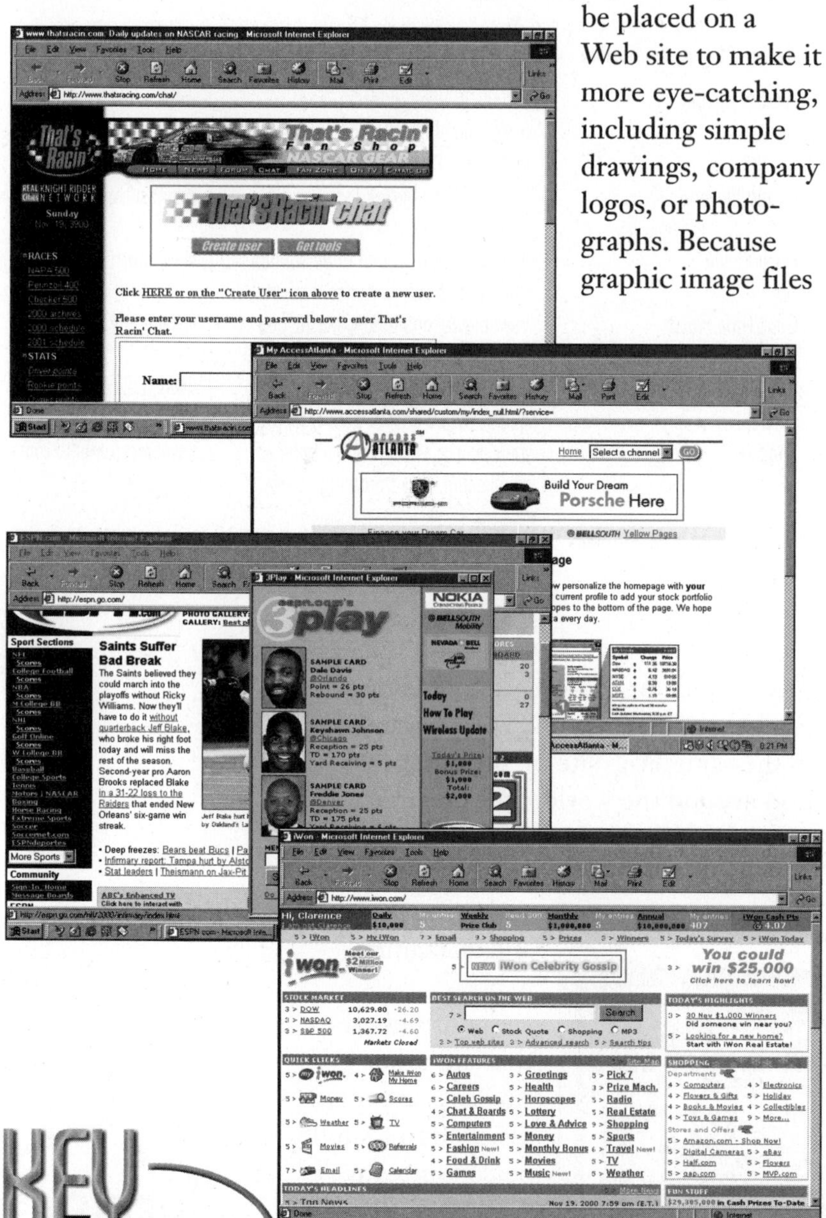

Numerous types of graphic images can be placed on a Web site to make it more eye-catching, including simple drawings, company logos, or photographs. Because graphic image files are sometimes quite large, they often take considerable time to download. To expedite file transfers, Web designers typically use a file format that uses **compression** to reduce the image into a more manageable size. The most popular of these compression formats are JPEG and GIF (see Table 6-6). Many software applications can perform JPEG (Joint Photographic Experts Group) format compression, but the **GIF (Graphics Interchange Format)** compression software is patented and requires the purchase of a license for use. However, a browser can display GIF format graphics without the need for a license. The World Wide Web Consortium has approved **PNG (Portable Network Graphics)** format as a GIF replacement graphics standard that does not require a license. Another popular visual tool on the Web is an animation file wherein sequences of still graphics are played iteratively, simulating motion. One of the most popular forms of animation files is called an **animated GIF** which combines several images into a single GIF file. When these files are displayed in a browser, the sequence of images animates the Web page. When used in Web sites, they often take the form of cartoons, animated company logos, or a marquee of information that scrolls across the screen in the manner of stock market quotes or sports scores.

Graphic Acronym	Name	File Extension
BMP	Bitmap	.bmp
GIF	Graphics Interchange Format	.gif
JPEG	Joint Photographic Experts Group	.jpg
PCX	PC Paintbrush	.pcx
PNG	Portable Network Graphics	.png
TIFF	Tagged Image File Format	.tif

Table 6-6: Graphics Formats in Use on the Internet

Web Audio

Web sites can also include multimedia forms such as audio and video. Sound files can be downloaded to a computer and then played back using the system's media player. Most of the audio files used on the Internet are created using one of the international standard file types called **WAV** for sound wave or **AU** for audio. **Streaming audio** is a recent and more

KEY Terms

streaming audio Technique that allows a listener to hear a file as it actually transfers over the Web.

advanced form of Web sound file transfer. Streaming allows the listener to hear the file as it actually transfers over the Web. This technology has opened the Internet to continuous real-time broadcasts such as radio, talk shows, sporting matches, and other live events. A widely used format for streaming audio is called **RealAudio**.

Another new technology application compresses sound files to approximately one-twelfth of their original size before they are downloaded. One of the most popular formats for this type of transfer is MP3, named for its origin in the Motion Picture Experts Group's (see below) MPEG-1, Audio Layer 3 standard. MP3 files can be downloaded to a variety of personal portable players for mobile entertainment. In fact, the recorded music industry has been significantly altered by the introduction of this digital sound format, and its use has been the subject of ongoing litigation as courts try to decide if using MP3 violates copyright laws.

Internet Telephone Service

Yet another innovative use of streaming audio is the evolving **Internet telephone service** and real-time **audio conferencing.** Internet communications allow participants in remote locations to converse using microphones connected to their computers' soundboards. These microphones then digitize the voices and transmit them over the Web (see, for example, Figure 6-10). The primary advantage of Internet telephone service is that, unlike traditional phone services, there are no long-distance toll charges. Sound quality and the inclusion of motion video to Internet telephone service will continue to develop as broadband connections expand in the future.

Web Video

Video applications on the Web are much larger than audio files. As a result, video

clips taken from television broadcasts or movies, or privately filmed content, must be compressed before being downloaded over the Web. The **Motion Picture Experts Group** (**MPEG**) compression standard is usually used for Internet video transfers. The newer streaming technology has also been applied to video applications. This technology permits the viewing of a file as it is being downloaded. It also creates opportunities for live videoconferencing, video telephony, and simulcasting television and other video over the Web. For streaming video, RealAudio has expanded its software to include **RealVideo** as a part of **RealPlayer**. This software is supported by most browsers.

Numerous video applications are available on the Internet. Clips may be obtained for such varied subjects as news, sports, travel, historical events, and countless other areas of interest. Streaming video is used by Fox News to broadcast features from its cable television news channel over the Web. Sporting events and concerts are also being broadcast over the Web, often with multiple camera offerings that permit each person to select the view that he or she prefers. Visual presentations on the

Motion Picture Experts Group (MPEG)
Compression standard created by a professional organization, widely used for Internet video transfers.

 Figure 6-10: PhoneFree.com, an Internet Telephone Service

Web can be further enhanced by the use of three-dimensional graphical displays called virtual reality (VR). VR presentations use either a plug-in for regular applications or a special **VRML browser**. The majority of Web virtual-reality applications are developed in **virtual reality modeling language (VRML)**. This programming language defines the way in which three-dimensional images are displayed and enables a developer to empower users with controls to manipulate the graphics. VR technology has numerous practical and entertainment uses. For instance, architects can use VRML to "fly through" (see Figure 6-11) models of buildings to examine features prior to construction. Auto manufacturers can use VR modeling to develop and test new ideas before production. Marketing professionals, too, use VR techniques in their Web sites to enhance the promotion of their products. VR is used widely in computer games to provide a stimulating and fun environment.

Publishing to the Web

Creating a Web site is not difficult, and it is becoming easier all of the time as software-authoring programs increasingly do the required coding. As we have seen, Web sites are created by the use of HTML, or Hypertext Markup Language (see Figure 6-12). This relatively simple programming language uses a collection of codes to indicate page parts, text characteristics, and the location of links. These codes are called **tags,** and they tell the viewing browser how to display the words and data that appear on the page.

Computer users can customize typeface and colors for viewing Web pages in their computer's browser application. As a result, each page a user views may appear slightly different from that of the author's originally created screen. To completely control the appearance of the page, a Web site designer must use Java or ActiveX. The final document is then saved as an ASCII binary file with a file name suffix of .htm or .html, which indicates a page created by HTML. Web HTML documents can be typed into any text editor that permits saving the file in ASCII binary format. Many site designers, however, prefer to use Web authoring software to do some or all of the code programming. A number of page-build-

Figure 6-11: Site with fly-through: The lower picture scans the restaurant interior.

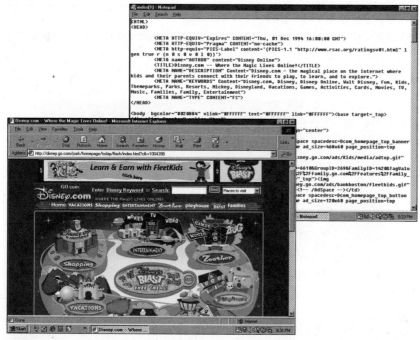

Figure 6-12: The Disney Web Site and the HTML Code for the Same Page

EXPANSION CARD

Netiquette is a word created by combining "Internet" and "etiquette." Netiquette can be defined as a set of informal guidelines for proper behavior when using the Web. As in all forms of interaction with others, annoying, belligerent, mean-spirited, or otherwise inappropriate behavior on the Internet can disrupt communication and lead to ill feelings. Always remember that there is a human being on the other end of your communication. Treat that human being with respect, and do not transmit any message other than what you would be willing to communicate face to face. Here are a few Netiquette pointers:

- Show others the courtesy that you would like to receive from them.
- Never use profanity or offensive language.
- Avoid **shouting**, or the use of all capital letters, in your message.
- Never post insulting or abusive attacks on others, called **flaming**.
- Avoid posting irrelevant messages, referred to as **spam**.
- Be brief in all communications, and use proper spelling and grammar.

Since Internet communications are usually brief and concise, they often make use of acronyms and abbreviations. Many people who communicate frequently over the Internet recognize these shorthand items easily. Those new to such communication may not understand them, however, so only use such abbreviated forms if you are sure your audience knows what they stand for. Here are some common ones:

AFAIK	As far as I know	GF	Girl friend
ASAP	As soon as possible	IC	I see
BF	Boy friend	IMHO	In my humble opinion
BTW	By the way	L8R	Later
CYA	See ya	OIC	Oh, I see
FYI	For your information	TTFN	Ta ta for now
FWIW	For what it's worth	TYVM	Thank you very much

Some Internet users also add **emoticons** to their messages. An emoticon, a word derived from "emotion" and "icon," is a shortcut that conveys common emotions or feelings. Some software applications even replace the keystrokes typed in (on the left in the list below) for "face" pictures (on the right). Here are the most common emoticons:

:)	Smile	☺
:(	Frown	☹
:|	Indifference	😐
:\	Undecided	
: o	Surprised	

Finally, it is always a good idea to announce to readers beforehand if your message contains a spoiler. A **spoiler** is a fact that, when related, ruins the result of an activity for the reader. For example, if a reader views a message that exposes the winner of a tape-delayed sporting event that he or she plans to view, it would spoil the viewing fun. By placing a warning in the subject line that a message contains a spoiler, a user can alert readers and they, in turn, can decide whether or not to read the rest of the message.

ing application programs such as Microsoft's FrontPage and Adobe's PageMill are available, and updated versions of word processing, spreadsheet, and graphics programs, such as found in Microsoft Office, also permit automatic program coding for Web sites. Once the Web documents are complete, they must be placed on the server so that viewers can access them. Many ISPs offer **Web hosting services** for the storage of site files at a nominal charge. To permit more users to locate their Web sites, designers also typically register their site's URL and the keywords that describe its content with some of the more popular search

tags Series of codes used in Web pages that tell the viewing browser how to display the words and data on the screen.

engines. Or, they will employ a submission service to perform this task. These services register a site with numerous search engines for little or no charge.

Communicating over the Internet

E-Mail

One of the most popular Internet features is electronic mail (e-mail). Businesses and individual users have quickly adopted e-mail as their primary mode of communication due to its many advantages. It is, for one thing, almost instantaneous. While telephone communication is also instantaneous, it requires that all parties be free at the same time to talk to one another. By contrast, e-mail does not require both parties to be available to communicate at exactly the same time. It can be answered many times per day, if needed, and it can be worked into the schedule of all users. E-mail also costs much less than overnight or second-day mail delivery and does not involve long-distance telephone charges, as faxing does.

E-mail uses the Internet to transfer message files to one or more recipients anywhere in the world. To send or receive e-mails, a user must have an e-mail program and a connection to the Internet. E-mail programs may be obtained through ISPs, and they are also included with Microsoft and Netscape browser software. E-mail programs allow users to create, send, receive, forward, and delete messages. Messages can also be filed for future reference or printed if hard copy is needed.

A user's **e-mail address** is made up of the user name and a domain name that identifies each distinct mailbox (see Figure 6-13). The ISP or the **mail server** that makes the connection to the Internet holds a **mailbox** that is the repository for all newly received messages.

As messages come in, they are stored in the appropriate mailbox until called for by the user. The mail is transmitted over the Internet using **Simple Mail Transfer Protocol (SMTP),** a standard communi-

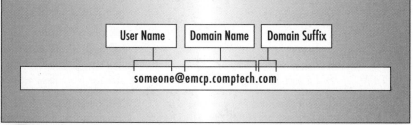

| User Name | Domain Name | Domain Suffix |

someone@emcp.comptech.com

Figure 6-13: Components of an E-Mail Address

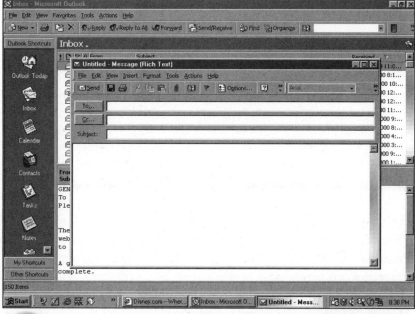

Figure 6-14: Outlook E-Mail Client Open

KEY Terms

Simple Mail Transfer Protocol (SMTP) Standard communications protocol used to transfer e-mail over the Internet.

cations protocol. When received, messages are transferred to a **POP (Post Office Protocol) server** or a **POP3 server** (Version 3, the newest form of POP). When the user executes the e-mail program, access to the mailbox is made available. The messages are downloaded from the mailbox to the e-mail program so that the user can read and react to them in whatever way is desired (see Figure 6-14).

Mailing Lists

Mailing lists are a logical extension of e-mail. They make possible the sending of messages to multiple receivers with a single command. Mailing lists are sometimes called **Listservs** because of the name of the early popular software application used for this purpose. There are literally thousands of mailing lists on the Internet to which individuals can subscribe to receive information on every type of special interest, including automobiles, sports, politics, health matters, entertainment, and so on (see Figure 6-15). Mailing list topics can be found by searching with any Web browser. Once an interest area is located, a user can request that her e-mail address be added to the mailing list. If the user later wishes to cancel the subscription, she can easily unsubscribe by following the instructions usually included with all mailing list e-mails. To create a mailing list, a user collects e-mail addresses under a single designator for ease of distribution. For example, if a hundred people subscribe to a computer club, all of their e-mail addresses can be stored under one name, such as "C-CLUB." This name is then used as an alias through which e-mail information can be sent to all of the club members at once.

Mailing lists have numerous e-commerce advantages as well. Businesses rely on them to inform customers about product changes and availability. Entertainers maintain lists to provide

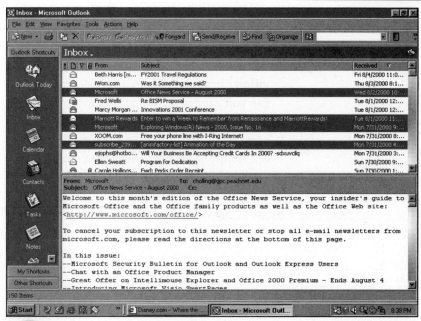

Figure 6-15: Listserv Examples in Outlook E-Mail Client

their fans with announcements of public appearances or souvenirs for sale. Software firms use mailing lists to send users updated information about their products or alert them to new virus threats. These are just a few areas where mailing lists provide important marketing and advertising advantages.

Chat Rooms

In Internet **chat rooms**, users can participate in conversations with people from anywhere in the world in real time (see Figure 6-16). Participants type their messages alternately into a **chat client** program in order to post them to the **chat server**. Or, users can simply opt to observe rather than enter into the discussion. Some Web sites also support chat rooms that allow users to enter into "private" rooms that limit general public participation. While chat rooms can be fun and informative, there is, of course, no guarantee that participants will stay on the room's designated subject matter, present themselves truthfully, or use nonoffensive language, even in moderated sites (see next page).

The earliest chat sessions were text only. More recent chat software used in some sites also supports **voice chat,** a feature that lets the users hear one another, and **video chat,** technology that adds video to the voice transfer. Voice and video chats require substantial bandwidth to carry large amounts of data so as to avoid breaks or choppy transfers. Since chat client software is included with most operating systems, many computers are already geared for chat room participation.

Newsgroups and Message Boards

Unlike chat rooms, **newsgroups** are used for the exchange of communication between users who may not be online at the same time. Participating in a newsgroup requires a **newsreader**, a feature found on most Web browsers. A vast number of newsgroup sites covering every conceivable topic can be found on the Internet (see Table 6-7 for some representative categories). Broad subject areas of newsgroups are subdivided into smaller and smaller subtopics, each divided by a period (.). For example, some popular newsgroups are alt.fashion, soc.college.financial-aid, rec.collecting.sport.baseball, and rec.photo.equipment.35mm. Once a desired subject has been located, a user can subscribe to it. Members of a newsgroup can post messages to a particular group and read messages posted by other members. When a member posts a question or comment, it is called an **article**. Other members can reply to the user's article in what is known as a **threaded discussion**, so named because newsgroups are presented in a hierarchical arrangement with articles and their subsequent responses following a common thread or thought. Article postings are made to a **news server**, which is often provided by businesses, educational institutions, ISPs, or other organizations. Some newsgroups have a **moderator** who first examines each article for its appropriateness to the discussion before it is posted for the general public. This filtering process can add to participants' confidence that material being posted is relevant to the topic and of some degree of quality.

A Web-based form of content posting that does not require the use of a newsreader is called a **message board** or **discussion board**. Thousands of these

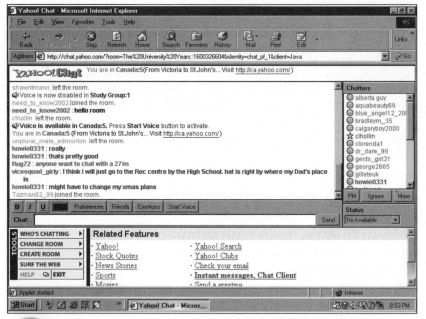

Figure 6-16: Yahoo! Chat Room Client Open

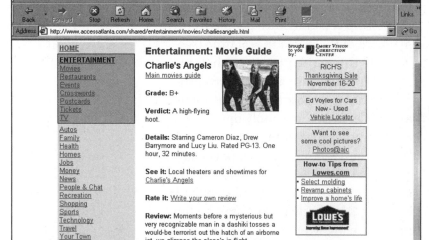

Figure 6-17: Message Board with Movie Reviews from AccessAtlanta (Cox Newspapers)

discussion locations, which allow users to comment on issues of common interest, can be found on the Web (see Figure 6-17). Since message boards are generally easier to use than newsgroups, they are expected to grow rapidly in the future.

News Category	Content Description
Alt	Alternative
Biz	Business
Comp	Computer
k12	Education
Misc	Miscellaneous
News	Newsgroups
Rec	Recreation
Soc	Social
Talk	Talk
usenet	News Postings

Table 6-7: Sample Newsgroup Categories

Sending Files over the Internet

A common way to transfer files over the Internet is by **File Transfer Protocol**, or **FTP**. All types of files, including data, graphics, sound, and video files, can be sent over the Internet, and transfers are possible in either direction. Files are stored at so-called **FTP sites** on **FTP servers** attached to the Internet. In order to upload files to a remote FTP site, an **FTP program** on the sending computer is required. ISPs make this software available to subscribers, or shareware software can be downloaded at no cost from Internet Web sites. FTP servers often require that users log in by entering an e-mail address and a password. Many servers allow any user to log in by typing the word *anonymous* at the password prompt. Such a server is called an **anonymous FTP site**. One can find FTP files by using a search engine, and many FTP archives are connected by links to Web sites. To download an FTP file, a user follows the instructions given in the documentation or online help provided with a browser. Computer hardware and software companies often use FTP for downloading upgrades and corrective software

to users of their products.

Telnet sessions are a type of protocol over the Internet that lets a computer connect to a remote system so that it can operate as though it is an on-site terminal. This type of connection is frequently used to access personal data files, reference articles, and other forms of databases held by the remote computer. Libraries have long used this format to give remote users access to their collections. Some telnet connections restrict user access by using login identifications and passwords, while others allow users to enter with generic entries. As more sites make their databases accessible on the Web, however, the need for this type of connection may decline. Still, many salespersons and company representatives in our connected economy today carry handheld systems that use telnet sessions with the main office to place and follow up on orders and to carry out other business functions.

Security and Privacy on the Internet

Someone once described the Internet as electronic anarchy. Indeed, the lack of a single owner or regulatory authority makes it impossible to control content on the Web. The Internet is, in a sense, the ultimate source of free speech where any person can post anything. However, the lack of regulation means that some Internet content can be inappropriate for young surfers and offensive to persons of any age. The U.S. court system has ruled that free expression in both words and pictures on the Internet is protected by the Constitution. But because the Internet connects the entire world and legal guarantees do not extend beyond any single nation's borders, offensive text and images will continue to be posted. Parental guidance, therefore, must be used to protect children. While parents can use **filtering software** to stop most objectionable content from being displayed, the surest preventive measure is

File Transfer Protocol (FTP)
Common way to transfer files over the Internet.

telnet sessions Type of communication protocol over the Internet that lets a computer connect to a remote system so that it operates as though it were an on-site terminal.

filtering software Software designed to stop most objectionable content on the Internet from being displayed on a browser.

for them to monitor closely their children's Web surfing activity.

Guarding against Viruses

As discussed in Chapter 5, computer crime in on the rise. To ensure against harmful viruses, virus protection software should also be installed on all business and home computers and updated frequently (see Figure 6-18). Such software automatically scans disks, files, and programs, and alerts users to detected viruses. Viruses often spread through e-mail attachments or through applications offered free on the Internet. Users who regularly download free games, for instance, need to be careful to check each download for viruses since they are often embedded in such applications.

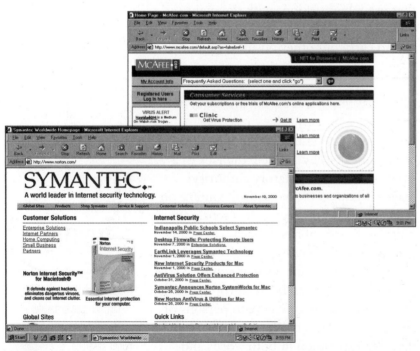

Figure 6-18: Norton and McAfee Virus Protection Sites

Ensuring Personal Security

Another issue surrounding Web safety is that of personal security. E-mail and chat rooms are an easy way for persons with malicious intent to lure children or vulnerable adults into personal relationships. After developing trust through written communication, such perpetrators often arrange to meet their victims privately, and some of these contacts end tragically. Although it is now illegal in the United States to collect names and personal information from minors over the Internet without parental consent, it is imperative that parents or other responsible adults be aware of their children's activity on the Internet and talk to them about such hazards. Adults, too, need to be extremely cautious when arranging a meeting with a person with whom they have only had Internet contact, since e-mail communication can well disguise a person's true nature or intent.

Protecting Credit Card and Other Personal Information

E-commerce also opens the Web to fraudulent transactions, such as the taking of money without delivering a product and the improper use of credit card information. As the volume of e-commerce grows, more people will likely become vulnerable to the unscrupulous practices of those who use the Internet dishonestly. In fact, the large number of recent consumer complaints about promised yet undelivered purchases made over the Internet has given rise to third-party guarantee firms whose job it is to ensure the correct fulfillment of the expected order. Issues of providing personal information in e-commerce are also of concern today and have yet to be fully resolved. E-commerce activities and other services such as online banking need to assure their users that information such as credit card, bank account, and social security numbers are protected from inappropriate use, computer hacking, or theft. Consumers on the Web also tend to enter personal information on Web sites that permit customized or user-chosen views of content. This information is stored on the computer in small files called cookies. Web content providers are able to access the information about their visitors in these cookies during the Web viewing process (see Figure 6-19). The collection and sharing of this personal information is a major privacy violation issue. While it is possible to set up the computer's operating system to reject the receipt of cookie files, one then forfeits the ability to use these special Web viewing features.

In the near future, we can expect that these security and privacy concerns will continue to take center stage as this aspect of Internet use is developed. Users are justifiably wary about entering personal data on the Internet, and e-commerce will not advance to its full potential unless these matters are resolved. The financial services industry has already taken the lead in adopting **secure Web site servers** to ensure the protection of users' data. A secure Web site automatically encrypts the personal data being communicated for the mutual protection of the server as well as the user. A secure Web site can be easily identified by its URL, one that begins with **https://** as opposed to the traditional non-secure site prefix http://. The "s" in the protocol instruction stands for "secure server" for data transmission. Encryption is also available for e-mail and other forms of data transfers.

An Internet Code of Ethics

Because the Internet is an unregulated public forum, our society is faced today with developing a code of ethics, or conduct, for its use. All mature organizations have developed and enforce some type of a professional code of ethics, a set of rules that help guide the appropriate behaviors of members. Figure 6-20 gives an example of possible guidelines that might appear in an Internet code of ethics. Many schools have developed their own codes, and have students and parents sign them before the student can access the Internet. In order for our connected world and economy to prosper, it will be increasingly important in the future that the public adopts the Internet Code of Ethics.

The Internet of the Future

More than half of all Americans are now connected in some way to the Internet. A recent survey of U.S.

Figure 6-19: Cookie Contents—Note the Personal Information

The following guidelines represent an update of a code of ethics developed by the Computer Ethics Institute of the Brookings Institute of Washington, D.C., in 1992. This code of ethics has been updated to reflect the expanding use of networks today. Firms and other organizations often produce and distribute similar rules to guide the Internet behavior of their employees.

1. Never use computers or systems to cause harm to other people.
2. Never interfere with the computer or network work of others.
3. Never scrutinize, alter, or erase another person's files or computer settings without his or her permission.
4. Never use computers or networks for any fraudulent reason.
5. Never use computers or networks to spread malicious or defamatory information about another person or organization.
6. Never use software in a manner that abuses the licensing agreement under which it is authorized.
7. Never use another person's computer or network resources without proper authorization.
8. Never use another person's computer or network intellectual property without permission.
9. Never use computers or networks to create systems or programs without first assessing the impact of such actions upon society.
10. Always use computers or networks in a manner that is considerate and respectful of others.

Figure 6-20: Internet Code of Ethics

EXPANSION CARD
Internet 2 and Beyond

Today's Internet is based on technology that is beginning to show its age. Even the fiber-optic cable is approaching its thirtieth anniversary. A network communication channel is only as fast as its slowest link or connection, and there are many bottlenecks in our current configuration. Imagine what a network would be like if the entire system was created with state-of-the-art technology. This is the objective of **Internet 2 (I2)**, a testbed for the development of advanced technology that involves more than 170 U.S. research universities, a number of industry partners, and some governments. Internet 2 is a private network that was launched in 1998 for research purposes only; it cannot be accessed by the public. This network can operate at transfer speeds a thousand times faster than today's Internet, approximately 9.6 billion bits per second. At this speed, an entire 30-volume encyclopedia can be transmitted in one second. The Internet 2 project plans to create and deploy new technologies that can be implemented on the existing public Internet.

The U.S. government wants Internet access available to all citizens regardless of their economic situation. Our nation does not want to foster a technology-deprived underclass. The government's **Next Generation Internet (NGI)** initiative is working on this goal. NGI wants to bring the technological promise of Internet 2 to the general public. A debate is continuing as to whether the implementation of NGI should be provided by the government or be the product of private enterprise. The government wants a network that it can control, whereas the private sector wants the Internet to remain free from such intervention. We can expect much more debate on this important issue in the near future.

KEY Terms

Internet 2 (I2) Extremely high-speed private network launched in 1998 for research purposes only.

Next Generation Internet (NGI) U.S. government-sponsored initiative designed to bring the technological promise of Internet 2 to the general public.

Figure 6-21: Internet-Linked Devices

employees' computer use found that 70% of respondents use computers at work, and 23% of their computer time is spent on the Internet. Moreover, it is estimated that 75% of the world's population will use the Internet by the year 2020. Besides desktop or laptop computers, there are now literally dozens of wireless devices on the market that deliver e-mail and Internet capabilities, such as handheld computers, cell phones, and media screens (some examples are shown in Figure 6-21). In the future, we will be a "pervasive computing" and "information-everywhere" society. In addition, as we have seen, the Internet is suddenly big business, with enormous e-commerce profit potential, and companies large and small are scrambling to get their share of this huge market. As a result, the Net is changing rapidly, and in some directions that are controversial.

Increasing Commercialization

In the past, the Internet was used primarily for noncommercial purposes—for research, for education, for correspondence through e-mail, and for news. But this situation has changed drastically as commercial traffic has taken over much of the territory. Along with this commercialization comes, naturally, increased advertising. Numerous online services now offer users free e-mail and access to the Internet, a deal that can only occur when advertising and other revenue streams pay the cost. Many commercial Web sites today contain a distracting amount of advertising that, to get users' attention, increasingly relies on animation, banners, video, or sound.

With growing commercialization on the Net, its traditional **open architecture**, or free-range access to users, is disappearing as companies create sites open only to their employees, corporate partners, customers, or subscribers. Internet 2, now being developed by some 170 college, industry, and government participants, was initiated in response to the growing number of commercial and private users. Access to Internet 2 will be restricted to member institutions for educational and research purposes only. Large corporations are also looking into setting up private alternatives to the Internet. In the future, therefore, the highest-speed, highest-bandwidth connections may be available only on private, alternate networks that charge premiums for their services. Under such a scenario, a slower successor to the current Internet would remain available to the average user. On the other hand, the creation of alternate Internets will bring about numerous improvements in speed and capability that eventually will be incorporated into the commercialized Internet. Such developments will pave the way for greater expansion of large-file applications such as full-motion video and virtual reality.

Pull or Push?

Traditionally, the Internet has been a **pull medium**, one in which specific connections to information on host computers were instigated by users. In effect, the user would decide that he or she wished to get some particular information—a newsgroup posting, or a particular Web site—and pull that information to his or her computer. Commercial firms and nonprofit organizations have now, however, begun moving toward implementing a **push medium** model for Web content delivery. A typical push operation works like this: a person interested in information on some topic requests that such information be automatically sent to his or her e-mail address. So, for example, a user can subscribe to *Wired News*, from the editors of *Wired* magazine, and have high-quality daily news regarding developments in computer technology posted to his or her electronic mailbox. A problem occurs, however, when irresponsible organizations resort to spamming, pushing unsolicited and unwanted materials into people's mailboxes.

Better Search Engines

Future technology will continue to improve search engines. Typically, today's search engines work by making use of **Web crawlers**, software that continually searches the World Wide Web and other parts of the Internet to identify new pages. These pages are then downloaded to the search engine company's site and examined for key words that are placed in an index. Searching by key words is problematic, however, because such a search does not screen out unwanted materials. A search using the word *modem*, for example, will turn up millions of entries, including those in which modems are

mentioned only incidentally. Another approach to preparing a search engine, the one used by the search engine Yahoo!, is to employ human operators to search the Internet and place new material into an existing classification system, or catalog. Unfortunately, this manual approach is far too slow and expensive.

One way to improve the current system is to create a standard for posting **metadata**, similar to the information provided by a library catalog entry, for all materials that appear on the Net. Such metadata would include the creator, title, date, and subject of the material and would vastly improve the efficiency of automatic indexing of Net contents. The most recent HTML standard, **HTML 4,** contains specifications for such metadata to be placed in the headings of the HTML documents that create Web pages. Such metadata will allow the crawler programs used by search engine providers to index Web pages more rationally. In the future, voice and image recognition systems may become intelligent enough to read and classify materials on their own. Although they may be some years in coming, we can expect to see such intelligent search engines in the future.

Many other changes will no doubt occur in the Internet's future. Special software called the **.Net** initiative is currently being developed by Microsoft that links Web sites automatically, allowing users to organize every aspect of their lives, from education to financial matters to what to prepare for dinner. One click of the mouse will open site after related site of importance to the user, without the user needing to search for information or open separate sites. In addition, images have now fully entered the once text-based-only Net. The next stage is the delivery of real-time, high-bandwidth audio and video over broadband channels into homes and businesses. Increasingly, people will communicate not only in text-based e-mail, but also through audiovisual means over intranets, extranets, and the Internet.

open architecture Traditional structure of the Internet that allows free-range access to users.

Web crawler Software that continually searches the World Wide Web and other parts of the Internet to identify new pages.

metadata Technique to place into Web pages data that would vastly improve the efficiency of automatic indexing of Net contents.

Chapter
SUMMARY

The Internet grew out of the Pentagon's 1969 defense-related project, ARPANET. By the 1990s, it had added extensive commercial applications, a graphical user interface, and the World Wide Web. These changes helped increase Internet user numbers to some 170 million worldwide in early 2000. Some major uses of the Internet today are e-mail, the Web, mailing lists, chat rooms, newsgroups, message boards, file transfers, and telnet sessions. No single person or organization owns or regulates the Internet; rather, it is overseen by a voluntary coordination effort of individual, public, and private enterprises.

A global network of networks, the Internet employs the client-server model of connectivity. Large networks connect by using high-speed data lines leased from local telephone companies. Smaller networks or individuals connect by establishing links to the larger networks or through Internet Service Providers. A variety of types of connections are available at varying transfer speeds and costs. Each Internet-connected computer is assigned an IP address, a series of numbers that define its location routing. Since domain names are easier to remember, they are usually substituted by users for the IP number. Creating a Web site is not difficult, and a number of types of Web authoring software are available to do the code programming. Web sites are created by the use of HTML, which codes content that is displayed as a system of links between otherwise unrelated documents. This permits users to explore the content of the Web by simply clicking a link in a Web site. To search for items, users can employ a variety of search engines that scan sites for information. Today, the Web also supports all types of audio, visual, and three-dimensional displays. Downloading complex graphical content or other multimedia files from some Web sites, however, requires a plug-in application to be first loaded so as to achieve the full effect of the multimedia content. In addition, large multimedia files usually need to be compressed before they are downloaded.

Besides searching for information, communication with others by e-mail or through other messaging activities such as mailing lists, chat rooms, newsgroups, and message boards is the most popular way to use the Internet. These services are expanding to include audio and visual capabilities as broadband connections continue to grow. Files can be transferred directly between computers using File Transfer Protocol. Remote computer connections can also be made over the Internet to a host system by the use of telnet sessions. This type of connection is often used by salespersons and company representatives to connect with the main office.

Since the Internet is unregulated, its content is not always suitable for children and other vulnerable persons. Filtering software may be purchased to screen viewing content. In addition, the growth of the Internet poses other important security and privacy issues, such as viruses, theft of personal information, and invasions of personal privacy. In the future, such issues will need to be resolved in order for users to feel confident enough to use the Internet to its full capacity in e-commerce and other activities. Our society struggles today and will continue to grapple with the need to develop a code of ethics that all Internet users can embrace.

Key Terms

Key terms are presented here in the order in which they are cited in the text. A complete list of key terms in the text, in alphabetical order with definitions, can be found in the Glossary at the end of the book.

Changes, *Challenges,* and CHOICES

CONFIGURING KNOWLEDGE

Multiple Choice Questions
Choose the best answer from those provided.

1. The Internet began with four linked computers in a 1969 Pentagon networking project called _____.
   a. NSFNet
   b. ARPANET
   c. the World Wide Web
   d. FTP
   e. W3C

2. The primary high-speed data connections that carry the majority of Internet transmissions over distances are called the _____.
   a. ISP
   b. trunk lines
   c. skeleton
   d. TCP/IP
   e. backbone

3. The volume of data transfers over the Internet is often referred to as _____.
   a. crowding
   b. traffic
   c. flows
   d. business
   e. compression

4. The _____ is the organization directed by Tim Berners-Lee that oversees issues concerning the development of the Internet.
   a. International Standards Organization
   b. CERN
   c. Federal Trade Commission (FTC)
   d. World Wide Web Consortium (W3C)
   e. Motion Picture Experts Group

5. To connect to the Internet, users need to establish a relationship with a(n) _____.
   a. ISP
   b. Webmaster
   c. client computer
   d. Internet client
   e. TCP/IP

6. The use of very high-speed data lines such as fiber-optic lines for data transmission is called _____ service.
   a. super speed
   b. DDSL
   c. broadband
   d. dynamic
   e. LDLS

7. In data transmission, routers determine the fastest available pathway for small units of data to reach the desired recipient in a process called _____.
   a. FTP
   b. HTML
   c. data forwarding
   d. PBX switching
   e. packet switching

8. A(n) _____ is an assigned number used to identify each computer that is connected to the Internet.
   a. IP address
   b. URL
   c. http
   d. sysno
   e. login

9. The "com" found in *dot com* commercial Web sites is called a(n) _____.
   a. URL
   b. top-level domain
   c. IP address
   d. domain name
   e. connector

10. When a person uses the Internet for browsing the World Wide Web, he or she uses a(n) _____ such as *www.disney.com*, which consists of several parts identifying protocol, format information, domain name, and organization type.
    a. IP address
    b. Webmaster
    c. FTP
    d. TCP
    e. URL

11. When a Web page user clicks on an image or line of text to transfer to another Web page or site, he or she is using a(n) _____.
    a. IP address
    b. transfer site
    c. URL
    d. hyperlink
    e. top-level domain name

12. The software program with graphical user interface that makes Web surfing accessible even to novice users is called a(n) _____.
    a. browser
    b. hypermedia
    c. IP ware
    d. server program
    e. chat client

13. Web users make use of a(n) _____ such as Yahoo! or Alta Vista to locate information when they do not know a specific URL.
    a. Internet address book
    b. card catalog
    c. search engine
    d. resource guide
    e. domain name system (DNS)

14. Loading some graphic and multimedia Web content requires a(n) _____, a small program that enhances the capabilities of the browser software.
    a. multimedia package
    b. plug-in application
    c. hypermedia tool
    d. VRML browser
    e. interpreter

15. Responsibility for Web site authoring and maintenance in an organization is assigned to a person or team of persons known as the _____.
    a. Webster
    b. newbie
    c. moderator
    d. browser
    e. Webmaster

16. Which of the following graphic file formats is *not* used in Web site design?
    a. .jpg
    b. .gif
    c. .wav
    d. .png
    e. .bmp

17. Which of the following is a file format that can compress sound files to approximately one-twelfth of their original size before they are downloaded?
    a. ASCII
    b. MP3
    c. TCP/IP
    d. HTML
    e. JPEG

18. Web sites often place a small file called a _____ on a user's computer to store viewing preferences.
    a. deposit
    b. data file
    c. record
    d. cookie
    e. view

19. A Web site that supports interactive conversation between users is called a _____.
    a. chat room
    b. browser
    c. client computer
    d. chat client
    e. communicator

20. A Web site that permits the posting of questions, answers, and comments about particular topics is called a discussion or _____ board.
    a. communication
    b. data
    c. user
    d. chat
    e. message

True or False?
Rewrite each false item to make it a true statement.

1. The World Wide Web and the Internet are two terms for the same thing.
2. The Internet can be defined as a very large and growing network of networks.
3. ISPs that provide dial-up service use a PPP, or local telephone number, for access.
4. Tim Berners-Lee created the World Wide Web based on an original program he developed called "Enquire."
5. The first page that appears when a user types a URL in a location box is called the home page.

6. The graphical browser that marked the beginning of the World Wide Web as we know it today was called Explorer.

7. Some commercial Web sites build in an attractor to capture attention and draw return visits.

8. In the transfer called streaming audio, a user must first download a sound file and then play it back.

9. Playing a three-dimensional virtual-reality presentation doesn't require helper or other special applications.

10. The programming language used for Web virtual-reality applications is called VRML.

11. Some rules of Netiquette include avoiding shouting, flaming, and spamming.

12. Creating a Web site is difficult and should be reserved for professional designers.

13. The codes used in Web page construction to indicate page parts, text characteristics, and the location of links are known as JPEG.

14. RealPlayer is a plug-in application that can be used to play audio and video applications over the Web.

15. With a mailing list, a user can send messages to multiple receivers only after executing numerous commands.

16. Today's chat software can support voice chat but not video chat.

17. To participate in a newsgroup, a user needs the newsreader feature that comes with most Web browsers.

18. A common way to compress files for Internet transfer is with File Transfer Protocol (FTP).

19. Telnet sessions are often used by sales representatives working at remote locations to connect with their main office.

20. A secure Web site can be identified by its special URL.

TECHNOLOGY IN CONTEXT

Prepare to discuss each of the following questions, drawing upon the material presented in this chapter, as well as your own experience and additional information you may have researched on your own.

1. Why has the Internet become so popular in recent years? How might use of the Internet change people's personal and work lives?

2. Describe the organization of the Internet and explain why there is not a single owner or regulating authority governing its content and operation. What are the advantages and disadvantages of no central ownership or regulation?

3. Explain how a Web site is created. How and why has the use of HTML in Web site design contributed to the fact that the Internet is filled with computer novices? What are the advantages and disadvantages of this situation?

4. Should the federal or state governments make Internet access available in all parts of our country? Who should pay for this service?

5. Describe the major concerns that should be addressed when considering a code of ethics for Internet use. What rules might be added to the possible Internet Code of Ethics presented in the chapter? How can our global society expect users to respect and adhere to these principles? What are the possible consequences for adopting or not adopting a code of ethics?

DEVELOPING MINDSHARE

1. Identify at least six Internet Service Providers that are available to you where you live. Create a chart or table that compares the features provided and their costs. Write a paragraph or two that describes the advantages and disadvantages of each feature, and choose which ISP is best for your situation.

2. Select a topic that interests you. Then, choose any four of the search engines that are presented in the chapter. Look up your topics using each of these four search engines and compare the results. Explain how the results are similar and how they differ, and why such differences might occur.

3. At a computer store, on the Web, or in computer magazines, research new devices besides desktop or laptop computers that provide Internet-related functions. For example, locate MP3 devices, Internet-capable cellular phones, handheld personal data managers, and connected automobile equipment. In a written report, examine and compare the capabilities and features of each of these devices. Identify the type of user who would most benefit from each device.

4. Locate some Web sites that have advertising on the screen. Find and identify any attractors present, such as games and message groups, that are designed to capture consumers' attention. Explain why such advertising might be important to the owner of the Web site, and discuss its impact on users.

5. Use any search engines to locate free Internet telephone service. What hardware and software is required for such free long distance communication? If you have the equipment to try the service, do so. Then, comment on the quality of the transmission. What effect will this new type of phone service have on traditional long distance phone service?

THINK TANK

The ongoing development of Internet 2 has the potential of creating at least two different Internets: one for the academic and government research institutions and a second (the existing Internet) for consumers and businesses. This possibility raises several issues. Is there a need to have separate Internets? Should the research community have a more powerful network that is inaccessible to the general public? Will the existing Internet become primarily a marketing and advertising medium? How could the privatization of the most current research results affect individuals' personal and work lives?

Team Challenge: Research the thinking of Internet experts and social philosophers on the issues identified above. Develop a position paper that presents your group's findings and its stand, or position, on the issues related to separate global networks.

The following search terms may help you find appropriate background information:
"Internet 2"   "separate Internets"   "equal Internet access"

Answers to Configuring Knowledge Questions

Multiple Choice: 1 – b; 2 – e; 3 – b; 4 – d; 5 – a; 6 – c; 7 – e; 8 – a; 9 – b; 10 – e; 11 – d; 12 – a; 13 – c; 14 – b, 15 – e; 16 – c; 17 – b; 18 – d; 19 – a; 20 – e

True-False: 1 – F; 2 – T; 3 – F; 4 – T; 5 – T; 6 – F; 7 – T; 8 – F; 9 – F; 10 – T; 11 – T; 12 – T; 13 – F; 14 – T, 15 – F; 16 – F; 17 – T; 18 – F; 19 – T; 20 – T

Glossary

access controls (p. 125) Systems such as passwords and eye, finger, or hand scanners that can be programmed into a computer to guard against unauthorized use.

alignment (p. 87) The position of text on a page, either side-to-side or top-to-bottom.

alphanumeric (p. 89) Entries into computer programs that include all keyboard characters, including text or numbers, that are not to be used for calculation.

American Standard Code for Information Interchange (ASCII) (p. 31) A standard code used internally to represent the entire standard keyboard's characters with a binary equivalence.

analog waves (p. 35) Sounds in nature that are made up of vibrations oscillating at different rates for high or low pitches; they must be converted into digital information to be stored in a computer.

animated GIF (p. 148) A popular form of animation that combines several images into a single file to simulate movement.

animation (p. 38) A succession of still images that are shown rapidly to simulate moving action.

anonymous FTP site (p. 155) A network server that permits access to its files by anyone through the use of a generic password prompt, the word *anonymous*.

applets (p. 73) Small application programs designed to do specific jobs, originally developed in Java programming language, that can be run on any computer platform.

application (p. 12) Software that performs a particular kind of function, such as a word processor.

application service provider (ASP) (p. 102) Firm that makes software available for rental or lease over the Internet.

applications software (p. 84) Computer programs for carrying out specific functions not related to the operation of the computer itself.

arithmetic logic unit (ALU) (p. 39) The component of the CPU where all mathematical and logical operations are performed.

ARPANET (p. 140) The Internet traces its origin to this Cold War-era technology project that was initiated by the Pentagon's Advanced Research Projects Agency (ARPA).

article (p. 154) A question or comment posted by a member of a newsgroup.

artificial intelligence (p. 12) The field of study within cognitive science that involves modeling intelligent or learning behaviors on computers.

asymmetric digital subscriber line (ADSL) (p. 119) A high-speed data transfer line that supports a faster speed when downloading or receiving data than when uploading or sending data.

asynchronous transfer mode (ATM) (p. 129) A data transfer method that can carry voice, data, multimedia, and motion video at very high speeds.

asynchronous transmission (p. 122) A technique in communications that permits the data to flow at any time from either end of the line.

attractor (p. 148) An attention-gathering device in a Web site, such as games, chat rooms, or information not readily available elsewhere, designed to draw return visits; also known as a hook.

AU (p. 148) One of the types of audio storage file format used on the Internet.

audio conferencing (p. 149) The use of streaming audio to create a real-time communication network link between multiple participants in remote locations, using their computer's microphones and speakers.

audit-control software (p. 127) A form of security protection that keeps a running log of all computer transactions and provides periodic reports that can be analyzed for unusual activity.

authentication (p. 125) A step in computer security that ascertains if the user making an access request is actually authorized to do so.

backbone (p. 141) The high-speed data connections that provide the primary connections to the Internet.

backed up (p. 127) The act of making duplicate copies of data files at regular intervals as a protection against loss.

bandwidth (p. 115) A measure of the number of bits of data that can be transferred in a given second over a medium in a network.

barcode readers (p. 36) Scanning devices that use light reflectivity to sense patterns of lines that represent data and can be digitally stored.

base-10 (p. 30) A counting system made of ten elements, 0 through 9, also known as the decimal system.

base-2 (p. 30) A counting system made of two elements, 0 and 1, also known as the binary number system.

binary code (p. 30) A system of numbers comprised solely of the symbols 0 and 1.

binary digit (p. 31) A single piece of data, which can be either a 1 or a 0, is referred to as a *bi*nary digi*t*, or bit.

binary number system (p. 30) A number system containing only two digits, 0 and 1. A person counts from 0 to 1 and then, to represent the number 2, carries a 1 to the two's place and writes a 0 in the one's place: 0, 1, 10, 11 (0, 1, 2, 3 in decimal).

binary numbers (p. 30) A numbering system constructed solely of the symbols 0 and 1.

biometric scanning device (p. 127) Access control hardware designed to recognize a characteristic of an authorized human user, such as the eye, finger, or thumbprint.

bit (p. 31) A single piece of data, which can be either a 1 or a 0, is referred to as a *bi*nary digi*t*, or bit.

BitMap (BMP) (p. 96) A commonly used standard graphics file format.

bitmap- or raster image-based graphics (p. 95) A common graphics storage format that represents pictures by changing the individual pixels that comprise the image.

bits per second (bps) (p. 115) Unit of measurement of the speed of digital data transmission.

Bluetooth (p. 129) A new radio frequency specification that will let portable devices communicate with each other by way of an embedded transceiver.

boilerplate (p. 97) A component of a software program that includes standardized specifications for recurring elements.

booting (p. 60) The step of starting a computer when the operating system is loaded and other initialization steps make the computer ready for use.

bridge (p. 123) The device that permits the connection of computers into a larger network where the protocols for each of the local networks are the same.

broadband (p. 115) A high-bandwidth network pipeline that is sufficient to carry extremely large data transmissions.

browser (p. 113) Software used to view hypertext documents on the World Wide Web.

bus (p. 38) One of a number of electronic pathways through which signals travel inside a computer, allowing communication among the various components of a system.

byte (p. 31) An eight-digit binary number that can be used to represent any one of 256 separate symbols or characters.

cable access television (CATV) (p. 115) The companies that provide traditional cable television services into homes and other subscribers.

cable modem (p. 115) A device that makes possible the connection to coaxial cable media in order to access high-speed Internet services.

cache (p. 42) A chip memory holding area in which the data and instructions most recently called from RAM by the processor are temporarily stored for possible repeated use.

CAD/CAM applications (p. 14) Computer-aided drafting and computer-aided manufacturing systems that enable manufacturing companies to design and change products without having to redo drawings or old models.

callback system (p. 128) A security system for remote computer access in which a user dials into the system and is identified, whereupon the computer hangs up and dials back a previously provided phone number that is known to belong to the authorized user.

carpal-tunnel syndrome (p. 51) A medical condition or repetitive-stress injury that causes pain and numbness in the hands and lower arms.

cathode ray tube (CRT) (p. 45) A typical computer monitor that uses a large glass tube onto which the output is projected.

CD-ROM (p. 49) Compact disk method of data storage with read-only memory.

CD-RW (p. 49) Compact disk method of data storage with capacity to record, be erased, and then reused.

CD-WORM (p. 49) Compact disk method of data storage with capacity to record once and thereafter become read-only.

cell (p. 89) The element that makes up the rows and columns of a spreadsheet.

cell address (p. 89) The location of a cell in a spreadsheet, consisting of a letter designating the column and a number designating the row occupied by the data.

central processing unit (CPU) (p. 28) The part of the computer that transforms the data; the microprocessor or "brain" of the system.

chart (p. 88) Results of calculations or data in a spreadsheet that can be presented as a pictorial graphic.

chat client (p. 153) A software program used by participants who type their messages alternately in order to post them to a location where their comments are shared.

chat room (p. 153) An Internet site in which users participate in conversations with people from anywhere in the world in real time.

chat server (p. 153) The computer that is the host system in a chat communication session between participants.

cladding (p. 116) A wrapping and insulating material used in the manufacture of fiber-optic cable.

client (p. 113) A single computer or node of a network that is served by one or more servers that control all of the major functions of that network.

client-server network (p. 113) A network of computers in which one or more clients are provided data and remote connections through one or more server systems.

coaxial cable (p. 116) A communication medium commonly used for cable television connections, in telephone networks, and in some computer networks.

command (p. 63) A string of abbreviated codes that tell a computer what to do.

command-line interface (p. 63) Environment of early personal computer operating systems in which the user would key a command as an instruction to perform a desired activity.

communications channel (p. 112) The communication linkage in a network made up of the hardware, software, and connecting media needed to effect transfers between individual computers.

communications port (COM) (p. 43) A computer connection that typically transmits one bit of data at a time.

communications software (p. 123) The software in a networked computer that manages the transmission of all data and information that flows between the linked computers.

compatible (p. 38) A condition that is met when all of a computer's components, such as the system board with its CPU and memory, and additional peripheral devices for input, output, and storage, are designed to interact correctly and efficiently with one another.

complex instruction source code, more commonly known as **complex instruction set computer (CISC)** (p. 40) Traditional programming method for computer processors that includes several different machine language instructions.

compression (p. 148) The process of reducing a file into a more manageable size for storage or transfer purposes.

computer literate (p. 4) The ability to understand fundamental computer concepts, operate a personal computer, and navigate the Internet.

computer virus (p. 124) Small program with a buried code that is sent to computers with the intent to do damage to hardware or software.

computer-aided design (CAD) (p. 14) Sophisticated computer system used to design and test products before manufacturing.

computer-aided manufacturing (CAM) (p. 14) Computer system that enables manufacturing companies to control and change production processes to meet design specifications.

continuous waves (p. 35) Sounds in nature made up of vibrations that oscillate at different rates for high or low pitches.

control systems (p. 14) Mechanical, arithmetic, or computerized regulating devices that are used to ascertain if systems are functioning as anticipated by managers.

control unit (p. 39) A part of the central processing unit in a computer that coordinates all of the functions and activities of the system.

convergence (p. 6) The recent trend toward merging of the data, entertainment, and communications industries.

copyrighting (p. 84) The act of documenting through the U.S. Copyright Office the originality of a written or artistic effort. Commercial software is copyrighted to reduce the likelihood of illegal copying and to provide a legal basis for enforcement.

country code (p. 144) A part of the domain name used in Internet transfers that carries specific identifiers for international locations.

cursor (p. 33) A symbol, usually blinking, that appears on a monitor to show where in a document the next keystroke or change will appear.

cursor keys (p. 33) Directional arrow keys that allow the user to change the location of the cursor.

customer management software (p. 102) A type of software that helps retailers and manufacturers learn exactly what their customers want and will purchase even before the products exist.

data (p. 10) The basic element that can be captured and organized into useful information.

data compression (p. 38) The process of shrinking the size of binary data files for long-term storage or transfer.

data mining (p. 92) The examination of current or warehoused data to discover potentially useful new information.

data processing (p. 28) The process of collecting basic data and converting it into useful information upon which decision makers can act.

data warehousing (p. 92) The process of storing data files for future examination for reasons unrelated to their original creation.

database management systems (DBMS) (p. 91) Software programs that efficiently store, organize, and manipulate large amounts of information.

databases (p. 13) Software used for storing and manipulating large amounts of information.

Datacenter Server (p. 69) The most advanced version of the Microsoft Windows 2000 operating system.

decision support systems (DSS) (p. 82) An arrangement of hardware and software that models the reality of a problem to assist a manager in making decisions.

decrypt (p. 126) To decode data that has been put into an indecipherable format as a security measure during transfers.

demodulation (p. 115) The act of translating analog signals from a communication line into digital signals that a computer can process.

desktop (p. 33) The basic workspace screen of the Microsoft Windows and the Macintosh environments, a place where the user can click icons or buttons to execute a command, drag items to other locations, and call up menus of options.

desktop publishing programs (p. 13) A type of software for composing, designing, and printing professional-level documents; page layouts can include graphic items that come from external sources.

dialog boxes (p. 65) A type of window used in applications software to give users various options in completing the desired tasks.

digital storage (p. 35) The capacity to store binary data for future applications or usage.

digital subscriber line (DSL) (p. 119) Broadband communication line that operates economically by using existing copper wire connections.

digital video disk, recently changed to **digital versatile disk (DVD)** (p. 49) A format for arranging and saving digital data onto a CD-sized optical disk to provide a much higher capacity than the standard CD.

digital video recording (p. 98) Multimedia presentation format that permits the mixing of multiple images and other objects that are then stored in binary form.

digitized photograph (p. 96) A photograph that has been stored as a raster image, or collection of black, white, or colored pixels.

digitizing pen (p. 34) A type of tactile input device used for creating images that are transferred digitally to a computer, thus giving greater control to engineers and artists who need to simulate precise drawing on paper.

direct access (p. 48) The dominant form of data storage today; information on disks or chips is accessible to the CPU almost immediately, no matter the order in which it was recorded.

directory (p. 60) A file management organization tool, listing names and locations of files, that permits the user to access programs and documents quickly.

documentation (p. 84) Instructions and guidance for software installation and use; sometimes available in printed form, but today more commonly built into the program itself.

domain name (p. 143) Easy-to-remember text name used to replace the numeric Internet address.

domain name system (DNS) (p. 144) Storage location of all domain names and their associated numeric addresses on Internet computers.

domain name system server (DNS server) (p. 144) Server that translates a domain name into its numeric IP address for routing to the chosen site.

domain suffix (p. 143) An abbreviation that indicates the type of organization that is operating a Web site. See table 6-2 (p. 144) for examples.

dot matrix (p. 46) A printing technique that arranges dots to create letters and numbers, similar to the arrangement of light bulbs that show numbers on a scoreboard at an athletic event.

dot pitch (p. 45) The space between the pixels of which an image is composed that measure the resolution or image quality of a monitor.

double (or dual) in-line memory module (DIMM) (p. 41) RAM chips that are mounted in double rows onto small boards that snap into place on the motherboard.

drawing tablet (p. 34) Paper pad used as the medium for providing digital graphical input for which engineers and artists need to simulate precise drawing on paper.

dumb terminal (p. 10) A keyboard or keyboard and display that have no CPU but are connected to a mainframe or other computer and used, generally, to input raw information.

DVD-RAM (p. 49) A high-capacity optical storage medium that includes both recording and playback capability.

DVD-ROM (p. 49) A high-capacity optical storage medium that includes playback capability only.

e-commerce (p. 15) Business conducted on the Internet either between firms or directly with customers through Web sites.

electronic mail (e-mail) (p. 13) Capability of networked computers with appropriate software to send and receive messages.

e-mail address (p. 152) A user's identification for sending and receiving electronic mail, made up of the user's name and a domain name that identifies each distinct mailbox.

embedded computer (p. 16) Computer that performs its work behind the scenes to automate tasks without special human training or intervention.

emoticons (p. 151) A word derived from "emotion" and "icon"; denotes a keyboard entry shortcut that conveys common emotions or feelings.

Encapsulated PostScript (EPS) (p. 96) A commonly used standard graphics file format.

encryption (p. 125) A process that converts data into an indecipherable code to protect sensitive information during transfer.

encryption key (p. 126) The key or code that allows the user at the receiving end of an encrypted data transfer to decrypt the message.

erasable programmable read only memory (EPROM) (p. 42) A type of specialized memory ROM chip that is reprogrammable.

ergomatics (p. 51) The broad study of the issues of physical harm that can come to users from extended computer use, such as radiation and repetitive stress injury.

ergonomics (p. 51) The science of examining the design of a work environment to improve workers' safety and health, and thus their productivity.

Ethernet (p. 122) A simple local area network form that uses linear bus topology and a wide variety of media.

Ethernet network (p. 122) A network using Ethernet, the most widely used network protocol, which is a simple LAN form employing linear bus topology.

expansion card (p. 43) Any type of circuit board that plugs into one of a number of empty locations in a computer to add various capabilities to the system.

expansion slot (p. 43) An empty location in a computer into which additional circuit boards can be inserted to add various capabilities to the system.

exporting (p. 95) The act of transferring a data or graphic file to another location or computer.

extension (p. 64) The part of a file name following the period (.), used to identify the type of file.

extranet (p. 112) A network that connects an entity to one or more private external networks.

fax modem (p. 115) The circuit board that enables users to gain remote access to other computers, to transfer files, and to send e-mail, and also has the capability to send and receive faxes.

feedback (p. 28) The capacity of a system to allow users to compare results received with the results expected, for the purpose of effecting a change.

fiber-optic cable (p. 116) A communications medium made from a string of glass or high-quality plastic, used to transmit beams of light carrying data.

field (p. 91) A column in a database table.

file compression (p. 148) The process of reducing a file into a more manageable size for storage or transfer purposes.

file name (p. 64) The title by which a file is known.

file server (p. 113) A computer in a network that has the responsibility to provide storage, routing, or connectivity to subordinate machines in the system.

File Transfer Protocol (FTP) (p. 155) A common way to transfer files over the Internet.

filtering software (p. 155) Software designed to stop most objectionable content on the Internet from being displayed on a browser.

finance (p. 13) The area of business that use computers to maintain a company's accounting records, generate its financial statements and reports, and aid in the analysis of their quality.

firewall (p. 126) Hardware and software designed to limit access to computer systems and data.

flaming (p. 151) The act of posting insulting or abusive attacks on others through Internet connections.

flash memory (p. 42) Chips whose memory content can be changed by the user but which continue to hold their data even without the use of electricity.

flat panel LCD (p. 46) A form of computer monitor that features a flat panel architecture, does not require a large glass tube for display, and requires less desktop space than a conventional monitor.

flexible work schedule (p. 16) A work schedule whose hours and times may be changed to accommodate the time and availability of the worker and the needs of the workplace.

floppy diskette (p. 48) A magnetic disk used for data storage that is direct-access and therefore accessible to the CPU almost immediately.

folders (p. 60) Subsidiary elements in a computer's directory that permit the user to access programs and documents quickly.

font (p. 87) A collection of keyboard characters and symbols in a consistent style.

footers (p. 87) Documentation or other information that is to be printed at the bottom of each page of a document.

freeware (p. 99) Software that can be copied and distributed with no payment to its author, though the author retains the copyright and the program may not be altered or sold without permission.

FTP program (p. 155) A program that is required in order to upload files to and download files from a remote FTP (File Transfer Protocol) site.

FTP server (p. 155) A computer on a network that facilitates upload and download file transfers between remote sites.

FTP sites (p. 155) Sites on a network that permit the uploading and/or downloading of files from remote locations.

full-duplex transmission (p. 122) Communications channel in which the data flows in both directions concurrently.

function keys (p. 33) Specialized keys on a keyboard that allow the user to issue commands by pressing a single key; for example, those labeled F1, F2, F3, and so on.

functions (p. 89) Programmed capabilities included in a software package to ease the performance of complex actions or calculations, such as mathematical, statistical, or financial measures.

gateway (p. 123) The device that connects computer networks when the protocols for the LANs are different.

geosynchronous communications satellite (p. 118) A satellite for transmitting data that orbits the earth at the equator at an altitude and speed that allow it to remain in a constant position relative to the earth.

gigabyte (p. 32) A measure of data volume: 1,024,000,000 bytes or about 1,000 MB.

graphical user interface (GUI) (p. 33) The technique through which the user can click icons or buttons to execute a command, drag items on the screen to other locations, and pull down menus of options.

Graphics Interchange Format (GIF) (p. 148) A format for file compression whose software is patented and requires the purchase of a license for its use.

graphics programs (p. 13) Software for producing drawings and other types of illustrations.

groupware (p. 13) A collaborative form of software that allows multiple participants to use standard Internet communication techniques to work on the same project simultaneously, no matter where they are located.

half-duplex transmission (p. 122) A form of communications transfer in which the data flows in one direction at a time, so the users must alternate in their usage in order for the data to flow in both directions.

handheld PC (HPCs) (p. 70) Small, dedicated systems such as personal digital assistants that use the Windows CE operating system.

hard copy (p. 44) A permanent printed version of information contained on a computer.

hard disk drive (p. 48) A magnetic disk or pack of disks used for data storage on which the information is available via direct access, and therefore accessible to the CPU almost immediately.

hardware (p. 12) The tangible machinery that is used to create computer systems.

headers (p. 87) Documentation or other information that is to be printed at the top of each page of a document.

helper application (p. 147) A small program that enhances the capabilities of a computer's browser software.

hertz (Hz) (p. 115) A time measurement used in computer analog transfers measured in the number of machine cycles per second.

home page (p. 145) The first page that appears when accessing a Web site.

hook (p. 148) An attention-gathering device designed to draw return visits to a Web site, e.g., games, chat rooms, or information not readily available elsewhere (also known as an attractor).

host computer (p. 141) A computer that provides networking or data services to subordinate computers to which it is connected.

HTML 4 (p. 159) Version 4 of Hypertext Mark-up Language, the programming language that supports the World Wide Web.

https:// (p. 157) The prefix that identifies a secure Web site, as opposed to the traditional nonsecure site prefix http://. The "s" in the protocol instruction stands for "secure server" for data transmission.

hub (p. 122) A device that serves as the location where the individual connections to a group of computers are centralized for further routing and for sharing of information (also known as a concentrator).

human resources (p. 14) The area of any enterprise that identifies job candidates, develops wage scales and benefit plans, keeps employee records, creates training materials, and monitors hiring and promotion data for compliance with fair employment laws.

hyperlink (p. 144) Link in a Web document that enables immediate jumping to other pages or Web sites with the simple click of a mouse.

hypertext documents (p. 113) Documents written in the code language HTML, used on the World Wide Web and viewed with browser software.

Hypertext Markup Language (HTML) (p. 85) The programming language used to create documents that make up the World Wide Web.

Hypertext Transfer Protocol (HTTP) (p. 144) The set of data creation and transfer instructions used to support the World Wide Web.

icons (p. 33) Thumbnail pictures on a graphical user interface, representing familiar objects such as a trash can, a file folder, or a printer, used to direct computer actions to particular files or operations.

identification (p. 125) A part of a computer's security system that can be programmed to guard against unauthorized use.

impact printer (p. 46) A type of printer that prints by making contact with the paper through a carbon source, somewhat like a typewriter.

importing (p. 95) The act of receiving a transfer of a data or graphic file from another location or computer.

information (p. 28) The end product of the data that is collected, processed, delivered, and stored by a computer system.

information age (p. 4) Our current time period, when work is dominated by the manipulation, analysis, and dissemination of information via computers.

information systems (IS) (p. 28) The process through which data is collected, processed, delivered, or stored.

information systems theory (p. 28) The study of how components in a system interact to create information from basic data.

infrared (IR) (p. 118) A format for wireless transmission over short distances, accomplished by using technologies that carry digital signals on light waves beyond the visible spectrum in line-of-sight applications.

ink-jet printer (p. 46) A type of printer that sprays ink in tiny dot form to create text and graphics equally well in black and white and in color.

inputting (p. 28) The process of capturing data and entering it into a computer for further processing into useful information.

Integrated Services Digital Network (ISDN) (p. 117) A high-speed communication line specially installed by a telephone company, for which a user pays a monthly usage fee.

intelligent agents (bots) (p. 102) Small programs that can be sent on Internet searches to locate desired information and then deliver it to the user on demand or on a schedule.

interface (p. 63) An environment displayed on a monitor with which the user interacts when working on a computer.

Internet (p. 4) The network of linked computers that has created a worldwide electronic community for communications, research, commerce, and entertainment.

Internet service provider (ISP) (p. 68) An organization that provides connective service to the Internet and access to communications software, usually for a fee.

Internet telephone service (p. 149) Internet communications that allow participants in remote locations to converse just as if on a telephone, using microphones connected to their computers' soundboards.

Internet2 (I2) (p. 158) An extremely high-speed private network that was launched in 1998 for research purposes only.

intranet (p. 112) A network that is used within a single organization.

IP address (p. 143) The identifying number that is assigned to every computer network on the Internet.

JavaOS (p. 73) A multiplatform operating system growing in popularity among technically competent users.

Joint Photographic Experts Group (JPEG) (p. 96) A format for saving and transferring graphic files that compresses the data; created by a group within the International Standards Organization.

joystick (p. 8) A computer input device used to direct the mouse pointer or software actions, especially when playing computer games.

just-in-time inventory (p. 14) Efficient method of automating the purchase and delivery of raw materials, ensuring their delivery to assembly lines exactly when needed.

kerning (p. 87) The space between letters in a word or sentence.

keyboard (p. 28) A tactile input device used to enter text, numbers, and symbols into software applications on a computer.

kilobyte (p. 32) A measure of data volume: 1,024 bytes or 2^{10}.

knowledge worker (p. 4) One whose work consists of the manipulation, analysis, and dissemination of information.

laptop or notebook computer (p. 11) A computer that is small and light enough to be placed on a lap or carried by its user from place to place; usually powered by batteries.

laser printer (p. 46) A printer that uses technology similar to a photocopier wherein a laser beam creates points of electrical charge on a cylindrical drum and toner, composed of particles of ink with an opposite electrical charge, sticks to the charged points on the drum to create an image.

leading (p. 87) The space between lines on a page.

licensing agreement (p. 84) The terms to which you consent for the right to use a software program.

limited warranty (p. 84) As applied to most software sales, manufacturer's guarantee of replacing a defective disk or CD-ROM for a specific period of time while disclaiming any responsibility for lost data.

line printer (p. 46) A type of impact printer that prints a complete line of output at a time by making contact with the paper through a carbon source.

linear bus network (p. 119) A network that connects all of its parts to a single primary cable connection.

Linux (p. 72) A variant of the UNIX operating system; considered an open-source program, in that the internal programming instructions are available freely via the Internet so that anyone can add to, or improve, it.

liquid crystal display (LCD) (p. 45) A type of visual display, made up of chemicals responding to polarized light, widely used in digital watches, calculators, and laptop computers.

Listserv (p. 153) A popular early software application used to maintain mailing lists.

local area network (LAN) (p. 112) The kind of network used to connect computers within an office, building, or other relatively small geographic area, permitting the sharing of programs and data as though they were on the same system.

Macintosh OS 8 (p. 71) The operating system for the Apple Macintosh, released in 1997, that added improved multitasking abilities, enhanced multimedia support, and numerous interface enhancements.

Macintosh OS X (p. 71) Operating system software (Beta version released in September 2000) that has a new interface called Aqua and is based on the Unix operating system, making it likely to be highly stable.

magnetic disk (p. 48) The direct access technology for data storage that makes content accessible to the central processing unit (CPU) almost immediately.

magnetic ink character reader (MICR) (p. 36) The device that can read and process at high speed somewhat strangely shaped numbers printed with magnetic ink, as on the bottom of a cancelled check.

magnetic storage device (p. 47) Data storage hardware that works by applying electrical charges to iron fillings on magnetic media, orienting each filing in one direction or another to represent a 0 or a 1.

magnetic tape (p. 48) A type of data storage that uses continuous tape to store content; inexpensive but slow because the tape may require unwinding to find the storage location of particular data.

mail merge (p. 92) A feature in word processors that collects personal data from one file, layout information from another, and then combines them in a third, merged document to create labels and form letters.

mail server (p. 152) A server computer that makes a connection to the Internet for e-mail.

mailbox (p. 152) The repository for all newly received messages on a server computer that makes a connection to the Internet for e-mail.

mailing list (p. 153) An extension of e-mail that makes possible the sending of messages to multiple receivers with a single command.

mainframe (p. 10) A very large-capacity computer, typically used in a large organization to handle high-volume processing.

management (p. 15) The gathering, allocation, and direction of human, financial, and material resources to achieve an organization's objectives.

management information systems (MIS) (p. 88) The use of computer-based models that provide a flow of information from everyday actions to assist decision makers in carrying out their tasks.

manufacturing (p. 14) The act of designing and producing products.

marketing and sales (p. 14) The process of creating opportunities for selling the output of a firm.

megabyte (p. 32) A measure of data volume: 1,024,000 bytes, or about one million bytes.

megahertz (MHz) (p. 40) The unit of measurement of the speed of a computer's internal clock, determined by the number of electric pulses it creates reported in units of millions of cycles per second.

memory (p. 28) Chip storage area used by the CPU as workspace while it transforms data.

message board (discussion board) (p. 154) A Web-based form of message content posting that does not require the use of a newsreader helper program.

metadata (p. 159) A technique to place into Web pages data that would vastly improve the efficiency of automatic indexing of Net contents.

Metcalfe's law (p. 123) The value of a network increases exponentially with the number of users (and machines) connected to it.

microform (p. 47) Space reduction form of photographic storage of data output in microfilm roll or small sheets.

Microsoft Windows (p. 65) The Microsoft operating system with a graphical user interface that is used on the majority of desktop and laptop computers today.

microtechnology (p. 19) The research into the tiniest designs of computers and robotic machines, with sizes approaching a millionth of a meter.

microwave (p. 118) Comparatively short electromagnetic transmission signal, broadcast by earth-based towers to receiver locations.

minicomputer (mini) (p. 10) A midsize computer used, typically, in universities, research labs, and smaller corporations.

modem (p. 115) A device that converts the digital output signals of a computer into analog signals to be sent by telephone or other communication lines.

moderator (p. 154) A person in some newsgroups who first examines each article for its appropriateness to the discussion before it is posted for the general public.

modifier keys (p. 33) Keyboard keys that enable the user to change the symbol or character that is entered when they are pressed; e.g., the *shift* key makes a letter uppercase.

modulation (p. 115) A process that converts the digital output signals of a computer into analog signals that can be sent by telephone lines.

monitor (p. 44) A device that receives output from a computer and displays it visually.

Mosaic (p. 146) The first graphical Internet browser that gained wide distribution; developed at the National Center for Supercomputing Applications (NCSA).

motherboard (system board) (p. 38) The main circuit board in the computer, consisting of a collection of electrical pathways and connected chips.

Motion Picture Experts Group (MPEG) (p. 149) A compression standard created by a professional organization, widely used for Internet video transfers.

mouse (p. 33) A device that moves the cursor on the computer screen to correspond to directional movements; also contains switches for activating commands.

MP3 (p. 99) A data-compression standard for music file creation.

MS-DOS (p. 620) Microsoft operating system for the earliest IBM and compatible personal computers.

multimedia (p. 47) Applications that can mix sound and motion video to produce stimulating presentations.

multimedia authoring software (p. 47) Software used to create multimedia applications.

multiplatform (p. 71) The capacity of a software product to be used on computers with different operating systems.

multiplexing (p. 119) The communications capability to support numerous signals over a single carrier.

multitasking (p. 61) A feature of operating systems that enables a user to have multiple software programs running concurrently.

multiuser OS (p. 66) An operating system that provides the capability to permit effective time-sharing, or simultaneous access by many users.

musical instrument digital interface (MIDI) (p. 98) A standard connection through which musical instruments such as keyboards can be attached to computers.

National Science Foundation (NSF) (p. 141) U.S. government-supported agency that fosters scientific research.

native format (p. 95) Instructions that enable users to save files so they can be read by the application in which they were created.

.Net (p. 159) An initiative currently being developed by Microsoft that links Web sites automatically, allowing users to organize every aspect of their lives.

network (p. 11) A system of computers interconnected so they can share data and programs.

network computer (NC) (p. 11) A computer that accesses programs and data over a network but, like a personal computer, has processing capabilities of its own.

network interface card (NIC) (p. 115) A circuit board that is placed into an expansion slot within the CPU case to provide a port to which the network cabling can be attached.

network operating system (NOS) (p. 124) The software that takes overall responsibility for how the network communicates and performs all of the administrative and file management activities necessary to coordinate the individual computers or nodes that are connected.

network topology or architecture (p. 119) The physical arrangement of the computers that are connected in a network.

networked economy (p. 4) The series of linked computers that have redefined the worlds of business, education, and entertainment.

newbies (p. 145) A term used to refer to new users of the World Wide Web.

news server (p. 154) A computer that permits news postings, often provided by businesses, educational institutions, ISPs, or other organizations.

newsgroup (p. 154) A message-posting system used for the exchange of communication among users who may not be online at the same time, usually devoted to a specific topic.

newsreader (p. 154) Software that is required for participation in a newsgroup, a feature found in most Web browsers.

Next Generation Internet (NGI) (p. 158) A U.S. government-sponsored initiative designed to bring the technological promise of Internet 2 to the general public.

NeXT Step (p. 72) The operating system created by NeXT for use on the company's RISC-based computers, based on UNIX; NeXT Step provides a superb graphical user interface.

node (p. 113) A site on a network.

NSFnet (p. 141) The network of supercomputers created by the National Science Foundation that provided a high-speed communications backbone for the modern Internet.

object- or vector-based graphics (p. 95) Computer graphic images made by creating, editing, and combining mathematically defined geometric shapes.

online (p. 17) Performing tasks of work, communications, commerce, or entertainment while connected to a network.

online searches (p. 145) Research conducted by programs called search engines, which find information based on key words typed into a query box.

online service (p. 142) An organization that provides connective access to the Internet and to communications software, usually for a fee.

open architecture (p. 158) The traditional structure of the Internet that allows free-range access to users.

operating system (OS) (p. 60) The software that includes the step-by-step instructions that control all of the functions necessary for a computer to carry out its tasks.

optical character recognition (OCR) (p. 5) The process by which computer software is used to translate hard-copy text into a computer-readable file.

optical mark recognition (OMR) (p. 36) A scanning system that uses light reflectivity to sense the presence or absence of a mark; a binary condition that can be digitally stored.

optical network (p. 129) All-digital fiber-optic network that will result in communication channels with incredible speed and superior accuracy.

optical storage device (p. 48) Storage medium that operates by directing a laser light onto the surface of the disk and then back to an opto-electronic device that detects changes in light.

optical storage media (p. 49) The discs and cartridges that hold the data read by optical storage devices.

outputting (p. 28) The process of making available the information created from the capture of data and subsequent processing by the computer.

packet switching (p. 143) The actions of routers along the Internet that determine the fastest available pathway for a message to reach the desired recipient.

packets (p. 122) The small sections into which a message is broken in order to facilitate efficient transfers of data.

page layout program (p. 97) An application program used to combine text and graphics and to design and lay out pages for publication.

palmtop computer (p. 11) A computer that is small enough to fit into a pocket.

parallel port (p. 43) A connection on a computer that transmits multiple bits of data concurrently.

password (p. 125) A secret code, usually containing both numbers and text, that allows a user access to something, such as a file, a secure network site, or an online service.

pathname (p. 63) A command that specifies the route to a document's location on a storage medium.

PC card (p. 43) A type of credit card-sized expansion card used in portable computers as adapters to connect networks, telephone connectors, auxiliary storage, or other peripheral devices.

PC-DOS (p. 62) IBM's version of the disk operating system used with its earliest personal computers.

PCMCIA card (p. 43) A type of expansion card widely used in portable computers to connect to networks, telephone connectors, auxiliary storage, or other peripheral devices.

PDF (Portable Document File) (p. 97) A format for file creation and transfer that enables a document to appear identical on any computer, no matter what platform is being used; viewable with Adobe Acrobat software.

peer (p. 113) A member of a workgroup with whom resources are to be shared.

peer-to-peer network (p. 113) A form of network in which the controls and the program software must be installed on all the linked computers, but any shared peripheral devices need to be connected to only one location.

peripheral output devices (p. 44) External devices, such as a monitor or printer, that are used to receive output from a computer.

personal communications services (PCS) (p. 118) Devices, such as the Palm Pilot, that are capable of a wide range of communications, including Internet connections, e-mail, voice mail, and cellular phone transmission.

personal computer (PC) (p. 11) A desktop computer that has the capability to run programming applications to solve a wide variety of problems.

personal digital assist (PDA) (p. 11) A palm-sized computer specialized to store telephone numbers, calendars, schedules, and other personal information; some offer fax, e-mail, and Internet capabilities.

personal information manager (PIM) (p. 94) Software program that offers the same calendar and address book functions that one might find in a pocket calendar.

personal productivity program (p. 13) A type of software used for scheduling and project-planning tasks.

photons (p. 116) Beams of light, such as those transmitted over fiber-optic cables.

pixel (p. 44) The tiny picture element that creates the display seen on a computer monitor's screen.

Plain Old Telephone Service (POTS) (p. 117) The traditional wire-based telephone system used throughout the world.

platform (p. 60) A hardware or software standard that serves as the basis for computer operation; the two popular hardware platforms for personal computers are PCs and Macintoshes; the software platform is determined by the operating system used by the computer.

platform-independent software (p. 101) Software that can be run on any kind of computer at any time, used for documents that can be read on any platform.

plotter (p. 46) A computer output device that uses ink to draw designs, diagrams, maps, and blueprints, and prints them onto large format paper.

plugged in (p. 5) To be a computer user or connected to the Internet.

plug-in application (p. 147) A small program that enhances the capabilities of a computer's browser software.

point of presence (POP) (p. 142) A local telephone number provided by Internet service providers that offer dial-up service.

point of sale terminal (POS) (p. 36) Computer terminal that serves as a cash register as well as a data collection device.

point-to-point protocol (PPP) (p. 142) One protocol used by Internet service providers for dial-up connections.

POP (Post Office Protocol) server (p. 153) A server computer that uses a standard set of instructions or protocol for the handling of e-mail accounts.

POP3 server (p. 153) An e-mail server using version 3, the newest version of POP protocol software.

port (p. 43) A connector, generally found on the back of a personal computer, that allows a user to attach peripheral devices.

Portable Network Graphics (PNG) (p. 148) A graphics file format that does not require a license, designed to be a GIF replacement graphics standard.

presentation software (p. 93) An application program that allows a user to create presentations that combine text, numbers, graphics, sounds, and movies.

printers (p. 46) Computer output devices that provide hard copy, a permanent record of a computer's output.

processing (p. 28) The organization and manipulation of data into useful information by a computer.

processor (p. 10) The brain of the computer, the part that actually carries out the instructions fed into the machine.

productivity (p. 6) The measure of output per unit of input.

programs (p. 61) Sets of instructions for manipulating data to be executed by a computer.

project management software (p. 93) Application that enables users to collaboratively plan and track projects and deliver the results in any format that the business needs.

protocol (p. 121) A standard set of rules and settings for computers, peripherals, and communications devices that enables them to perform specific functions.

pull medium (p. 159) An Internet linkage in which specific connections to information on host computers are instigated by users.

pull-down menus (p. 65) Menus in software applications that open downward and enable the user to carry out functions by clicking the alternative choices provided.

push medium (p. 159) An Internet connection in which a user interested in information on some topic requests that such information be automatically sent to his or her e-mail address.

QBE (p. 92) A method for making an inquiry of a database by giving an example to be replicated.

query (p. 92) Search of a database for records that meet certain criteria.

QWERTY (p. 32) A name for a standard typewriter keyboard, so named for the first six keys at the left of the first row of letters.

radio frequencies (RF) (p. 117) Electromagnetic wave frequencies, assigned by the Federal Communications Commission (FCC), used for several kinds of wireless communication.

random access memory (RAM) (p. 41) The primary memory of a computer, consisting of chips that can be accessed and changed directly at any time but require a power source to maintain the data's integrity.

read only memory (ROM) (p. 42) A type of computer memory that is permanent, programmed into the chip by the manufacturer, and cannot be changed or erased by the user.

RealAudio (p. 149) A widely used format for streaming continuous audio over the Internet.

RealPlayer (p. 149) A software application that includes streaming video and audio over the Internet.

RealVideo (p. 149) A widely used format for streaming continuous video over the Internet.

record (p. 91) A row in a database table.

reduced instruction source code, more commonly known as **reduced instruction set computer (RISC)** (p. 40) Simplified programming method for computer processors that can be executed quickly because there are fewer instructions from which to choose.

relational database program (p. 92) Software that allows users to link database tables in ways that can then be combined into useful information while reducing data redundancy.

relational field (p. 92) Field that appears in common in multiple tables in a database, allowing tables to be linked.

repeater (p. 122) Device in a communications system that enhances the signal to keep it accurate and strong enough to continue transmission.

research and development (p. 14) The activities that lead to the design of new products and services.

resolution (p. 45) The image quality on a computer monitor.

RGB (p. 37) Computer pictures stored as a combination of the primary colors red, green, and blue.

ring network (p. 120) A common network topology so named because a connecting cable forms a closed circle, or ring, through all of the networked computers.

robotics (p. 14) Computerized control systems that regulate assembly lines and often do the actual assembly and testing.

router (p. 123) Network hardware that can connect multiple networks regardless of the protocols used; a router can determine the best route to a distant site.

sampling (p. 35) The digital storage process of taking many thousands of samples of a desired analog sound in fractions of a second, recording the binary number that each represents, and then replaying them in the same time sequence.

scanner (p. 37) An optical input device used to convert text and images into computer-readable form.

search engine (p. 145) An Internet application for finding information on the Web in response to key words typed into a query box.

Secure Digital Music Initiative (SDMI) (p. 99) Technology that allows no more than three copies to be made of a music file for personal use.

secure Web site server (p. 157) Site that automatically encrypts the personal data being communicated for the mutual protection of the server as well as the user.

sequential access (p. 48) A form of data storage in which content stored in a medium such as magnetic tape is available only in the order in which it was recorded.

Serial Line Internet Protocol (SLIP) (p. 142) A protocol used by Internet service providers for dial-up connections.

serial port (p. 43) A computer connection that typically transmits one bit of data at a time.

shareware (p. 100) Software that can be freely copied and distributed, but for which the author retains the copyright.

shell (p. 65) An overlay program that essentially converts choices selected by a user into system-equivalent commands.

shielded twisted-pair (STP) cable (p. 116) Typical communication line that consists of two parallel copper wires, each individually wrapped in plastic and bound together by another plastic casing, with additional insulation to reduce the likelihood that line interference or noise will corrupt the signal.

shielding (p. 116) The additional insulation used in communications cable to reduce the likelihood that line interference or noise will corrupt the signal.

shortcuts (p. 65) Icons or underlined letters that provide a link to files or programs elsewhere on the same computer; they can be used to open the activity with a simple mouse click, rather than having to select it from a menu.

shouting (p. 151) The use of all capital letters in an Internet message, implying exclamation.

Simple Mail Transfer Protocol (SMTP) (p. 152) The standard communications protocol used to transfer e-mail over the Internet.

simplex transmission (p. 122) A form of communications transfer that permits the data to flow in only one direction.

single in-line memory module (SIMM) (p. 41) RAM chips that are mounted in single rows onto small boards that snap into place on the motherboard.

soft copy (p. 44) Computer output viewable only on the computer monitor.

software (p. 12) Computer program containing instructions that tell the computer what to do to perform a particular kind of function; programs and applications are examples of software.

software convergence (p. 101) The industry trend toward combining features of multiple software packages into a single program.

software piracy (p. 84) Making unauthorized copies of copyrighted commercial software or using it in other ways that violate the licensing agreement.

software suites (p. 13) Collections of commonly used computer application programs.

sound capture and editing program (p. 97) Specialized software used for recording and editing sounds for computer use.

spam (p. 151) The posting or sending of irrelevant and unwanted messages over the Internet.

spikes (p. 128) Brief electrical surges that can burn out system circuitry and cause damage to computer hardware.

spoiler (p. 151) A fact or information that, when revealed in e-mail or a message board, ruins the result of an activity for the reader, such as exposing a surprise ending to a movie.

spreadsheets (p. 13) Tables arranged in rows and columns for doing accounting and other types of mathematical calculations.

SQL (Structured Query Language) (p. 92) A standard set of syntax used to perform database queries.

standard graphics file format (p. 95) A standard set of instructions that enables users to save files so they can be read by many applications.

star network (p. 120) A topology for a network whose configuration resembles the hub and spokes of a wheel.

storage (p. 28) Permanent location of programs and data, primarily hard and floppy magnetic disks and optical media.

storage address (p. 41) A machine location known to the operating system through which data held permanently, usually on magnetic or optical media, can be recovered for future use.

streaming audio (p. 148) A technique that allows a listener to hear a file in real time as it transfers over the Web.

subdirectory (p. 63) Subsidiary element in a computer's directory that permits the user to access programs and documents quickly.

subfolders (p. 60) A file management organization tool that permits the user to access programs and documents quickly.

supercomputer (p. 10) A mainframe computer capable of very high volume and very fast processing, typically used in research and defense applications.

surfing (p. 145) Moving from place to place on the Web, a term suggesting speed, excitement, and continual motion through the sea of information one finds there.

surge protector (p. 128) Hardware that protects computer circuits from extraordinary and damaging surges in electrical current.

S-VGA (p. 45) The monitor specification Super-VGA, which can display 1,024 columns and 768 rows of pixels, and thus is said to have a 1,024 x 768 image.

switched network (p. 116) A standard telephone network in which each location has a number that is used to connect to the system on an as-needed basis.

symmetric digital subscriber line (SDSL) (p. 119) A type of digital subscriber line used if transmission distance longer than standard DSL connections is needed.

synchronous transmission (p. 122) Data transmission in packets of more than one character, requiring sophisticated equipment to schedule the synchronized timing of the flow.

system board (motherboard) (p. 38) The main circuit board in the computer, consisting of a collection of electrical pathways and connected chips.

3-D modeling program (p. 96) Software used to create images that give the illusion of being three-dimensional and can be rotated or viewed from different angles.

table (p. 91) Database concept that consists of rows, called records, and columns, called fields.

tags (p. 150) A series of codes used in Web pages that tell the viewing browser how to display the words and data on the screen.

T-carrier lines (p. 119) Telephone communications lines that have extremely high capacity and speeds.

telecommute (p. 16) Using a computer and networking to work at a distance from one's office.

telnet sessions (p. 155) A type of communication protocol over the Internet that lets a computer connect to a remote system so that it operates as though it were an on-site terminal.

terabyte (p. 32) A measure of data volume: 1,024,000,000,000 bytes, or about one million MB.

threaded discussion (p. 154) A concept in newsgroups in which articles and their subsequent responses are presented in a hierarchical arrangement following a common thread or thought.

token (p. 120) An all-clear code that is circulated around a token-ring network until a given node sends a message.

token-ring network (p. 120) A common network topology so named because a connecting cable forms a closed circle, or ring, through all of the networked computers; a code called a *token* circulates around the network.

top-level domain (p. 143) A Web site domain name abbreviation that indicates the type of organization that is operating the site.

touchpad (p. 34) A form of input device, an alternative to a mouse or trackball, consisting of a pad on which the user moves a finger to manipulate a cursor on a computer screen.

touchscreen (p. 34) A computer monitor that enables the user to perform tasks by simply placing a finger on a point on the screen.

trackball (p. 33) A stationary pointing device containing a ball that the user moves with his or her fingers or palm in order to change the position of a cursor on a computer screen.

traffic (p. 141) The volume of data transfers on the Internet.

transceiver (p. 120) A device that sends messages along a network bus in either direction.

transmission control protocol/Internet protocol (TCP/IP) (p. 122) Data transfer protocol, developed for use with the ARPANET, that manages transfers by breaking messages into small sections called packets.

true color (p. 45) 24-bit display on a monitor creates a palette in excess of 16 million shades.

TrueType (p. 85) An outline font format for text scaling or sizing that makes it possible to have virtually limitless control over the look of any document.

twisted-pair cable (p. 116) Typical communication line that consists of two parallel copper wires, each individually wrapped in plastic and bound together by another plastic casing.

Unicode (p. 32) A system for coding symbols and characters as binary numbers using two bytes, or 16 binary digits, that can represent more than 65,000 separate characters.

Uniform Resource Locator (URL) (p. 144) An Internet address; the combination of necessary Internet routing information that enables a specific Web site to be located.

uninterruptible power supply (UPS) (p. 128) Hardware that maintains the flow of electric current from its batteries for a period of time after a loss of power, and also has circuitry to reduce the likelihood of electrical spike damage to the protected system.

Universal Product Code (UPC) (p. 36) The barcode made up of lines and spaces that appears on virtually every product sold in the United States, which the computer translates into a useful product number.

UNIX (p. 71) Operating system developed in the mid-1970s and widely adopted by laboratories and universities; it has a complex command-line interface and provides effective time-sharing, or simultaneous access by many users to a single computer.

upgrade (p. 84) A newly released version of software or hardware.

user interface (p. 60) The environment displayed on the computer screen with which the user interacts to cause actions to occur.

utility program (p. 61) A type of program used to enhance the operating system, such as antivirus software, that may be added at any time.

vertical application (p. 12) Integrated software that performs functions central to many different parts of a business at many different levels.

very high rate DSL (VDSL) (p. 129) A faster form of DSL data communications that is beginning to compete with other broadband connectivity forms.

video adapter (p. 44) An expansion board on or attached to the motherboard that creates the monitor display from the flow of data from the CPU.

video chat (p. 154) Chat software used on some sites that also supports technology that adds video to the voice transfer.

video digitizing card (p. 98) An expansion board that allows a user to capture and digitize video images and sounds from such sources as television, videotape recorders, and camcorders.

video display terminal (VDT) (p. 44) A typical computer monitor that uses a large glass tube onto which the output is projected.

video editing software (p. 98) A program that allows the user to edit sound and video and output it in various digital formats, such as QuickTime, Motion Picture Experts Group (MPEG), and Video for Windows.

video port (p. 43) A computer connection that is used to provide data to a monitor; may be built into the computer or provided by a video card or graphics card.

video RAM (VRAM) (p. 44) A type of random access memory used to store information traveling to and from monitors.

virtual reality (p. 14) Software and hardware used to create simulated three-dimensional environments and provide a method to view versions of finished products prior to manufacture.

virtual reality modeling language (VRML) (p. 150) A programming language that defines the way in which three-dimensional images are displayed and enables a developer to empower users with controls to manipulate the graphics.

virus protection software (p. 127) Products that check for unusual activity, such as bits of operating system code being rewritten, and either prevent such activity outright or provide warnings through dialog boxes.

VisiCalc (p. 82) An early innovative software program, the electronic spreadsheet that changed the direction of personal computing in 1979.

voice chat (p. 154) Internet chat feature that lets the users hear one another through the computer's microphone and speakers.

voice recognition software (p. 35) Software and technology that recognizes and interacts with human speech.

volatile memory (p. 41) Memory that is erased when the computer is turned off; e.g., RAM chips lose their data if the flow of electricity is interrupted.

VRML browser (p. 150) A software application that can view virtual reality images.

wand reader (p. 36) An input device that looks like a pen and can interpret alpha and numeric data preprinted onto sales tags, charge slips, or inventory records.

WAV (p. 148) A digitized audio storage file format that is used on the Internet.

Web authoring software (p. 97) An application that allows users to create HTML pages that incorporate multimedia elements to be posted on the World Wide Web.

Web crawler (p. 159) A program that continually searches the World Wide Web and other parts of the Internet to identify new pages.

Web hosting service (p. 151) Computer system or server that performs the centralized function of making Web site files available over the Internet; Internet service providers often provide this service.

Web page (p. 145) An element of a Web site; a file containing data, links, or other information, and available for viewing as a single page on the World Wide Web.

Web site (p. 15) An Internet location for a file or group of files whose home page is represented by a single uniform resource locator (URL).

Webmaster (p. 147) The person or team responsible for the creation and maintenance of a Web site.

what-if factor (p. 88) The act in business decision making of changing and recalculating variable quantities to view their impact.

wide area network (WAN) (p. 112) Widely separated computers that are connected together; often can include two or more LANs.

Windows CE (p. 70) Operating system developed for use in small, dedicated systems such as personal digital assistants (PDAs) or handheld PCs.

Windows 95 (p. 66) August 1995 release of the Microsoft operating system that adopted a version-naming convention tied to the year of release; it was a 32-bit operating system that replaced the DOS and shell concept with a completely new integrated approach.

Windows 98 (p. 68) An upgrade and update of the Windows 95 operating system.

Windows NT (p. 66) A sophisticated multi-user operating system widely used by network administrators and professionals in MIS.

Windows platform (p. 60) A computer or computer system whose operating system is one of the Windows family.

Windows 2000 Millennium Edition (Me) (p. 69) An upgrade of the Microsoft Windows operating system developed primarily for the home computer market, featuring an enhanced capability to work with digital media and making the creation of a home network easier.

Windows 2000 Professional (p. 69) An upgrade of the Windows NT mainstream operating system for desktop and notebook computing, used primarily in organizations.

Windows 2000 Server/Advanced Server (p. 69) An advanced version of the Microsoft Windows 2000 operating system.

wired (p. 5) To be a computer user or connected to the Internet.

wireless communication (p. 117) Transmission link that makes use of data encoded as electromagnetic signals, such as radio waves, microwaves, or infrared light.

wizard (p. 68) Software that includes step-by-step instructions that guide the user through some task process, or that anticipates what the user wants and does all or part of the task automatically.

word processors (p. 13) Applications software that is used for entering, formatting, and otherwise manipulating documents that consist primarily of text, but can also include graphical materials.

works program (p. 91) A single computer program that combines scaled-down and interrelated versions of several different applications, typically a word processor, a spreadsheet, a database application, and a graphics function.

workstation (p. 10) A desktop computer powerful enough to rival the performance of a minicomputer or, in some cases, a small mainframe; widely used for scientific, engineering, and research applications.

World Wide Web (the Web) (p. 113) A very popular part of the Internet that consists of linked documents that can display text, graphical, audio, and video content.

World Wide Web Consortium (W3C) (p. 143) Organization with the responsibility to oversee research and development of the World Wide Web; sets many Web standards.

WYSIWYG (p. 85) Acronym taken from "What You See Is What You Get," which means that the view on a screen is exactly how it will appear when printed.

Index

Photo Credits